Investigating Cryptocurrencies

Investigating Cryptocurrencies

Understanding, Extracting, and Analyzing Blockchain Evidence

Nick Furneaux

WILEY

Investigating Cryptocurrencies: Understanding, Extracting, and Analyzing Blockchain Evidence

Published by
John Wiley & Sons, Inc.
10475 Crosspoint Boulevard
Indianapolis, IN 46256
www.wiley.com

Published simultaneously in Canada

ISBN: 978-1-119-48058-7
ISBN: 978-1-119-48057-0 (ebk)
ISBN: 978-1-119-48056-3 (ebk)

Manufactured in the United States of America

10 9 8 7 6 5 4 3 2 1

For general information on our other products and services please contact our Customer Care Department within the United States at (877) 762-2974, outside the United States at (317) 572-3993 or fax (317) 572-4002.

Wiley publishes in a variety of print and electronic formats and by print-on-demand. Some material included with standard print versions of this book may not be included in e-books or in print-on-demand. If this book refers to media such as a CD or DVD that is not included in the version you purchased, you may download this material at http://booksupport.wiley.com. For more information about Wiley products, visit www.wiley.com.

Library of Congress Control Number: 2018939042

To Claire, Toby, and Loulé

I love you

Nick

About the Author

Nick has been playing and working with computers since his parents gave him a Sinclair ZX81 when he was 12. By the age of 14, Nick had designed a computer program to convince his teacher that he had gained access to his bank account.

In the past 20 years, he has provided cyber security, forensics consultancy, and training to companies and law-enforcement institutions in the UK and across Europe, the United States, and Asia, and has lectured on the subject to numerous groups and organisations.

Nick has been specifically involved in the development of data extraction and digital forensic analysis techniques that work on live, running computers, and has had the opportunity to work with some of the top security researchers in the world.

He is currently working with government and corporate teams throughout Europe in various forms of data acquisition, teaching computer memory analysis and carrying out cryptocurrency investigations.

Nick is the Managing Director of CSITech Ltd and Director of the online forensics training company CSILearn Ltd.

Throughout his career, family has always come first. He enjoys spending time and travelling with his wife and son as well as caring for his daughter who suffers with a rare genetic condition (https://www.kleefstrasyndrome.org). In his limited spare time, he enjoys running and sport climbing.

About the Technical Editor

David S. Hoelzer (MSc) is the Director of Operations for Enclave Forensics, Inc., the Dean of Faculty for the SANS Technology Institute, and a Fellow with the SANS Institute. He is well known in the field of cyber security in general and more specifically in intrusion detection and network monitoring circles as an international speaker/teacher on information security topics, having developed a number of both offensive and defensive tools and techniques. For the past few years, he has specialized in covert communications development and scalable back-end communications solutions coupled with threat hunting and counterintelligence. He has more than thirty years of experience in the information technology field, with more than twenty-five of those years engaged in information security, both defensively and offensively. He currently resides in New York.

Credits

Project Editor
Kathryn Duggan

Technical Editor
David S Hoelzer

Production Editor
Athiyappan Lalith Kumar

Copy Editor
Kim Cofer

Production Manager
Katie Wisor

Manager of Content Enablement and Operations
Pete Gaughan

Marketing Manager
Christie Hilbrich

Executive Editor
Jim Minatel

Project Coordinator, Cover
Brent Savage

Proofreader
Nancy Bell

Indexer
Johnna VanHoose Dinse

Cover Designer
Wiley

Cover Image
©allanswart/iStockphoto

Acknowledgments

Firstly, thank you to my Mum for not just teaching me to read as a child, but to learn to love reading and writing. One of the reasons I started writing this book in late 2017 was to take my mind off her finally going to sleep in the July after showing pancreatic cancer who was boss for four years. She would have been really happy that I eventually wrote a book, even if she didn't understand a word of it! (Although she would have tried and told me it was the best book ever!)

Secondly, my "brother from another mother," Chris Hadnagy, who suggested I write this book and has stood tirelessly at my shoulder through the extraordinary challenges of the past few years.

Next, thank you to the team at Wiley. Jim Minatel, I appreciate you giving me a chance—we need to go watch some racing sometime! And to Kathi Duggan, for your astonishing levels of patience dealing with my writing style and for your personal words of kindness over the past months.

Finally, Dave Hoelzer, thank you for being technical editor. Although we have been friends for years, your direct edits such as "Wrong" and "I don't know what you are talking about" were exactly what I needed and have made this book so much better.

Contents at a glance

Contents

Foreword

Any novel technology brings with it a wave of early adopters. While some of these are keen to explore the potential societal and economic benefits that may be had by leveraging the technology, others seek to apply the technology as a means to enable nefarious activities. Bitcoin and other cryptocurrencies are no exception. Indeed, it may be very reasonably argued that the first "killer-app" for Bitcoin—responsible for a large influx of users and a significant boosting of economic traction—was the Silk Road dark market, founded in February 2011. Other use cases thriving today include ransomware, unregulated gambling, Ponzi schemes masquerading as high-yield cryptocurrency investment schemes, in-person cryptocurrency muggings, and cryptojacking—that is, the practice of covertly hijacking computers to mine cryptocurrency.

Digital forensic experts need to keep pace with new technologies to ensure relevant objective evidence can be brought forward to throw light on investigations. They face tough challenges, not least an exploding array of new cryptocurrencies, many based on high-privacy foundations. Fortunately they are supported by the fundamental goal of blockchain technology—that is, to create an immutable, decentralised record of transactions. Thus evidence trails are perfectly preserved while both forensic technology and long-running legal processes have an opportunity to play catch up. Indeed, the clustering techniques pioneered by the likes of academic Dr. Sarah Meiklejohn in 2013, and built on by companies such as Chainalysis and Elliptic, have enabled the unmasking of the ownership of large numbers of Bitcoin addresses—including many associated with the Silk Road—something that had previously thought to be impossible.

Within this context, Nick Furneaux's book is both timely and relevant. Its comprehensive scope includes not only an accessible introduction to the technology and its history, but also an overview of relevant methods and the critical factors that should be respected in any forensic investigation. Indeed, I have personally observed on more than one occasion how a failure to apply proper methods can mean critical evidence is missed or lost, while a lack of a sufficiently deep level of understanding can mean incorrect conclusions are drawn from the evidence. In either case, the consequences for the integrity of the investigatory process are often terminal. I hope that you will enjoy reading this book, that you will find it as insightful as I did, and that you will find the opportunity to apply its wisdom to some real-world cases.

—Prof William Knottenbelt, Director of the Centre for Cryptocurrency
Research and Engineering, Imperial College London

Introduction

"The Times 03/Jan/2009 Chancellor on brink of second bailout for banks"

Those 69 characters should be much more famous than they are. In the very first Bitcoin block, the enigmatic Satoshi Nakamoto, the inventor of Bitcoin, encoded that message in hexadecimal (see Figure Intro-1).

```
00 00 00 00 00    ...............
00 00 00 00 00    ...............
B2 7A C7 2C 3E    ....;£íýz(.²zÇ,>
32 3A 9F B8 AA    gv.a.È.Ā˜ŠQ2:Ÿ¸ª
1D 1D AC 2B 7C    K.ˆJ)«_Iÿÿ...¬+|
00 00 00 00 00    ...............
00 00 00 00 00    ...............
04 FF FF 00 1D    ....ÿÿÿÿ..ÿÿ
73 20 30 33 2F    ..EThe Times 03/
61 6E 63 65 6C    Jan/2009 Chancel
6B 20 6F 66 20    lor on brink of
6F 75 74 20 66    second bailout f
FF 01 00 F2 05    or banksÿÿÿÿ..ò.
B0 FE 55 48 27    *....CA.gŠÿ°þUH'
28 E0 39 09 A6    (à9.¦.Ö.;ð.
3F 4C EF 38 C4    ybàê.aÞ¶Iö¼?Lÿ8Ä
F7 BA 0B 8D 57    óU.å.Á.Þ\8M+º..W
00 00             ŠLp+kñ._¬....
```

Figure Intro-1: Message in the Genesis block.

Either by design or coincidence (which seems unlikely), Satoshi both launched the first blockchain-based cryptocurrency and made the semi-covert statement as to the reasons for the development of his or her system (we do not definitively know the sex of Satoshi or even if Satoshi is an individual or a group). It seems that in Satoshi's view, the banks were failing, and his or her system could free people from the control of central banks and exchanges. On a cryptography mailing list, Satoshi wrote the following:

> **"You will not find a solution to political problems in cryptography.**
>
> **Yes, but we can win a major battle in the arms race and gain a new territory of freedom for several years.**
>
> **Governments are good at cutting off the heads of a centrally controlled networks like Napster, but pure P2P networks like Gnutella and Tor seem to be holding their own."**
>
> **Satoshi,** *https://www.mail-archive.com/cryptography@metzdowd.com/*
> *msg09971.html*

Although Satoshi wrote little about the Bitcoin system, the few comments on forums show that there was at least a small part of his or her motivation that wanted to enable people to step outside the traditional banking and currency systems.

Since those early days, Bitcoin has grown massively both in value and reach. Although at the time of writing, one could not assert that Bitcoin was a mainstream currency, it is certainly in the mainstream consciousness, regularly making headlines on conventional news channels and spawning thousands of column inches of editorial.

Aside from Bitcoin, hundreds of cryptocurrencies are now based on the blockchain concept. Some are very similar; others are trying to do things in very different ways. For example, although Ethereum is a cryptocurrency in its own right, it is based around a complex, programmable contract system. A transaction can include many contractual obligations and could be used for everything from buying a house to getting married. In fact, several couples have already embedded their marriage on the Bitcoin and Ethereum blockchains, including parts of their vows and links to an image of their marriage certificate. Blockchain technology is here to stay, and an investigation involving it is going to land on your desk soon, if it hasn't already.

Cryptocurrencies: Coming to a Lab near You

I've been working specifically in computer forensics and digital investigations for about 14 years. In that time, the equipment coming to the lab and the programs we have had to investigate have changed drastically. About 13 years ago, a computer investigation would focus almost solely on Internet activity in a web browser, perhaps some newsgroups or ICQ and, of course, good old e-mail. Fast-forward to 2018, and the equipment that lands on the check-in desk at the lab has changed beyond recognition. Most smartphones, such as the humble iPhone, have significantly more power and storage than the computers of the early 2000s, and instead of simply looking at visited websites, we now have encrypted chat, messaging programs that come in hundreds of flavors, and social media environments that are investigation centers in their own right, such as Facebook, Snapchat, and many others.

Throughout this time, criminals have continued to carry out nefarious deeds and have found ways to pay for illegal goods and acquire ill-gotten payments from the defrauded and unsuspecting. The problem for the 2005 criminal was the lack of options for sending or receiving monies in an anonymous, untraceable way. For example, criminals could easily carry out a "ransomware" attack where malware encrypts the victim's computer until money is paid and then they are "hopefully" provided with a decryption key. But to have the money sent to the criminal presented significant difficulties. You could publish a bank account number, but that's very hard to set up without ID, and when the money is transferred, the police can easily trace it and move in for the arrest. Because of these problems, criminals and criminal gangs took to setting up post-office (PO) boxes where money could be sent, but again, it was not difficult for the authorities to keep watch until someone turned up to collect the cash. Some went the route of using what amounted to cash mules, who would retain some percentage of the risk involved, adding a layer of misdirection to the payments and cutting into profits. The Internet, though, offered possibilities in the form of Western Union and PayPal, but those are also connected to real-world bank accounts, making it straightforward for the police to trace. I'm somewhat simplifying the methods used, but you get the idea: there was no easy way to pay or get paid without leaving a trail that is easily followed.

Then in January 2009, Satoshi launched the Bitcoin currency, based on a concept called the blockchain. This currency did not need any connections to the real-world banking system or require anyone to sign up to any central system—you could acquire a few bitcoin and pay for goods with seeming total anonymity. Add to this new ability the burgeoning underground marketplace the media loves to call the "dark web"—mostly because it has the word "dark" in it, which makes it sound mysterious, with a hint of evil. Of course, the dark web is anything but dark, with many legitimate services available to assist those in more restricted territories of the world to communicate and be informed online. It would be fair to say, though, that it certainly represents the rough side of town! Because of this association, Bitcoin became the bad guy of finance, and when a computer came into the lab with Bitcoin software on it, the owner was automatically viewed with significant suspicion.

> **NOTE** I often see this attitude amongst investigators when it comes to anything that obfuscates computer communication or hides data. When investigating a computer with a VPN client on it, if storage encryption is turned on, a Tor client is installed, or even if a browser cache has been recently purged, the assumption is that the owner "must have something to hide." I regularly argue that many reasons exist why someone would have all or any of these software tools on their computer—they may have something to hide, but it's not actually illegal or they just value their right to privacy. Sadly, I'm usually wrong, and the computer owner generally does have something bad to hide—but it's nice to think the best of people, isn't it?

In recent years, Bitcoin has moved out of the figurative shadows of the dark web and into the light of mainstream commerce. It seems most owners of bitcoins are just holding them for investment as the bitcoin-to-dollar price fluctuates wildly, but generally in an upward direction. If you go to `http://bit.ly/2td8ref`, you can see the bitcoin-to-dollar exchange rate from its inception in 2009 to now.

Although Bitcoin, Ethereum, and others could stand alone as a trading currency if enough traders accepted them, the reality is that even today, in 2018, what you can buy with a cryptocurrency is limited. Users wanted to be able to buy cryptocurrency with dollars and euros for use online and then sell coin that they had received for currency that they could use in Walmart, for example. To fill this void, currency exchanges began to pop up that would take your real-world money in exchange for commensurate Bitcoin. The process is the same as converting between any currencies. Head to an online site that offers conversion, pay your money by credit card or wire transfer, for example, and you will be credited with the Bitcoin or whatever currency you have asked for. As I discuss in this book, most sites have their own "wallet" system that stores your Bitcoin for you so you can then pay for goods using your coin directly from the website. This means that the company can both take your money and have access to your bitcoins.

> **NOTE** The volatility of Bitcoin compared to its dollar value in 2017 and 2018, aligned with the growing fees involved to make a Bitcoin purchase, have led some economists to question Bitcoin's use as a currency, rather terming Bitcoin a crypto-asset. Time will tell if Bitcoin or another cryptocurrency manages to become widely available on the high street.

The problems have been significant. Anyone who knows anything about setting up a website that includes a bit of code to accept credit cards could set up a cryptocurrency exchange in very little time. A developer could construct a professional-looking interface, host it on servers in Belize, register it on the primary search engines, and wait for customers. Those customers give money to the website host who in turn transfers bitcoins into his or her wallet on the servers, waits until the wallet contains lots of money and bitcoins, and then quietly closes the door and tiptoes away. This happened early in the life of Bitcoin with the fraudulent Bitcoin Savings and Trust in 2012, and Global Bond Ltd in 2013.

Alternatively, the person who sets up this type of online payment might be completely legitimate but get hacked and lose all their coins. Examples include Mt Gox in 2011, MyBitcoin in 2011, Bitfinex in 2016, Bitstamp in 2015, and NiceHash in 2017. This problem is not exclusively a Bitcoin problem as $500 million worth of a cryptocurrency called NEM coins were lost in a hack of Coincheck in 2018.

Or the person can lose access to his or her master wallet file and lose all the customers' coins. An example of this is Bitomat in 2011.

Suffice to say that there are large, legitimate exchanges out there. The key is to buy your bitcoin and then transfer it to your own wallet away from the exchange. Then remember to back up your wallet—twice. And add a password—a strong one! Alternatively, save the private key to paper-based cold storage, a method we will discuss later in the book.

No matter what happens to Bitcoin, cryptocurrencies are here to stay, and they will continue to be a strong contender for criminals to receive payments, pay for goods, and launder money. A cryptocurrency investigator does not need to be an expert in Bitcoin specifically, but needs to understand the concepts behind blockchain currencies in order to apply that knowledge to whatever becomes the next payment system of choice.

Who Should Read This Book

If you are like me and spend your life digging through other people's data, whether that is as a digital forensics investigator, a forensic accountant, or even an Open Source Intelligence gatherer, then you need to know about this subject. If not today, then you will tomorrow. Because this book covers a broad range of techniques, you may find that parts of it are very pertinent to your work and other parts are not so relevant. For example, I will teach you how to extract cryptocurrency-related data from hard drives and devices, as well as how to conduct a premises search for this type of information. Although you may never carry out a premises search in your work, being able to communicate your needs to a front-line officer or investigator may prevent vital information being missed.

It is worth downloading and reading the report "National risk assessment of money laundering and terrorist financing 2017," which you can find at http://bit.ly/2z9513x. Under the section "Money laundering," the report makes some excellent observations about the use of virtual, or crypto, currencies in international crime. Here's what the article says regarding terrorist financing in conclusion of this section:

> **"The NCA [UK National Crime Agency] has assessed the risk of digital currency use for money laundering to be relatively low; although NCA deems it likely that digital currencies are being used to launder low amounts at high volume, there is little evidence of them being used to launder large amounts of money."**
>
> —*UK HM Treasury,* *https://www.gov.uk/government/uploads/system/uploads/ attachment_data/file/655198/National_risk_assessment_of_money_laundering_ and_terrorist_financing_2017_pdf_web.pdf*

It is my experience that the reason that law enforcement and governments believe that terrorists are not using cryptocurrencies widely comes down to lack of technical expertise. But, as with all technologies, the skill levels needed to securely operate in a cryptocurrency space are decreasing quickly, and this will not be a barrier for long. Law enforcement bosses draw the same conclusions with money laundering—that the technical know-how needed is holding back many crime groups.

It is worth noting in the report regarding both terrorism and money laundering vulnerabilities they state the following:

> **"The rapidly developing nature of products and services in this sector puts an imperative on the ability for government, supervisors, firms and law enforcement to respond rapidly to both the opportunities and risks which they pose."**
>
> —*UK HM Treasury,* *https://www.gov.uk/government/uploads/system/uploads/ attachment_data/file/655198/National_risk_assessment_of_money_laundering_ and_terrorist_financing_2017_pdf_web.pdf*

You may be reading this and believe that your job role will never pit your skills against a Russian crime group or extremist Islamists, but the use of cryptocurrencies is trickling down into much lower-level and lower-value crime. One example is that of crypto-mining code that is being installed by hackers into websites. When a user browses to an infected site, processor cycles on the visitor's computer are used to mine cryptocurrency coins. Another example is the fraud that has become known as "ransomware," which I mentioned earlier in this introduction. Ransomware became media-worthy in May 2017 with the WannaCry outbreak. It simply encrypts a computer's files and then displays a message asking for payment.

Figure Intro-2 shows a WannaCry screenshot with a countdown timer (an excellent social-engineering ploy to generate urgency), instructions, and a Bitcoin address. (I particularly like the "bitcoin ACCEPTED HERE" logo!) Because the perpetrators were possibly linked to North Korea, no one thought that the bitcoins would move, but in early August 2017, over $100,000 worth of bitcoin were emptied from the wallets. Again, you may be thinking that this type of international and possibly politically motivated crime is outside your paygrade. But it was noteworthy with both WannaCry ransomware and the Petya/NotPetya virus that came later (see Figure Intro-3) that individuals and small companies were often the victims of these crimes that on a singular level only cost $300 or more dollars. Sadly, in the case of Petya/NotPetya, those who paid never saw a decryption key, and if the victim had no backups, then the potential loss was considerably greater.

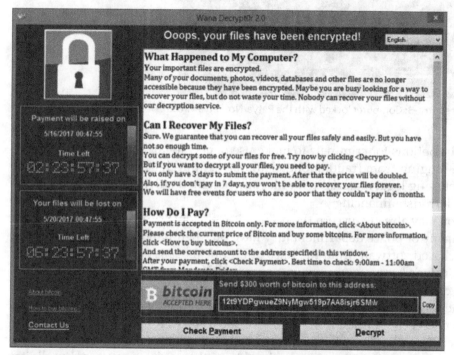

Figure Intro-2: Screenshot of a computer locked with the WannaCry ransomware.

The question that's raised with each of these examples is, are they international or local crimes? There is every reason to believe that Police Hi-Tech Crime units and private security firms would be receiving many calls from victims asking for help. In the simplest terms, it would be good to be able to monitor the payment addresses and trace any movement. You may reason that all the larger agencies will be doing exactly that, but you may have heard that it was a 22-year-old security researcher, Marcus Hutchins, who found a kill switch to stop the spread of WannaCry, not the US NSA, not the UK NCA, not even the European Anti-Fraud Agency—it was Marcus, from his bedroom in the south of England. We all have a part to play.

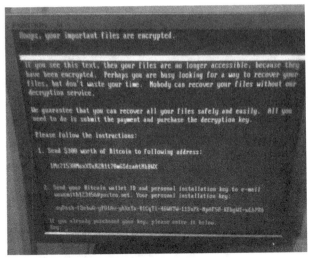

Figure Intro-3: Computer locked with the Petya/NotPetya virus.

The options for criminals to make use of cryptocurrencies are almost endless, ranging from fraud, money laundering, purchasing illegal material, or purchasing legal material with illegally obtained currency through to crime and terrorism financing.

You may already discern the need to learn about cryptocurrencies, but your company or police department may have put their hands in their pockets and purchased software from the likes of Elliptic (`https://www.elliptic.co`) or Chainalysis (`https://www.chainalysis.com`). If you can afford one of these tools, buy one—they are both excellent. However, I make that statement in exactly the same way as I would if we were talking about computer forensic investigations and referencing Encase from Guidance Software, FTK from AccessData, or the superb X-Ways. These tools are extremely useful, they take the heavy lifting out of an investigation, and you should use them where you can. But digital investigators should be able to explain to a manager, senior officer, tribunal, or court how they reached a conclusion and be able to interpret the raw data behind some intelligence or evidence.

To illustrate, I can click a button in the FTK forensics software, and the tool will carve deleted files from a hard drive. However, when challenged, I should be able to return to the drive and have the skills to locate the disk offset and carve that file by hand, without relying on the competency of the FTK programmer to have done his or her job right.

This book takes a similar approach. Although tools are available to help with some cryptocurrency investigations, this book will walk you through the manual processes including how to find wallets (payment addresses) on devices and online, how to gather intelligence about payment addresses, and then how to follow the money through to potentially de-anonymizing a user or seizing coins.

What You Will Learn—and Not Learn

It sounds terribly negative to tell you what you are not going to learn in this book, but it's important that you understand where this book will take you and what other reading may be useful for you:

- I am not going to tell you how to become rich trading cryptocurrencies.
- The book will not help you build your own cryptocurrency.
- The book is not a detailed technical deconstruction of the technologies behind cryptocurrencies, although I do cover them in sufficient detail for you to be able to understand the concepts and explain them to others.

What you are going to learn is much more important. Here's a brief walk through the chapters:

Chapter 1: What Is a Cryptocurrency? defines what a cryptocurrency actually is and describes where the value of the currency comes from and how it is traded. We will look at some of the leading currencies in the field today and talk about transactions, contracts, and the many possibilities that exist for the technology.

Chapter 2: The Hard Bit covers some rather unpleasant mathematics that form the basis for hashing and the cryptography protocols that are used in various cryptocurrencies.

Chapter 3: Understanding the Blockchain is a critical chapter where a blockchain and its functions are clearly defined. We will look at how to get at the raw blockchain data via API calls and how to deconstruct a block header from the raw hex.

Chapter 4: Transactions drills down to individual transactions, again extracting raw transaction data rather than the data we get from web interfaces online. We will examine how "change" works as well as fees and the Mempool.

Chapter 5: Mining covers the concept and technology behind mining and how blocks are added to the blockchain and new "coins" created.

Chapter 6: Wallets examines the many different types of wallets. This is an important chapter because investigators need to know what they are looking for in a premises search or a search on a computer or other device. This chapter also covers how a criminal might set up a covert wallet.

Chapter 7: Contracts and Tokens looks more deeply into how cryptocurrency contracts work and examines the difference between bitcoin and Ethereum scripts.

Chapter 8: Detecting the Use of Cryptocurrencies looks at detecting use of cryptocurrencies by a suspect, from house searches to searching online.

I will teach you, in detail, how to find wallets and payment addresses on a disk image or a live machine by extracting and analyzing computer memory (RAM).

Chapter 9: Analysis of Recovered Addresses and Wallets will take us into the analysis of recovered payment addresses and wallets, intelligence gathering, and using APIs to get to the raw blockchain data. We also look at utilizing recovered private keys to find public keys and discovering what has been used as well as how to crack encrypted wallets.

Chapter 10: Following the Money will help you to understand how to follow the flow of money, avoiding "address blindness" and following blocks through hard forks. This chapter also covers automatically monitoring addresses and using the Bitcoin Core command line to interrogate the blockchain offline.

Chapter 11: Visualization Systems explores tools you can use to visualize connections between transactions. Visualization can both help and hinder because it tends to create a lot of data, so we look at ways to manage the tools.

Chapter 12: Finding Your Suspect focuses on attempting to de-anonymize a user on the blockchain. You will learn clustering methods so you can identify groups of addresses owned by a single user. In this chapter, we'll look at logged IPs, how we can crawl for IP addresses of Bitcoin users, and even figure out if they are using Tor. We also consider how to use open-source methods to connect a payment address to a real-world person. A short section looks at the use of the blockchain to send micromessages.

Chapter 13: Sniffing Cryptocurrency Traffic covers extracting data from wiretaps and watching activity of nodes on the Bitcoin network.

Chapter 14: Seizing Coins explores methods for asset seizures once you have identified coins in use by a suspect.

Chapter 15: Putting It All Together helps you to use all the skills you have learned and apply them in a methodical way to investigate a crime involving cryptocurrencies.

About the Book's Web Resources

Code files to support this book are available at www.wiley.com/go/cryptocurrencies and at www.investigatingcryptocurrencies.com. The second site also contains a voucher code for the online course at csilearn.learnupon.com.

Understanding the Technology

As digital investigators, we have a tendency to want to get straight to the proverbial coal face and start looking at the data. However, with cryptocurrencies, it is important to understand the underlying technologies and how blockchains function to be able to effectively and accurately investigate the evidence.

What Is a Cryptocurrency?

Over the past few years, the term *cryptocurrency* has become a well-used term in financial circles, new business plans, and news headlines. Often the term is associated with criminal activity on the so-called "dark web," but more recently with the increasing value of currencies like Bitcoin, the word, concept, and products are entering mainstream consciousness.

But what really is a cryptocurrency and how does it work? In this chapter, we will examine the concept, the history, and the uses for cryptocurrencies and look at how to set up a Bitcoin trading node.

Why does an investigator need to know this? Understanding the concept of these online currencies can help you form a good foundation to build a more comprehensive technical understanding. It can also help you to see the criminal uses of these currencies.

A New Concept?

In the far western Pacific region of Micronesia is a tiny cluster of islands named Yap. Conspicuous against the deep blue of the ocean, this tiny group of "high islands" comprises rolling hills covered with dense, lush forest. The islands share a coral reef that provides sustenance for the islanders from the fish that seek protection from ocean predators.

As far back as the thirteenth century, the sultan of Egypt referenced islands at the far east of the Persian Empire, where the only currency was millstones. This was later confirmed by the Spanish when they "discovered" the island group in 1528. If you visit today, you can still see the stone coins that made up the primary currency of the islanders for many centuries; in fact, they are still used today in trades involving land or marriages.

The stones are a variety of sizes—some as small as 3.5 centimeters—but the ones that draw the most attention are up to 4 meters in diameter (see Figure 1-1). The Internet boasts many pictures of tourists standing next to these vast doughnut-shaped disks of calcite named Rai coins.

STONE MONEY OF UAP, WESTERN CAROLINE ISLANDS.
(From the paper by Dr. W. H. Furness, 3rd, in Transactions, Department of Archæology, University of Pennsylvania, Vol. I., No. 1, p. 51, Fig. 3, 1904.)

Figure 1-1: Stone money of Yap.

The stones do not originate on Yap but are mined and shipped from other islands such as Palau, which is 450 kilometers away. For centuries, these coins were loaded onto sail-driven rafts, and brought across the open ocean to the island, unloaded, and moved to a location somewhere on the island where they would generally stay put forever.

You may be wondering: How do the islanders use such huge coins in actual transactions? How do they value them? How do they know who owns each coin?

The Rai coins are interesting because they almost exactly prefigured the way a blockchain in a cryptocurrency works—in fact, similar questions can be asked about a cryptocurrency. How can you trade something that doesn't really exist, such as a Bitcoin? How is a blockchain-based coin valued, and how can you know who owns a coin with no central bank controlling the movement of funds? Examining the Yapese currency helps us to understand the blockchain currency concept.

So why does a large stone disk have value? Let's say that Bob from Yap wants a 3-meter coin. First, the coin must be mined. Consider the difficulty involved. Workers have to be employed and sent in boats to an island 450 kilometers away. Calcite must then be mined, and the resulting stone carved into the distinctive doughnut shape. This final "coin" must then be loaded onto a boat and sailed back across the stretch of Pacific Ocean with its obvious dangers. The work and considerable expense involved to mine the coin are what gives it its perceived and agreed value to the islanders. Indeed, the bigger the coin, the higher the difficulty—so the value is commensurately greater.

One of the first questions I am asked about cryptocurrencies is where does the money come from? The answer, of course, is that the money comes from nowhere, but that is not really a fair answer. If you know anything about any cryptocurrency, you will know that new coins are "mined." This concept will be discussed later, but in simple terms, computers work to solve really, really hard mathematical problems, and when they find a solution, they are rewarded with "new" coins. But just like mining a Yapese Rai coin, work is involved that carries a very real cost. Although Bitcoin miners, for example, are not chartering a ship and crossing oceans, they must spend real money on expensive, specialized custom ASICs (application specific integrated circuits) capable of carrying out trillions of calculations a second. They must then spend money on providing considerable amounts of electricity for running the computers and keeping them cool. Just like their stone counterparts, it's difficult and expensive to mine cryptocurrency coins, which gives them a perceived and generally agreed value due to their scarcity and the fact that eventually Bitcoin will "mine out," where all coins will be mined and no more can be produced.

It is notable that in 1874, a captain named David O'Keefe imported a large number of coins from Palau to trade with the Yapese. Interestingly, this "had its disadvantages, not least the introduction of inflation, caused by the sudden increase in the stock of money" (see https://www.smithsonianmag.com/history/david-okeefe-the-king-of-hard-currency-37051930/). In the same way, if the "difficulty of work" to mine cryptocurrency coins became easier, it would directly affect their accepted value.

How do the Yapese trade their coins? Most of the coins are too big to move, so the Yapese use a very simple but effective form of what we would now call a distributed ledger. For example, let's say there was villager named Bob, and when Bob's coin arrived by boat from Palau, it would be placed near a pathway or some other visible place. All the villagers would know that the coin "on the path by the beach" belonged to Bob, because everyone would be told this and would add it to their individual mental note that included the other large coins on the island. If Bob wanted to buy some land from Alice, they would agree on the transfer of coin for land, and they would then tell all the villagers that the coin "on the path by the beach" now belonged to Alice. With no centralized person keeping a record or ledger, the possibilities of fraud are massively reduced. If a pretender named Nick told others that he owned the coin "on the path by the beach," the majority of villagers could reject the claim due to their collective knowledge of ownership.

Amazingly, blockchain-based cryptocurrencies work in almost exactly the same way. When you wish to pay for goods or services, a record of the transaction is sent to every (full-node) user of the currency (covered in more detail in "Setting Yourself Up as a Bitcoin User" at the end of the chapter). This means that there isn't just one record of the transaction, but thousands all around the world. You are, in effect, saying, "Hi everyone, the coin you can find at this address now belongs to Alice." Should anyone else try to claim ownership of a coin, the large number of ledgers around the world can disagree, preventing any fraud.

It was reported that a coin being transported to Yap was lost overboard in a storm, but as all the villagers knew of the mishap, the owner was still credited with the coin, and although no one had ever seen it, it was still traded as "the coin in the bay." This demonstrates that a coin does not need a physical manifestation to be accepted as real, tradable tender. A cryptocurrency coin such as a bitcoin or Ethereum ether coin never has a physical representation, but because all the users of the currency trust its existence and accept the work that went into mining it, its value is accepted as real and hence it can be traded.

Now back to the original question: What is a cryptocurrency? There is considerable debate over the definition of a currency when related to so-called cryptocurrencies. The cryptology community is uncomfortable with the widening and often inaccurate use of the term "crypto" in news headlines and press releases and even financiers are suggesting that the term "currency" in cryptocurrency should be replaced with the word "asset." However, a currency is generally understood to be a tradable system of money. But in reality, anything can be a currency if it is accepted as representing an agreed value; effectively, we are using a barter system where we perceive value in the currency that we trade for goods and services. Although we tend to think of a currency as the monetary notes in our purse or wallet, we use many tradable "tokens" in our everyday life. Perhaps you recently paid for a flight with air miles or used a coupon to get a free item when you bought another. Although these "tokens" do not have a traditional monetary value in the same way as a dollar bill or euro note, they are still tradable at an agreed rate or even flexible rate.

Here's an analogy: A parent or teacher may use simple marks on a board to indicate when a child has behaved well or achieved something. There may be an agreement that 10 marks equal a certain treat, trip, or other benefit. In this situation, the marks on the board become a currency of sorts. They have a value that can be traded, even if it's in a very limited way.

As we have seen, a stone slab at the bottom of the ocean can be a tradable currency, so using the same reasoning, a block of text in a database that states that it carries a particular value—for example, one bitcoin—can also be traded. But that doesn't answer the "crypto" part of a cryptocurrency.

On Yap, the system of trust works because collectively the villagers are believed to be reliable witnesses. If many villagers clubbed together and formed a majority, they could then prove that a coin belonged to someone other than its rightful owner, but that would put their own coins at risk should they fall out of the new dishonest collective. This creates a paradigm of dependability where the majority can always be trusted. The same concept works in cryptocurrency. Users of a cryptocurrency such as Ethereum, Bitcoin, or others are encouraged to run a "full node"—that is, a complete record of every single transaction that has ever happened on the currency. This prevents individuals from dishonestly claiming ownership of currency, as the rest of the world's full nodes will disagree. The "crypto" part forms the underlying basis for authenticating the ownership of coins. In fact, cryptographic systems are used in every part of the process.

The definition of cryptography in its simplest form is from the Greek meaning "secret writing." Today, we define it as generating codes that allow information to be kept secret. With a cryptocurrency, we are not keeping information about a transaction secret—quite the opposite, every transaction can be read by everyone. We are using the techniques applied in messaging cryptography to enable people to prove that they are the rightful owner of monies, or more accurately, that they are the rightful owner of a transaction where they were the approved receiver of the money. Bitcoin, for example, uses a mixture of SHA256 hashing, Elliptic Curve cryptography, and others to not just secure a transaction but keep securing it repeatedly, forever. You will learn more about those systems in Chapter 2, "The Hard Bit."

The idea of being able to pay for goods and services over the Internet is not new. David Chaum developed Digicase in the late 1980s, which was arguably the first concept of Internet money. But it wasn't until 1998 that an attempt at public online payments based on the concept on an online wallet appeared and became successful with PayPal, which was led by the now hugely successful businessman Elon Musk. As I mentioned in this book's Introduction, PayPal still relies on the legacy banking world to handle the storing of money, and PayPal accounts are still primarily linked to real-world bank accounts today.

Interestingly, the crown for the first e-currency really goes to E-Gold, which was set up in 1996 by the unusual business pairing of an oncologist and an attorney. This system was based on stored gold, and users could make value transfers to other users of the system purely online. The E-Gold developers were way ahead of their time, using SSL (encryption) to move the payment data and an API for other developers to leverage the E-Gold system. Sadly, its demise came in 2013, after attention by the U.S. authorities regarding the use of the system for illegal payments. Ultimately, the owners were not implicated in any wrongdoing.

Leading Currencies in the Field

It was tempting to write an investigations book about Bitcoin since, at the time of writing, it is the brand synonymous with the word cryptocurrency in the public mind. However, as I spent more time with Monero, Litecoin, Ethereum, and others, I realized that although they were all subtly or sometimes significantly different and set out to provide certain abilities to their users, for an investigator, they all worked in the same fundamental way. When you consider that technology is a hard taskmaster and that online services hit the proverbial fan almost as fast as they spend their venture capital money (MySpace anyone?), will Bitcoin still be valuable and newsworthy in two years, or even a year? Could Ethereum be the next Facebook of the currency world and become the default choice for transactions and contracts of all types? Only the future will answer that question, but the methods of investigating crime involving a cryptocurrency will remain basically the same. So, although Part II of this book deals with investigations that are focused on tools for Bitcoin with its spin-offs and alt-coins, and Ethereum, this is only because tools are available for them. Should Monero take the limelight in a few years' time, undoubtedly an investigator will be able to find similar tools to help them investigate effectively.

In late 2017, investopedia.com, the world's largest financial educational website, named Litecoin, Ethereum, Zcash, Dash, Ripple, and Monero as the best investable cryptocurrencies aside from Bitcoin, but that should not necessarily drive research by an investigator. Some of the new breeds of currency lend themselves to criminal uses. For example, Zcash offers "shielded" transactions where the sender's and receiver's details are hidden, and Dash provides increased anonymity over Bitcoin. It is more likely that these features, rather than Bitcoins' burgeoning value, would attract someone with the need to hide his or her transactions for nefarious purposes.

I should be clear that I am in no way accusing these companies of deliberately attracting a certain type of client any more than Tor (which was partly developed and funded by the U.S. government) was designed to hide terrorists and pedophiles. However, if you, as an investigator, are aware of the specific security and anonymity features of a particular currency, you may be more prepared to research and ultimately exploit them during an investigation.

Due to these issues, I will decline from the obvious inclusion of a list of available cryptocurrencies, since by the time you read this, there may be a new pretender in town being used by our suspects. Instead, this book will try to both be specific as to investigation methods you can use now and look at the generic principles behind this type of analysis.

The website Coinmarketcap.com maintains a constantly updating list of the primary cryptocurrencies, almost 900 were listed at the time of writing.

If you are interested in launching your own cryptocurrency and becoming wildly wealthy, you will find an excellent tutorial at www.ethereum.org/token. (And once you are a billionaire, please remember who gave you the tip and at least invite me onto your boat!)

Is Blockchain Technology Just for Cryptocurrencies?

Although we look in detail at what a blockchain is in Chapter 3, suffice it to say that it is simply a list of transactions, distributed to many nodes on a network, grouped into clusters called blocks, and—using a physical analogy—stacked on top of one another like a Lego™ brick tower.

The concept of a virtually anonymous, distributed ledger, contract-led blockchain-based system certainly has some significant possibilities, but believing what you read in the press and in a company's marketing materials would be a major mistake. In 2018, you need to include two terms in your prospectus to float your company on the stock market or add to your brochure to sell your latest product: artificial intelligence (AI) and blockchain! In fact, throwing a bit of "cloud" in there couldn't hurt either. I saw the marketing headline "The First A.I. Big Data Marketing Cloud for Blockchain" on a software website recently. It seems that any system that adds up 2 + 2 or includes an "if . . . then" decision tree is now considered AI that may take over the planet at any moment. It's not and it won't, even if it's got a lot of "big data in the cloud"!

It is the same issue with the blockchain: Business analysts have watched the extraordinary rise in the value of Bitcoin, read an article on the technology it is based on, and then added the word to any system that needs to sound a bit more hip and cool (although I am well aware that the words "hip" and "cool" themselves are no longer considered "hip" or even "cool").

A quick search of the Internet reveals insurance companies that will put your insurance agreement on the blockchain, delivery companies that will use smart contracts to deliver your parcel, auction sites that use the blockchain to reduce fraud, and security companies that promise the blockchain will prevent you from ever being hacked again. Sound far-fetched? Most are. But consider the following auction-house example.

Several years ago, I bought an old book at auction—or at least I thought I had bought it since I was the final bidder. However, the auction house told me later that it did not have a record of my final bid, and since the previous bid hadn't reached the reserve, the book would be put up for sale again. Because the auction software was hosted in a single location and the auction house controlled it, I had no recourse or way of proving otherwise. However, I had taken a screenshot of my browser with my high bid and my successful purchase message. The auction house then told me that it had "lost the book." After a few choice words and threats of legal action from me, it "found" the book and honored the bid. It was clear that the auction house wanted more from the auction and simply wanted a chance to sell again with a better audience. How would a blockchain-based system have improved this situation?

A blockchain auction system could work as follows: Every bidder is a node on the blockchain. A product to be auctioned is set up as a token with a contract of sale connected to it, based, for example, on the Ethereum network. Each bid made is a transaction between the auction and the highest bidder with the "token" moving seamlessly from high bidder to high bidder. Whoever is the final bidder when the real or virtual gavel comes down is left as the owner of the token. Everyone on the blockchain can see the final transaction, and the contract is set. I own the item because I own the token, and it's proven by every node on the network. The sales contract can also form part of the blockchain contract, minimizing paperwork. (If anyone sets this system up and makes a million, please once again remember me when you are out on your yacht.)

How does this affect the investigator? Blockchain transactions on Bitcoin are one aspect of the technology and require a skill set that you will learn about in this book. However, in the future expect to find blockchain-based systems with transaction-centered contracts in a wide variety of business sectors. An analyst will need to have the skills to learn how a blockchain functions, and be able to decode contracts, and follow the flow of contract transactions. I will cover contracts in a little more detail later in the book, but if you choose to carry out further research on the smart contract-based platforms such as Ethereum, it would not be a waste of time.

Setting Yourself Up as a Bitcoin User

If you have not had a chance to either trade cryptocurrencies or just play around with the technology, I suggest that this would be a good time to just go and spend some time looking at transactions—perhaps by going to an online blockchain viewer such as `www.blockchain.info`, which we will use numerous times during the book. You will see block numbers—click one. Then you will see a long list of transactions. What can you figure out just from looking at this list? (We will cover everything in due course.)

Primarily, it would be a good time to set yourself up as a "full node" Bitcoin user. This will be necessary if you are to follow and practice some of the more advanced investigation techniques later in the book.

Here's the setup procedure:

1. Browse to `bitcoin.org/en/download` and download Bitcoin Core.

2. Install Bitcoin Core to the default locations.

As soon as you run Bitcoin Core for the first time, it will start to download the entire blockchain. This is fine, but at the time of writing, it takes up about 170 GB on the disk, so you will need to make sure that you have enough space for the initial download as well as the space for it to grow as it synchronizes with the Bitcoin network. It's also a good idea to experiment with the Bitcoin Testnet network where you can't lose any money. You will need another 80 GB or so for that.

If you wish to have the blockchain files on a different drive, it's easy to do. Just follow these steps:

1. Right-click your desktop and create a new shortcut. The path is usually:

   `C:\Program Files\Bitcoin\bitcoin-qt.exe`

2. Add the following to the end of the command:

   `-datadir=d:\Bitcoinfiles`

   where the path is the new folder where you would like the blockchain created (see Figure 1-2).

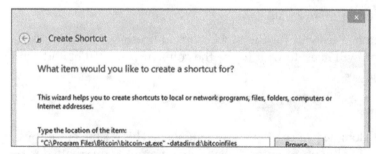

Figure 1-2: Dialog box to create a shortcut to run Bitcoin Core.

Remember to start Bitcoin Core from this shortcut each time. Start Bitcoin Core and allow a couple of days for the blockchain to fully download. You can stop and start it as you wish, and it will carry on from where you stopped it.

Initially it will be beneficial to use Bitcoin Testnet. This is a fully working Bitcoin environment, but the coins are free, and you can send them around and analyze the results exactly as if you were on the actual live Bitcoin environment. Follow these steps to access and use Testnet:

1. Locate the Start Menu Bitcoin Core group and the green shortcut to start the testnet version (see Figure 1-3).

   Again, you can edit this shortcut with -datadir if you wish to change where the blockchain will be stored.

Figure 1-3: The three options in the Bitcoin Core program group.

TIP If your path has a space, remember to enclose it in double quote marks. For example: -datadir="d:\bitcoin files"

2. Start Bitcoin Testnet and allow the blockchain to download.

   You can run the main core and the Testnet at the same time.

3. Send your wallet some coins.

   You do not need to wait for the blockchain to finish before doing this, although you will need to wait to see the coins in your wallet and send them on again.

4. While you are waiting, select **File ⇨ Receiving Addresses** on the Bitcoin Testnet wallet.

   You will see a long sequence of letters and numbers. This is a bitcoin address. (It's actually a value represented in Base58, but more about that later.)

5. Right-click and copy the address onto your clipboard.

6. Browse to http://bit.ly/2fcuEEl and paste in your address.

   Two testnet Bitcoins will be sent to your wallet. Once the blockchain has finished downloading, you will see a balance that you can now spend.

7. Go back to the Receiving Addresses dialog box and click the New button.

8. Copy the new address onto the clipboard and click the Send button on the menu bar (see Figure 1-4).

Figure 1-4: The Send screen in Bitcoin Core.

9. Paste the new address into the Pay To box, choose how much Bitcoin to send, and click the Send button (see Figure 1-5).

You have just sent yourself some Bitcoin. Congratulations.

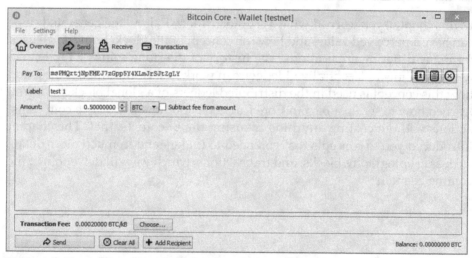

Figure 1-5: The Send screen with send address filled in.

10. In the Transactions dialog box, you will be able to see the transaction you just did. Double-click the transaction line, and a box will open that includes a long string titled `Transaction ID`. Copy this long value onto the clipboard.

11. Browse to `http://bit.ly/2jKBPso_` and paste the value into the Address search box at the top of the screen.

You should see a representation of your transaction taken from the blockchain (see Figure 1-6). Again, congratulations.

Details

1 Input Consumed

387.55928546 BTC from
mp87sgmyxiUs88a3vk8cdShnut7nwt2Wf3 (output)

2 Outputs Created

1.79576774 BTC to
mxnn5V6GPaaqXTYWzsaqhc12SzS5Rwv9BW (spent)

385.76238772 BTC to
n17MCfdfEPmp3B9R8jqaN4JNx8SHMiqJaZ (spent)

Figure 1-6: Blockchain viewer showing a transaction.

I will explain every aspect of what you can see on this screen in a future chapter, but for the time being, you now know how to send bitcoin and find your transaction on the blockchain.

Summary

In this chapter, you learned what a cryptocurrency is, how the generated coins can have a perceived value, and how the concept of the blockchain can be used for many differing applications. The history of the stone coins of Yap helped to explain how a decentralized ledger can work in a community setting and how this concept is used in the distributed ledgers of a global blockchain. You learned how to set up a Bitcoin Core full node and how to practice coin transactions without costing anything by using the Bitcoin Testnet. The chapter introduced you to concepts that you need to understand in much more detail, such as cryptography, blocks, and transactions, which we will delve into in the coming chapters.

The Hard Bit

I think it's only fair to apologize for this chapter. You probably didn't become an investigator because mathematics was your strong point or you wanted to spend your workdays enjoying the beauty of hashing algorithms and Elliptic Curve Cryptography schemes. On the other hand, you may be a complete geek like me and enjoy learning about something that is outside your comfort zone. If you have been involved in digital forensics or any information security role for any length of time, many of the concepts described in this chapter will already be familiar to you.

You may be thinking, "Is this crypto stuff really needed?" To be honest, it is. The very fundamentals of a cryptocurrency are based around the relationship between a private key and public keys derived from it, and if you do not understand this central relationship, you will be at a disadvantage from the start. In fact, every element—from the keys just mentioned to the hashing of block headers to the Merkle Tree—requires a reasonable understanding of the subject. I recommend sticking with it.

Why does an investigator need to know this? I have always believed that investigators or analysts need to be able to provide a reasonable explanation not only of the intelligence or evidence they see, but the lower-level interpretation of that evidence.

Here's an example that will resonate with digital forensics people and may help you to understand my thinking. As I alluded to in the Introduction, a forensics person may run a carving tool over a hard drive, memory dump, or other storage device and extract a JPEG file that is the smoking gun: the proverbial nail in the coffin for the suspect. However, can we trust the tool? How did the file get there in the first place? A good analyst will know, or be able to discover, the header of a JPEG file, return to the offset address on the storage device, and extract the file manually. With key evidence, one tool should never be trusted or the evidence taken at face value. In my RAM Analysis class, I teach students the possibility that an image file could be discovered in computer memory by a carving tool, but that several explanations exist for the image being there without the knowledge of the user. This would completely change the interpretation of that evidence in the case. I demonstrate that in those circumstances, the carving tool could not be trusted. If this image was an illegal image of a child, for example, the provenance of that image—how it got there—is critical to the suspect's guilt or innocence. As you examine blockchain evidence, you may be tempted to rely purely on a tool to interpret the data, but a good investigator should be able to explain how a tool came to its conclusion and provide an appropriate technical explanation to a senior officer, manager, or even a court of law.

However, if you do a Google search for "bitcoin crypto" or "understanding public/private key infrastructure" the results are often inaccessible to anyone without a mathematics degree, with lots of equations and words like "inference" and, probably least helpfully, a good smattering of the word "obviously" when describing something that, to my eye, it is not obvious at all! This chapter covers the subject to the extent necessary to hopefully enable you to understand the concepts without the need for the detailed math.

Hashing

I was introduced to computer or digital forensics a little less than 18 years ago by an extraordinary physics professor named Haniph Latchman. I stood in his lab at the University of Florida while he described the process of imaging (copying) a hard drive and the new range of tools that were available to search and analyze the data within. It was also the first time I had heard the term *hashing*. A computer hard drive could be "hashed" to generate a string of characters, and to check if anything had changed in any subsequent copy of the data. The drive could be "hashed" again and if the value didn't match, something had changed and hence the evidence was not reliable. Although I had been programming computers since I was 13 and at the time was the boss of a company that specialized in building company intranets, I had never stumbled across this concept of a hash based on a one-way algorithm.

How a hash works is very simple to explain; however, the math is significantly more complex.

Take some data (for example, a word, a file, a hard drive, or the contents of the Library of Congress) and run it through a hashing algorithm, such as the popular MD5 algorithm. With the example of MD5, this will result in a fixed length of 32 hexadecimal characters. What makes this process really clever, though, is that the process cannot be reversed. If I take my first name, Nick, and run it through MD5, I get the following value:

```
fd144f65f19df1c7adaa116c44ce2617
```

However, if I take that value and try to reverse the process mathematically, I can never find the original value. I will talk about using brute-force methods to crack hashes later in the chapter, but the fact remains that I can give you a hash value, but you cannot work out the original input value using any mathematical function. My colleague Dave Hoelzer uses the illustration of turning a pig into a sausage using a sausage machine. You can never turn the sausage back into a pig by sending it back through the machine. Gross I know, but a good analogy.

In computer forensics, this is useful in a number of ways. First, you can prove that a file or a drive has not changed by hashing it and then checking a previous hash to ensure they are the same.

> **NOTE** Yes, I know that MD5 was broken by Chinese researchers, but creating collisions by making two files that have the same hash or deliberately creating a file with a particular hash means having full control over the input files. In digital forensics, you do not just hash the drive and drive image; you hash each individual file too, even using multiple hashing algorithms so that if one is undermined the other should be fine.

Second, you can use a hash to detect if you have a particular file on your computer or in a set of evidence. This is very useful in detecting the presence of illegal material such as child pornography. The UK police had a program a few years ago to hash child abuse images from Hi-Tech Crime Units and combine them in a master list. The benefit of a one-way hash is that the police can send that list to any investigator to check if illegal images form part of a case, with no risk that anyone can re-create the original images from the hash values.

As mentioned previously, MD5 was successfully attacked by Chinese researchers and others, so we generally use other types such as SHA, RIPEMD, and others. In this book, SHA256 is referenced quite a bit. A number of different versions of SHA exist, including SHA1 (which is not really an improvement over MD5), 224, and 256. What do the numbers mean?

First, here's a quick tutorial about how anything digital works, which will help you understand some aspects of hashing:

- A *bit* is a 1 or a 0 signifying on or off, respectively.
- 4 bits is a *nibble*. (I'm not kidding—it really is. It will come up in a quiz one day, and you will thank me!)
- 8 bits is a *byte* (2 nibbles).
- 1024 bytes is a *kilobyte*.

> **NOTE** Actually, a kilo is a factor of 1000, but that doesn't divide by factor 2 (2, 4, 8, 16, 32, and so on), so it's 1024.

- 1024 kilobytes is a *megabyte*.

> **NOTE** *Mega* means a factor of 1,000,000, but again it doesn't fit the 8 bits to a byte model. But does it mean 1024×1024 bytes or 2^{20} (which is 1,048,576 bytes), or does it mean exactly 1 million (1000×1000) bytes? Helpfully again, they are used interchangeably; the larger calculation is sometimes used by hard drive manufacturers to make their drives seem bigger.

Thankfully, cryptocurrencies use tiny sizes of data, so all you need to concern yourself with are bits, bytes, and the odd kilobyte.

Now back to SHA256. The 256 signifies the number of bits: literally 256 1's and 0's. If I run my name and address through a binary SHA256 generator, I get the following value:

```
00110111 01100110 00110000 01100010 00110110 00110010 00111001 01100011
01100010 01100010 00111001 01100100 00110111 00111001 00110100 01100010
00110011 01100100 01100001 01100110 00110001 00111001 01100110 01100011
01100100 00110110 00111000 00110110 01100001 00110011 00110000 01100001
```

That is rather tricky to read, so to make it easier, we convert it into hexadecimal. Hexadecimal is Base16 and uses the characters 0–9 and then A–F.

256 bits divided by 8 gives us 32 bytes. Each computer character uses 4 bits (1 nibble), which gives us a hexadecimal value with 64 characters in it that looks like this:

```
7f0b629cbb9d794b3daf19fcd686a30a039b47395545394dadc0574744996a87
```

That's a bit easier to read, but it does take a bit of work. Fortunately, calculator programs can do this work for you. For example, try this out:

1. Open a web browser and go to `http://bit.ly/1oRH4Ct`. This is a SHA256 calculator.

2. Type your name in the text box and click the Calculate 256 Hash button.

This will generate the SHA256 hash of your name.

Cryptocurrencies such as Bitcoin use SHA256 throughout their implementation, so knowing what a SHA256 hash looks like, its length, and the fact that it's hexadecimal can be helpful later on in your learning.

Let's stop talking about digital forensics, which has nothing to do with this book, and start looking at how hashing is used in security. A good example is the storage of passwords. In applications written with security in mind, passwords are stored in a database as hashes rather than the raw password.

When you type in your password, it is hashed and compared with the hash in the database. The idea is that as and when the database is hacked (and experience shows that many databases are stolen eventually), the nefarious hacker only gets away with mathematically irreversible hashes. Also, the system administrator never actually sees the original password, so he or she can't go rogue and use it to log in to your super-secret account (except the administrator knows the hash so can usually log in anyway).

So, if you were to steal a database, and all the passwords were hashes, is there a way to reverse the irreversible? Not mathematically, but it turns out we can attack these hashes another way, and it's rather simple.

Imagine if in an even more insecure world than the one we live in, a website recommended that your password was simply your first name. You enter your name, and the website hashes it with something lovely and strong like SHA256 and stores that in its database. Then you, in the role of the hacker, closeted away in your dark bedroom in London or office block in Beijing, steal the database. How can you break the hashes?

If you went to the SHA256 calculator website and typed in the name **Annie**, calculated the hash, and then checked to see if the hash exists in the database, you would probably have no success. Then if you just start trying names in alphabetical order (for example, **Arnie**, then **Alfie**, and so on), it's going to take a *really*, *really* long time. That assumes you are doing this manually, which of course you most likely would not. Instead of typing and hashing each name individually, you could just find a dictionary online that contains every name in the world, write a program to hash each name, and then check the database for each hash (see Figure 2-1).

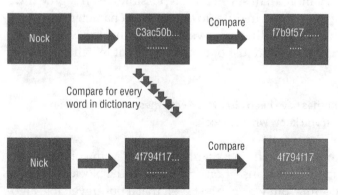

Figure 2-1: Hash a value from a list and compare with the leaked database.

Surely real-world companies don't store their passwords like this, do they?

In 2012, LinkedIn was hacked, and six million SHA1 password hashes were leaked to the Internet with their associated account details. Simply using a large

English dictionary file of common words and passwords, a friend of mine cracked almost 60 percent of the passwords in just a few days on his work computer using exactly the process I just described. What about the rest of the hashes? For that, you can use a technique called brute-forcing. This means you ask the computer not to use a dictionary but instead hash and then try the letter *a*, then *b*, then *aa*, then *ab*, and so on. Even using very fast computers with modern GPUs (Graphical Processing Units) that handle password-cracking well, the time it can take is significant.

NOTE In 2017, Google released a method for cracking SHA1 more quickly, but the issues around brute-forcing hashes apply to other hashing algorithms.

The problem with brute-forcing is the key space involved. The key space is the total number of possible values. Let's assume that an English keyboard has 26 lowercase letters, 26 uppercase letters, 10 numerals, and 32 special characters such as <, >, ?, :, @, and so on. So, a one-character password has 94 possible permutations. What about a two-character password? That's a calculation of $94 \times 94 = 8836$ permutations. And on and on it goes:

- Three letters = $94 \times 94 \times 94 = 830,584$ permutations
- Four letters = $94 \times 94 \times 94 \times 94 = 78,074,896$ permutations
- Five letters = $94 \times 94 \times 94 \times 94 \times 94 = 7,339,040,224$ permutations

And so on.

The numbers get big quickly, don't they? To find the password "Nick1" this method would have to try more than seven billion possibilities. Imagine if we multiply this by 94 three more times in order to obtain an 8-character password. The numbers quickly increase so that even very fast computers would take weeks, months, or even years to find just one password that matches the hash in the database.

NOTE Most LinkedIn hashes have been discovered with these techniques, and they're available publicly if you know where to look.

Why is this relevant to hashing within a cryptocurrency? Many of the checks and balances carried out within a transaction or indeed on the blockchain itself are based on SHA256 hashing, but we have just seen that a non-reversible algorithm can be reversed to its original input, which surely makes it inherently insecure. Let's think about that for a moment. It's only insecure in that we can use either a dictionary attack or a brute-force attack to calculate the hash of every possible permutation and look to see if the hash matches. We have also seen that the possible permutations for just a five-letter input are over seven billion.

In fact, if you kept doing the calculation of 94 × 94 for 10 letters, you would get a number somewhere around 50,000,000,000,000,000,000!

Now imagine if you were going to write down the details of a computer-based transaction between two parties. This would likely include a sender ID, a receiver ID, a unique ID for the transaction itself, a value, and a date and time. Let's visualize it like this:

```
Transaction ID - 12345
Sender ID - ABCDE
Receiver ID - FGHIJ
Value - 2 coins
Date - 25/6/2018
Time 06:26 UTC
```

Hashing these values (which you can try yourself using the calculator mentioned previously) would result in the following:

```
1df77ead6565bfaa82339ae75ba6bcd858a8c1fa870bb0f633984479a2ff6ef4
```

Now that you have a hash, think about how you would reverse this. That data contains 103 characters, which would never exist in that form in a dictionary. So, the only way to reverse it would be to brute-force this 103-character string. Some quick math on a scientific calculator provides possibilities of 17 with over 200 zeros after it. That's more than twice the number of atoms in the universe, so good luck cracking that. This demonstrates that as long as the input to a hash is long enough, reversing it with current technology is impossible.

We will look at hashing within a cryptocurrency in detail later, but this is one of the reasons that hashing in this environment can be trusted. (This is somewhat simplistic, but this is only Chapter 2, and there's a lot more to come!)

If you can understand the concept of a one-way algorithm used in hashing, you can apply this to the fascinating math involved in public and private key encryption.

Public/Private Key Encryption

Cryptography, which literally means "hidden writing," is a fascinating subject, and many books have been written on the topic. The concept of obfuscating a message has been recorded since the dawn of time. Some types of hidden writing in Egypt and ancient Mesopotamia have been discussed and disputed, but systems used by the Greeks and Romans were certainly simple attempts at sending secret messages. The problem of a hidden writing system is not just the strength of the encryption method or even the transmission of the message—it's the key!

If I encrypt a message to you using some code, I may be able to send it to you with confidence—perhaps I can email it, send it by courier, or call you and read it over the phone. The problem is that the message is useless without the key to unlock it. The key could be a password, but how do I transmit that to you securely? I can't encrypt it or it too will need a password, and so on. Even if there is no password but a method of obfuscation, such as moving all letters in an alphabet three places to the right as in the example of a Roman Caesar cypher, I still need to communicate those details to you. Even with the incredible Enigma machines used by the German military during the World War II, the receiver of the encrypted message still needed a key: the start positions of the rotors and plugboard positions (see Figure 2.2). These positions had to be encoded into code books, which became a weak link.

NOTE If you'd like to read more about the history of Enigma machines, I recommend *Enigma, the Battle for the Code* by Hugh Sebag-Montfiore (Weidenfield & Nicolson, 2000).

Figure 2.2: Military World War 2 Enigma machine

However, in 1976, two researchers in Stanford—Whitfield Diffie and Martin Hellman—came up with the concept of being able to generate a key that included a public key, which could be distributed to others and used to encrypt data; and a private key, which could be used to decrypt data, essentially an extension of a one-way algorithm.

> **NOTE** In 1969, James Ellis, who worked for the UK covert government department GCHQ, had an idea that would allow a master or private key to derive another key that could be shared with anyone and be used to encrypt but not decrypt data—an extension of a one-way algorithm. In 1973, Clifford Cocks, who also worked at GCHQ, solved the outstanding mathematical problems, three years before the U.S. researchers. However, because he was working in a covert facility, the information didn't find its way into the public domain until 1987 (see `https://cryptome.org/ukpk-alt .htm` if you'd like to read more about this). So, I'm sorry my American buddies, the Brits got there first.

The process of how a public/private key system works is quite simple and is important to understand as it builds upon hashing to provide a fundamental understanding of cryptocurrency systems. Let's take a look at a simplified process of the RSA algorithm.

RSA Cryptography

Building on the research of Diffie and Hellman, in 1977, Ron Rivest, Adi Shamir, and Leonard Adleman published a paper that detailed an asymmetric cryptographic system that, in simplistic terms, would use the product of two large prime numbers to generate a public and private key. The public key can *only* be used to encrypt data, so you can send that key to anyone you wish. That person can encrypt data using the key and send it to you. If you have the private key, you are able to decrypt the data.

Take a look at Figure 2-3.

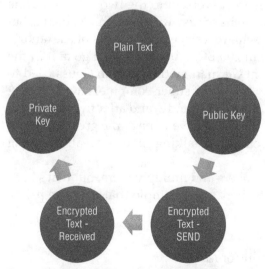

Figure 2-3: The encryption/decryption life cycle.

Are you ready to learn your first bit of technical know-how about cryptocurrencies? Here we go:

- A Bitcoin address that is used to send or receive bitcoin looks like this:

  14JYksKoNzDV98JocdJNPVgY9LQ12ZRM9s

- *A Bitcoin address is just a public key.*

- The key was derived from a private key in a user's wallet.

So, the key points for an investigator are as follows:

- If you have the private key, you can decrypt or resolve any public keys and/or Bitcoin addresses that came from it.

- This means you control the contents, or the value, of the address.

- If you only have a public key, you cannot derive the private key to take ownership of coins controlled by it.

One of the things we will be looking at later is how to recover a user's private key from his or her computer or device, because if you control the private key, you control all the funds associated with it. This can be critical in an investigation and if you want to seize funds.

How does a private key generate a public key in such a way as to be impossible to reverse the math? I will describe the RSA methodology processes in a very simplified manner, but I hope you will take the primary aspects away from it.

The first thing you need is two prime numbers (a prime is a number that can only be evenly divided by itself and 1). If you multiply two prime numbers, you get a result that isn't a prime, and here is the odd thing: there is no easy mathematical way to take the result and reverse it to the two original prime numbers, a method called *factoring*. It seems so easy when you think about it, but mathematicians have been trying to achieve it since Eratosthenes of Alexandria had a crack at it (no pun intended) in 200 BC. Fibonacci had a go at it in the 12th century, and finally, the eminent German mathematician Gauss tried to no avail in the 19th century. In today's world of super-computers, we still can't do it. Now, you might have tried multiplying 17 and 3, and after five minutes of trial and error with a calculator, thought you solved one of the great mysteries of mathematics, but the prime numbers we are talking about are really big, long primes—over 100 digits long.

We could take two large prime numbers and multiply them, but that's hard to visualize. So to keep this simple, here's an example that uses the prime numbers 23 and 11:

1. We multiply the two primes: $23 \times 1 = 253$

   253 becomes our maximum value or *MAX*.

2. Next, we choose any value below our *MAX* ceiling value.

   For the purposes of this example, let's choose the number 13. This becomes our public key or *PUB*.

3. We now apply the Extended Euclidean Algorithm. (I will not go into the mathematical details for this equation, but feel free to Google it.) The equation looks a bit like this:

   $ax + by = gcd(a,b)$ where gcd is the greatest common denominator.

   This calculates to a value of 17. This is our private key or *PRIV*.

   We now have the following three values:

   - *MAX* = 253
   - *PUB* = 13
   - *PRIV* = 17

4. Next, we compose the plaintext that we want to encrypt to send to our colleague.

   To keep things as easy as possible, we will send just the capital letter *C*. The ASCII code for *C* is 1000011 in binary or 67 in decimal value.

5. We take the value and multiply it by itself *PUB* times. We know that *PUB* = 13, so the math looks like this:

   $67 \times 67 \times 67 \times 67 \times 67 \times 67 \times 67 \times 67 \times 67 \times 67 \times 67 \times 67 \times 67 =$ [*a really big number*]

   We can just display this as 67 to the power *PUB* or 67^{13}.

   We now have an encrypted value of [*a really big number*] for the letter *C*, but the problem is that we can simply reverse it by factoring it back like this:

   $13\sqrt{}$ [*A really big number*] = 67 = C

   That would be fairly useless encryption.

6. The next step is a little complex but very clever. This is where our *MAX* value comes in. When we multiply 67 × 67, instead of the answer being 4489, the result cannot be more than our *MAX* value, which we know to be 253. When the result hits 253, it rolls around to zero, then back to 253, rolls around to zero, and so on, until 67 has been multiplied by itself *PUB* times.

   If we multiply 67 × 67, we get the result 4489. If we roll around to zero, we eventually end up with a value of 188 (see Figure 2-4). It works like this:

   4489 mod 253 = 188

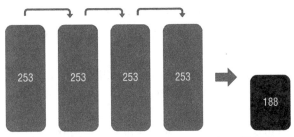

Figure 2-4: Every time we reach the max value of 253, we start from the beginning, providing a remainder of 188.

7. We then keep multiplying by 67 *PUB* times or 67^{13}, but this time rolling around when we hit the *MAX* of 253.

You can work this out with a scientific calculator by doing the following:

$$\text{Mod}(\text{remainder} \times \text{plaintext}, \text{MAX})$$

We can visualize this process in the following table:

CALCULATION NO.	SUM (MOD(253))	VALUE
1	67×67	188
2	188×67	199
3	199×67	177
4	177	221
5	221	133
6	133	56
7	56	210
8	210	155
9	155	12
10	12	45
11	14	232
12	232	111

We are left with the encrypted value of 111 representing the letter *C*. You may ask why there are only 12 calculations when *PUB* is 13. This is because 67^{13} only has 12 calculations. (Remember $67 \times 67 \times 67 \times 67 \times 67 \ldots$).

Here's how this works in practice:

1. We set up our calculation and derive a public and a private key.

2. We send the public key to our colleague Tom.

3. Tom can now use the public key to encrypt the letter *C* and send us the ciphertext *111*.

   If an attacker manages to intercept the ciphertext, he can only obtain the public key and therefore does not have enough information to reverse the message.

4. Once we receive the message, to reverse the value, we simply take the encrypted value, 111, and multiply it *PRIV* times or:

   $$value^{PRIV}$$

   So, in this case, we have 111^{17}.

You can do this with Mod again if you like. Remember that although *PRIV* = 17, you only do 16 calculations because the initial value counts as 1.

CALCULATION NO.	SUM (MOD(253))	VALUE
1	111 × 111	177
2	177 × 111	166
3	166 × 111	210
4	210 × 111	34
5	34 × 111	232
6	232 × 111	199
7	199 × 111	78
8	78 × 111	56
9	56 × 111	144
10	144 × 111	45
11	45 × 111	188
12	188 × 111	122
13	122 × 111	133
14	133 × 111	89
15	89 × 111	12
16	12 × 111	67

There we are, back to the number 67, which is ASCII for C.

You are now an expert in public/private key infrastructure!

It's worth imagining, though, what that calculation would look like with two initial prime numbers of perhaps 100 digits long, then multiplied to give an enormous *MAX* value. Then a public key maybe 80 digits long and a private key of similar length. The calculations involved are immense, and without the private key, trying to factor back without knowledge of the initial primes becomes computationally infeasible.

I hope that made some sense. It really is extraordinarily clever, and although I "high-five" the British inventors, the roles of Diffie, Hellman, Rivest, Adleman, and Shamir cannot be applauded enough.

Elliptic Curve Cryptography

Now that you've spent the last few minutes straining to twist your brain around the concept of prime numbers, powers, and factors, you are well prepared to understand the cryptographic system used by many cryptocurrencies such as Bitcoin, Elliptic Curve Cryptography (otherwise known as ECC).

You can compute how much energy is needed to break a cryptographic algorithm and compare that with how much water that energy could boil. By this measure, the technology website Ars Technica reported that breaking a 228-bit RSA key requires less energy than it takes to boil a teaspoon of water. Comparatively, breaking a 228-bit elliptic curve key requires enough energy to boil all the water on earth. In slightly easier terms to visualize, a 256-bit ECC key is comparable to a 3072-bit RSA key, a 512-bit ECC key is equal to a 15360-bit RSA key, and so on.

I will try to explain how ECC works in the simplest way possible. If you want to research this subject more thoroughly, numerous websites, YouTube videos, and books are available that will help you understand it more fully.

ECC works on the principle that computers find multiplication easy and division hard. In the RSA example, if you multiply a value by itself n number of times with a roll-around MAX value, it's easy for the computer to do the multiplication, but it's essentially a brute-force job to try every permutation to reverse the calculation to find n. ECC uses equations to plot points on a curve, and by connecting points, we can infer other values.

Many different types of ECC curves exist, but they all look visually similar and all reflect across the x-axis. Bitcoin uses the secp256k1 curve defined by the National Institute of Standards and Technology (NIST), which is often visualized in a similar fashion as what's shown in Figure 2-5.

The elliptic curve algorithm does not produce this clean line from Figure 2-5 but generates a vast number of points on a graph in the x-, y-, and z-axis, which can be joined in a large mathematical dot-the-dot game to form the pleasing-looking shape similar to Figure 2-5. The reality in a full implementation of ECC is that there would be a hugely complex pattern of dots on an incomprehensibly large graph.

If you take a private key, which is simply achieved by picking a number between 1 and 2^{256}, you can then plot values onto the graph using the following equation:

$$PUB = PRIV \times GEN$$

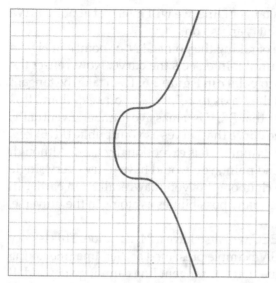

Figure 2-5: A visualization of an elliptic curve on a graph.

where *PUB* is the public key, *PRIV* is the private key, and *GEN* is the generator point on the graph (which is a known point in the Bitcoin implementation).

This is the same as adding *GEN* to itself *PRIV* times in a row. In ECC, adding a point to itself creates a tangent line that will intersect the curve at a new point.

Once we have a new point, this is then reflected across the x-axis to a new point and then repeated *PRIV* number of times. Figure 2-6 shows my attempt to visualize this.

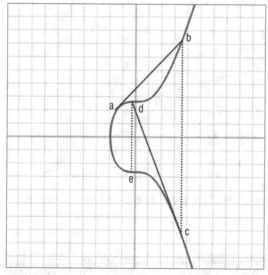

Figure 2-6: Intersecting lines on an elliptic curve and reflecting across the x-axis.

If we start at point *a* and create a tangent line, we will intersect at point *b*. We then reflect across the x-axis to point *c*, and so on.

If you can, play the mental game of taking the point *GEN*, or point *a* in Figure 2-6, and then drawing its tangent until it intersects the curve. Now, reflect the point on the curve across the x-axis to point *c* in Figure 2-6. Then take the tangent again to point *d*, and reflect across the x-axis to point *e*. As you keep doing this *PRIV* a number of times, remember that *PRIV* is a massive number. Eventually, you will end up with a point on the curve that serves as your public (*PUB*) key.

Reversing that to try to find *PRIV* from *PUB* is exceptionally hard. Although you know the start point and the end point, you would have to try every single possible value of *PRIV* to find the right one. As you may recall from earlier in the chapter, a 256-bit number has as many possibilities as atoms in the universe, so it's going to take a while!

To make life a little harder, the ECC will also have a *MAX* value. This is very similar to the *MAX* value in the RSA example presented earlier. Imagine taking the curve but defining a *MAX* value that our tangent line cannot go beyond. If it hits the *MAX* value, it re-enters the graph reflected across both the x-axis and the y-axis. As illustrated in Figure 2-7, the tangent leaves the *MAX* value of the graph and re-enters at the bottom before intersecting the curve at point *b* and then reflecting across the x-axis as normal.

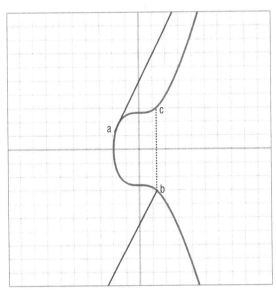

Figure 2-7: The *MAX* value means the tangent "leaves" the graph and re-enters reflected in the x- and y-axis.

Those of you who have been around computing for a while might remember playing the old computer game Asteroids. It was a simple game where you flew your little line-drawn arrow-shaped ship around and fired at asteroids, which became faster and smaller asteroids when they exploded. But the playing universe was only the size of the screen, so if you flew off the screen, exceeding the *MAX* value if you like, you re-entered the screen reflected in the x-axis and y-axis. If you are struggling to picture that, think of flying off the top right of the screen and re-entering at the bottom left (see Figure 2-8).

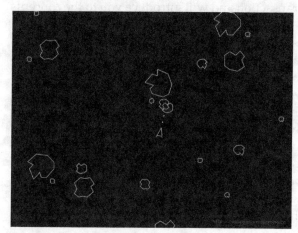

Figure 2-8: Asteroids!

Our *MAX* value does that for the graph and adds a further extraordinary level of complexity to reversing the calculation (see Figure 2-9).

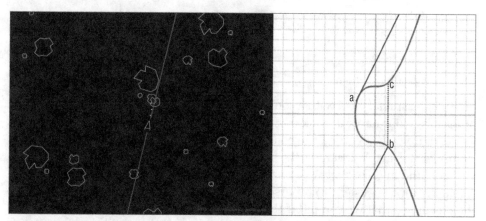

Figure 2-9: Ship leaving the screen and re-entering reflected in the x- and y-axis.

That, in the simplest terms, is how we derive a public key from a private key using Elliptic Curve Cryptography.

Building a Simple Cryptocurrency in the Lab

It's a fun practical exercise to build a simple cryptocurrency in the lab; you can then share it with your friends and colleagues and use it to buy and sell sweets and treats you bring into the office. To be honest you are not really going to do that but you could if you wanted to! This exercise will help you to see the role of hashing to secure each transaction and will introduce you to the concepts of blocks and mining.

You can use Google Spreadsheets to build a ledger that you can give others access to, which will simulate a distributed ledger. Remember, in the real world everyone would have a copy of the ledger but this exercise still demonstrates some useful principles. Once you have set it up, this works well if you can have two or three others sign into the Sheet so you can trade with them. If you have no friends, it's not essential—you can just pretend that you have friends and play the part of everyone! You can share it simply by using File ➪ Publish to the Web and giving the link to your group.

Set up a Google account if you don't have one, and browse to Google Sheets (`www.google.com/sheets/about/`).

Add the following column headings:

Date

Time

From

To

Amount

Hash

Block Hash

Close Block Hash

Save the spreadsheet with a cool coin-type name like NickCoin or EmilyCoin, assuming your name is Nick or Emily; otherwise, you will need to be creative.

Next, if you select the Date column, you can format it by going to Format ➪ Number ➪ Date. You can do the same with the Time column.

Each line in our Sheet will be a transaction between two people or a transaction from the system to a person. For each transaction, we want a hash to be created so that we can tell if the transaction is changed at any time. This is very simple to do, and we will use SHA1 for ease. First, add a script to Google Sheets by going to Tools ➪ Script Editor. Type in the following code, and save it as any name you choose:

```
function GetSHA1(input) {
  var rawHash = Utilities.computeDigest(Utilities.DigestAlgorithm.SHA_1,
```

```
input);
 var txtHash = '';
 for (j = 0; j <rawHash.length; j++) {
 var hashVal = rawHash[j];
 if (hashVal < 0)
  hashVal += 256;
 if (hashVal.toString(16).length == 1)
  txtHash += "0";
 txtHash += hashVal.toString(16);
 }
 return txtHash;
}
```

This code will take cells that you specify and generate a SHA1 hash, compensating for any negative values that may occur. Once that is done, return to your Sheet, and in the first cell of column F, enter the following equation:

```
=GetSha1(A2:E2)
```

When you hit Return you will likely get a hash that starts with 4e9e. This is because it is hashing the empty cells. You can drag and drop the little square in the corner of the cell and drag it down to add the hashing calculation to each cell in the column, perhaps about 10 to 20 cells for the time being.

Now, let's add a transaction. We will start with the system providing you with some "you" Coin. I'll call it NickCoin from now on to make me feel more "Nakamoto"! Fill in the date and time cells on the second row. In the From field, add the word **System**, and type your name in the To field. In the Amount field, enter the number **10**. The hash cell will now automatically update to hash the values in the cells (see Figure 2-10). You now are the proud owner of 10 NickCoin!

| 26/03/2018 | 13:23:00 | System | Nick | 10 | 3045e32ecc7c9b7772f63d6ece437f05 |

Figure 2.10: The line in the spreadsheet where the "system" has given you 10 NickCoin.

Next, add the following calculation to the cell in the Block Hash column on row 10:

```
=GetSha1(A2:E10)
```

This will generate a SHA1 hash of all 10 transactions. Go ahead and fill out nine more transactions from you to friends, between friends, and so on. Obviously, this very simple spreadsheet will not know whether you have enough coins to transact, but you are able to see the transactions build up. If you can have three or four other people logged into the Sheet, they can see the transactions take place in real time and add their own transactions. If anyone changes any transaction, the hash will change and other users of this ledger will be aware of this.

When you get to 10 rows of transactions, the Block Hash column will generate a hash of all the transactions completed (see Figure 2-11). We now want to close the block of 10 transactions so that no one can change them. We do this by mining.

Block Hash	Close Block Hash
4f6cee1982019416cbbd1f9672b9f2f0ab4e4e9d	000026d3250c942ffd44cebb8c663921d04808fd9ff037ff2b6c36cb58d65b56

Figure 2-11: Block hash.

We will discuss mining in much more detail in Chapter 5, but in very simple terms, we carry out calculations to try to find a solution to a problem. We are going to run a program to search, or *mine*, for a hash with a certain number of zeros at the start. This emulates almost exactly what is required for Bitcoin mining. I've written a small mining program in Python. This is what you need to do:

1. Install a good text editor. I strongly recommend Notepad++ from `notepad-plus-plus.org/`.

2. Install Python 2.7 from `www.python.org/downloads/`.

3. Open a new note in Notepad++ and type the following:

```
import hashlib

text = ("Copy Block Hash Here")

for nonce in range(10000000):
  input = text+str(nonce)
  hash = hashlib.sha256(input.encode()).hexdigest()
  print (input, hash)
  if hash.startswith("0000"):
    print ("Found Hash")
    break
```

4. Save the file as **miner.py**.

5. Go back to your NickCoin Sheet, copy the Block Hash value, and paste it where it says Copy Block Hash Here:

```
text = ("Copy Block Hash Here")
```

It should now look something like this:

```
text = ("e97e565b81b9752d8bddc5a5de1a6a60a95280cf")
```

We will review the code in Chapter 5, but essentially it is taking the hash, adding a value called a nonce, which will count from 1 until 10 million and create a SHA256 hash. Once it finds a hash that begins with five zeros, the requirement will be fulfilled and the solution is found.

6. To run the miner, open a command shell in the folder where you saved `miner.py`.

TIP To open a command shell in Windows already in the right folder, open the folder where you want, hold down the Shift key, and right-click white space in the folder window. This will provide an option to Open Command Window Here.

7. Run the following command:

```
python miner.py
```

The miner will run trying each hash one at a time until it finds the solution of a new hash value that has four zeros at its beginning (see Figure 2-12). How long this takes will depend purely on the speed of your computer.

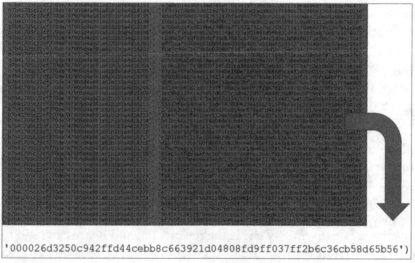

```
'000026d3250c942ffd44cebb8c663921d04808fd9ff037ff2b6c36cb58d65b56')
```

Figure 2-12: miner.py running to find a hash with four zeros at its beginning.

Eventually, the miner will finish, and you will have a hash that starts with four zeros. If you don't have the patience to wait for this, edit the code to have a requirement of just three zeros, save it, and try running it again. If you do not get a result, try changing the Nonce In Range value to 100000000:

```
if hash.startswith("000"):
```

8. You have successfully mined the block! Copy and paste the result into the Close Block Hash cell in row 10.

To make this more realistic, you can have a few friends copy the hash into their own `miner.py` on their computer and race to see who finds the solution quickest. Whoever wins, the next transaction in row 11 should "reward the winner" with 10 NickCoin! This is almost exactly how new coins are generated in Bitcoin.

| 27/03/2018 | 14:23:00 | System | Nick | | 10 | 1dc7811da01025f9cc31fa5cec89ad97 |

Figure 2-13: Awarding 10 NickCoin to the person who mines the fastest.

TIP If Python doesn't run as you expect, it may be a path issue. In the Windows Search or Run box, search for **env**. One of the options will be System Environment Variables. From the dialog click the Environment Variables button. In the bottom box, find the `path` variable and add the path to your Python installation folder at the end of the line. (You would likely add **;c:\python27\.**)

This simple exercise illustrated the following key points:

- Each transaction is hashed.
- Once there have been enough transactions, they are hashed as a block into a block hash.
- "Work" is then done on the block hash to find a solution to a problem, that is, find a hash based on the block hash with a certain number of zeros at the start. This introduces the concept of difficulty. Bitcoin, for example, adjusts the difficulty of closing a block to ensure that new blocks are only closed every 10 minutes or so.

It also illustrates a key lesson about cryptocurrencies. No one ever "owned" any coin on the Google spreadsheet. So how do we know how much each person currently has available to them? The only way is to look at each transaction and add how many coins have been sent to each person and subtract how many coins they have sent to others. There is no account balance, just a series of transactions that a person can say she is the recipient of and hence can send to others. You'll learn about wallets later in this book; however, they do not hold any coins either, but may calculate a balance for you based on coins received and coins sent on the blockchain.

Summary

This chapter dealt with some of the fundamental math that underpins a cryptocurrency. Hashing introduced you to one-way algorithms that are used in many areas of a cryptocurrency, as you will see in more detail in the upcoming chapters. We then extended the concept of a one-way algorithm into the creation of a derived public key from a private key. We are able to distribute a public key, which is only able to encrypt data. The private key can then be used to decrypt the data. You should now have a basic understanding of how RSA and Elliptic Curve encryption systems function.

In this chapter, you also learned that a Bitcoin address is merely a public key that can be used to carry out a transaction (as you will see in Chapter 4) and that if an investigator has access to a private key, he or she owns control of any funds available in derived public key addresses.

We also had some fun building a simple tradable currency on a spreadsheet, which introduced the basic concepts of a cryptocurrency that we will build on in subsequent chapters.

Understanding the Blockchain

As I discussed in Chapter 1, "What Is a Cryptocurrency?" the blockchain is not a specific type of software or installation, but rather a concept of recording contracts and transactions in a ledger that is distributed across many nodes on a network. It is easy to think of the blockchain in terms of a specific product such as Bitcoin or the many alternative coins or other startups that are beginning to use it to provide data security and proof of accuracy of data. Although in the short term, most investigations that an analyst will be presented with will be connected to online currency investigations, it is extremely likely that blockchain contracts and so-called ICOs (initial coin offerings) will make their way into cyber labs across the world.

It is also important for a detective to be able to explain the concepts when asked. I've often seen investigators made to look foolish and their competency called into question because they couldn't explain the fundamentals of a concept that they are being asked to give evidence about.

Understanding the blockchain in a conceptual way can also help an analyst better comprehend how criminals might leverage the technology to either facilitate a crime or hide their activities. This could be illegal purchasing, money laundering, or carrying out a fraud of some type—which can all be achieved on a blockchain system. When you understand the technology, you can better make the connection to understanding and predicting types of illegal activity.

A few years ago, I was working with a country's counterterrorism team that spent a huge amount of time learning how an attacker could potentially distribute a noxious chemical, even mocking up systems to see how they could work. In the same way, understanding the underlying technology and brainstorming how criminals could use it can help you stay ahead of the curve.

In this chapter, we will look at data in its raw form, which will help you understand how the blockchain works in its native view. We will also consider how to extract raw hexadecimal information from a block on the chain and analyze its key components. This enables the investigator to check the accuracy of what a tool is reporting.

In previous chapters, I have talked about the concept of a distributed ledger, given examples of the stone coins used on Yap, and played with a shared online spreadsheet. In this chapter, I will break this down to help you understand the following:

- The structure of a block
- The headers of a block
- The use of hashing and the Merkle tree
- Forks in the blockchain
- The role of the mempool

The Structure of a Block

So, what is a blockchain? Although this may sound overly simplistic, it is a chain of blocks with each block being made up of a number of transactions clustered into a block by mining. Once a block has been mined it is essentially locked, and nothing can be added or changed. Each transaction in the block is then said to have a "confirmation." In your mind, you can think of individual transactions making up a new block, the block being "locked" by mining, and then placed on top of the previous block. Of course, it's not really put on top of anything—the block is simply linked mathematically to the blocks that came before it.

In the case of Bitcoin, once a number of transactions have been made, they are "mined" into a block every 10 minutes or so by solving a mathematical puzzle as discussed earlier. Transactions are either in the mempool (which we'll look at in the next chapter) or part of a mined block.

Ethereum is a little different. Transactions can be in the transaction pool (txpool) or in a mined block. Blocks are mined on Ethereum about every 15 seconds.

You can see how many transactions are included in a block on Bitcoin by browsing to `http://bit.ly/2fyCoRs`. This will show you a live graph of transactions per block. If you choose the All Time option, you can see how the number of transactions per blocks has fluctuated over time, as shown in Figure 3-1.

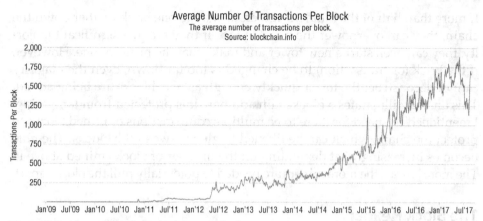

Figure 3-1: Live graph of transactions per block.

As you will learn as we progress, the block is hashed in several different ways, including being hashed together with the blocks that came before it. As more blocks are piled on top, it becomes mathematically more and more difficult to change any transactions further down the chain of blocks.

It is possible for an attacker who controls a significant percentage of all the cryptocurrencies mining capacity to launch what is known as the 51% attack. If the attacker controls over half the blockchain's mining capacity, it is theoretically possible to recalculate several previous blocks and create a new fork in the chain known as an orphan fork. So, it would be possible to "spend" 100 bitcoins, and then, using your mining majority, "fork" the chain to not include the transaction so it would never have been mined and could be spent twice (or "double-spent"). It is generally accepted that six confirmations, or six blocks that have been successfully mined on top of the block containing a certain transaction, make it practically impossible to change the chain. However, the BitcoinWiki (http://bit.ly/2x2Djjf) states that for large transactions, one hundred and forty-four blocks or one day is "required before completing the exchange."

To get a mental picture of a blockchain, I like to think of LEGO® bricks. Imagine the small bricks being transactions—they are clipped together to make a larger block. That block is then placed on the existing Lego™ tower of blocks you have made. If you wanted to change a single brick (representing a transaction in this analogy), the rules state that you must deconstruct the tower, brick by brick, until you get to the brick to change. If the brick you want to change is near the top of the tower, this deconstruction wouldn't be too hard, with not too much work to undo it. However, the further down the tower you go, the harder it becomes.

To complicate matters, let's say it isn't just you building the tower—many builders sat around, building bricks into blocks and adding them to the tower.

If more than half of the builders agreed to change one brick further down the chain, they can overpower the rest—in fact, if they are in a significant majority, they can even start a new tower and make that the primary one. However, if the brick (or transaction) to be changed is too far down, even the majority cannot deconstruct the tower quickly enough as new blocks are being added. This analogy illustrates a blockchain and how it is protected from tampering. I mentioned the need for there to be multiple confirmations or mined blocks to protect the chain, which can be likened to glue between the blocks. The glue becomes increasingly set depending on the number of blocks mined above it. The more blocks, the more miners are needed to potentially pull the blocks apart.

The Block Header

To help you understand block headers, I will focus on Bitcoin as an example. Every mined block has a header with a significant amount of information in it. The header in turn sits atop all the transactions that form the block as a whole. Transactions can be different file sizes depending on the platform. With Bitcoin, a block is always less than 1 MB. The Bitcoin Cash fork, which launched in late 2017, can have an 8 MB block size. This type of fork is different from the orphaned forks mentioned earlier and will be discussed later in the book. Ethereum works slightly differently by setting a cap on the "work" needed to process a transaction—a value known as "gas" (which you'll learn about in more detail in Chapter 4, "Transactions").

As illustrated in Figure 3-2, an entire block in its raw hex is made up of the following elements:

- The first 4 bytes describe the size of the block.
- The next 80 bytes make up the block header.
- The number of transactions takes up the next 1 to 9 bytes and is variable.
- This is followed by all the transactions.

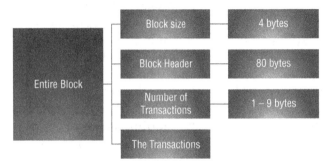

Figure 3-2: Block header and its constituent parts.

The 80 bytes of the block header are further broken up into the following parts (see Figure 3-3):

- Version
- Previous Block Hash
- Merkle Root
- Timestamp
- Difficulty Target

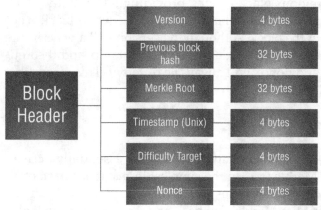

Figure 3-3: The block header.

Version

This value is a version number to track software and protocol upgrades. It's not unusual to see version numbers 2, 3, and 4, as follows:

- Version 1 was seen in the genesis block in 2009.
- Version 2 was introduced in Bitcoin Core 0.7.0 in 2012. Version 2 blocks required that the block height be recorded. This soft fork eventually rejected any Version 1 blocks.
- Version 3 blocks were introduced in Bitcoin Core 0.10.0 in 2015 as a soft fork.
- Version 4 blocks were specified in BIP65 and introduced in Bitcoin Core 0.11.2 in 2015 as a soft fork.

Unusual version numbers, on the other hand, could be an attempt to create a fork in the blockchain.

> **NOTE** BIP stands for Bitcoin Improvement Proposals. Bitcoin users can recommend adjustments, improvements, and additions to the Bitcoin environment. BIPs become "active" when the entire community gives mutual consent by adopting the proposal. You can review all the BIPs by visiting bitcoinbips.org. For example, BIP 151 details recommendations to encrypt Bitcoin traffic. When miners do not agree, you end up with forks such as Bitcoin Cash.

Previous Block Hash

This is the hash of the previous block header, providing a link to the block that sits directly "below" it on the blockchain. Note that the whole block is not hashed—only the header of the block. Although the version will always be the same, the previous block hash, the Merkle root, the timestamp, and theoretically, the difficulty target and nonce, will always be different. This means that the block header hash will always be a unique value.

Merkle Root

The Merkle root is a tricky one to explain but is a value essentially derived from a construct called a Merkle tree. In the simplest terms, it is a hash of all the transactions in the block. Of course, this means that if any transaction in the block changes, it will adjust the Merkle root hash and, by extension, will also adjust the block header hash, providing data protection and resilience. However, the transactions are not simply collated and hashed. There is a structure used that has some very special qualities. This is the way it works:

1. The transaction IDs (TXIDs) are paired.
2. The new value is created by the pair of ID values.
3. This new value, termed an intermediate hash, is double-hashed as follows:

   Hash=SHA256(SHA256(Intermediate Hash)

   In other words, the intermediate hash is SHA256-hashed, and then the result is hashed again, which results in a new SHA256 hash.
4. The result is then paired with another hash created from another TXID pair and then double-hashed, and so on, until you are left with a single hash for the block: the Merkle root. If there is an odd number of transactions, the odd transaction is hashed with itself.

Figure 3-4 shows how four transactions, including the Coinbase, are hashed.

> **NOTE** Coinbase is the value of coins (currently 12.5 bitcoin) that are rewarded in the first transaction of a new block for the successful mining of the previous block.

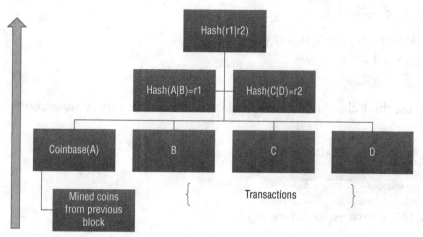

Figure 3-4: Visualization of the Merkle tree.

As you can see in the figure, A and B are paired, and C and D are paired. They are then hashed, and those hashes are combined and hashed.

This method is extremely efficient if you want to check the accuracy of a single transaction, because you only have to download and verify a single "branch" of the tree. The alternative is to hash every transaction in bulk, but that would require you to re-hash every transaction to check just one. This also allows you to verify the order of the transactions by evaluating just the intermediate hashes rather than accessing the entire blockchain.

Imagine having 32 transactions as "leaves" on the tree, where the root value is only separated five steps from any one transaction. This method requires only five (rather than 32) calculations, which is extremely efficient.

Timestamp

The timestamp is recorded in something called UNIX time. It is quickly recognizable as a 10-number string that starts with 15 (until September 2020, when it will start with 16). This value represents the number of seconds from 00:00:00 1 January 1970. The timestamp is the moment the successful miner started hashing the header (see `http://bit.ly/2fDmLrG` for more details from the Bitcoin developer reference).

To reverse the UNIX time into human-readable time and date information, you can use an online calculator such as the one at `www.unixtimestamp.com/`.

Alternatively, you can use Excel to carry out conversion on a list of UNIX timestamps by doing the following (see Figure 3-5):

1. Put your UNIX value into cell A1.

2. In cell A2, type

```
=(((A1/60)/60)/24)+DATE(1970,1,1)
```

3. Format cell A2 as

```
Custom - dd/mm/yyyy hh:mm
```

You can use this technique to convert multiple UNIX timestamps simultaneously.

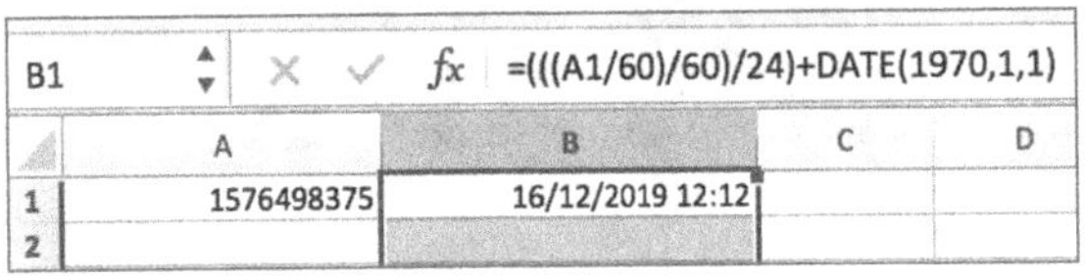

B1		×	✓	*fx*	=(((A1/60)/60)/24)+DATE(1970,1,1)		
	A		B			C	D
1	1576498375		16/12/2019 12:12				
2							

Figure 3-5: UNIX time conversion in Excel.

Difficulty Target

The difficulty target and the nonce work together and define what the miner is trying to find in order to solve the mathematical puzzle, or proof of work, and close the block. The difficulty target is the encoded version of the maximum value that the block's header hash must be less than or equal to.

To visual this, open the Python file you wrote in Chapter 2, "The Hard Bit." The text field where you put your block hash from your Nickcoin spreadsheet would be a similar value to the difficulty target:

```
text = ("Copy Block Hash Here")
```

The nonce is the value that the miner will change to in the Block Header Hash in order to try and fulfill the difficulty target. For example, to try and find a value with a certain number of zeros before it, the miner might enter the following:

```
for nonce in range(10000000):
    input = text+str(nonce)
```

This part of the code sets a nonce value by counting from 0 to 100000000. The value is incremented on each loop and concatenated with the hash from the text variable. This new, longer value is SHA256 hashed as follows:

```
hash = hashlib.sha256(input.encode()).hexdigest()
```

The code then looks to see if the target prefix of five zeros is present in the resulting hash. If it isn't, the code loops around and tries the next nonce value. When the target prefix is found, the result is printed. In the real world, the value is double-hashed but the principle is the same, when the proof-of-work has been found, the block is considered to be mined. It's then added to the chain, and the Bitcoin reward is given to the miner.

Deconstructing Raw Blocks from Hex

With this information about the makeup of a block, we are able to deconstruct the data without the need for an interpreter to do it for us. We can extract the raw hexadecimal from the blockchain and derive the data we need. Why would we want to do that?

It may be possible to extract raw blocks from a memory dump, or extract data from a wiretap. It may even be that you want to interpret the data personally so that you are not relying on the website or software to do it for you. Is the software interpreting the block correctly? How would you know if it wasn't?

The problem with the raw hex from a block is that it looks like this:

```
0200000066191da95594aeda1a98a19ff054a88a510754e2a4d93e0a00000000000
000008485ae797312b2cb37dfb1aac11d7c5ad9dd84364bbe26ffa781853996587d
9b10a06555f586161898a9870dfd0704010000000010000000000000000000000000
0000000000000000000000000000000000000000ffffffff1b0356770506cbcde1b6e
3fb084e8b873474fe192306457336e3ffceffffffffff012143069600000000001976a91
47f8723c3a5e64d6e1d47511863aca2f146b0a85588ac00000000010000001418be
bf3dfe21ea57f50863195e6cdef756aa755087c36aa2c6d597c573892a5010000006a
47304402207b9e4d1c1e126f47db3d74f981b8ee9c124f44a92637a657dc94cd4b0521
6a9a022014fe5df34c6e2c3b1bb1de3f69097873e220b97c0beefd29cc714abeb8180c
880121030e1e08f6d4ba2b71207c961109f9d0b7eaad24b106ecc9b691c297c732d47f
ccffffffff0200e40b54020000001976a914a31e71f2cfc0327c55cc4026073f06f3e9
e1a21a88ac00e40b54020000001976a914d6bbf4f08d2df7ea32b2930ae4b7436d4ca
6fe4b88ac000000000100000003c4b4dda5204f1796e65a5d740b87d2c4540c2a6bf85
fd7e779ad4b789126b94d010000006b483045022045666fd6805ab5264acdc3d2fcbff
c27d0482ef1e0d5dcdb958b18db50767f05022100f53d0fd0ce7951f45beaaa835fbcf
503a167026a685aed83c54dddceafdd58a401210270f83fc138312056466b13236680
642afcffd493fe1866cc74baddee2cf79ba3ffffffff58a0e67c144d64408cc6fa
b19f8131a02ca6a46c0c1ebf4643349b0b4dc0fc7f010000006c493046022100aee71
752f67d3af1bc599a30b9642765b57a59e7eaf4b4eaa41417689b662eb8022100c49
d9f48d26a96
```

And this is only a very small part of an entire block! However, the block header is, as you would expect, at the top, so it's nice and easy to find. Most of the data is the raw transactions, which we will look at later.

To carry out analysis on the header, you will need to install or open a hex viewer or editor. For Windows, I recommend HxD, which you can download from mh-nexus.de/en/hxd/.

Once you have installed HxD, I recommend you set it up as shown in Figure 3-6, Figure 3-7, and Figure 3-8. If you are using any other Hex reader you will benefit from adjusting the byte width to 32, the byte grouping to 4, and the offset base to Decimal.

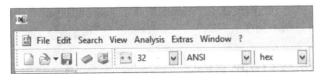

Figure 3-6: Set the byte width to 32 bytes wide.

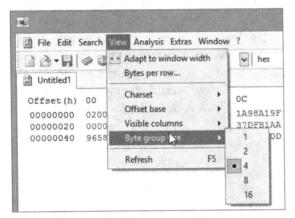

Figure 3-7: Set the byte group size to 4.

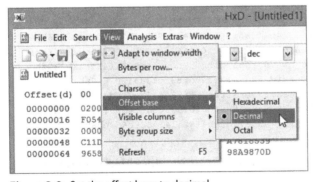

Figure 3-8: Set the offset base to decimal.

We know that the header is 80 bytes, which corresponds to 160 characters. Browse to `http://bit.ly/2xcEmP5`, which is a raw block from the Bitcoin blockchain, and copy and paste more than 160 *characters* into your hex editor. Highlight some of the hex code, and the editor will tell you when you have highlighted 0 to 159 (or 160) blocks. It also gives you the length, which will be 160. See Figure 3-9.

Offset (d)	00	04	08	12	16	20	24	28
00000000	02000000	66191DA9	5594AEDA	1A98A19F	F054A88A	510754E2	A4D93E0A	00000000
00000032	00000000	8485AE79	7312B2CB	37DFB1AA	C11D7C5A	D9DD8436	4BBE26FF	A7818539
00000064	96587D9B	10A06555	F5861618	98A9870D	FD070401	00000000	00000000	00000000
00000096	00000000	00000000	00000000	00000000	00000000	00000000	FFFFFFFF	1B035677
00000128	0506CBCD	E1B6E3FB	084E8B87	3474FE19	23064573	36E3FFCE	FFFFFFFF	01214306
00000160	96000000	001976A9	147F8723	C3A5E64D	6E1D4751	1863ACA2	F146B0A8	5588AC00
00000192	00000001	00000001	418BEBF3	DFE21EA5	7F508631	95E6CDEF	756AA755	087C36AA
00000224	2C6D597C	573892A5	01000000	6A473044	02207B9E	4D1C1E12	6F47DB3D	74F981B8
00000256	EE9C124F	44A92637	A657DC94	CD4B0521	6A9A0220	14FE5DF3	4C6E2C3B	1BB1DE3F
00000288	69097873	E220B97C	0BEEFD29	CC714ABE	B8180C88	0121030E	1E08F6D4	BA2B7120
00000320	7C961109	F9D0B7EA	AD24B106	ECC9B691	C297C732	D47FCCFF	FFFFFF02	00E40B54
00000352	02000000	1976A914	A31E71F2	CFC0327C	55CC4026	073F06F3	E9E1A21A	88AC00E4
00000384	0B540200	00001976	A914D6BB	F4F08D2D	F7EA32B2	930AE4B7	436D4CA6	FE4B88AC
00000416	00000000	01000000	03C4B4DD	A5204F17	96E65A5D	740B87D2	C4540C2A	

Figure 3-9: Raw hex from a block on the Bitcoin blockchain

Once you have 160 blocks highlighted, delete the rest of the hex that you had copied into your editor.

Before delving into this melee of hexadecimal, you need understand a computing concept called Endianness. This section describes the three types of Endianness: Little Endian, Big Endian, and Internal Byte Order.

Big Endian

Endianness is simply the order in which a value is written. We take for granted in Western languages that everything is written to be read from left to right on the page; however, numerous languages are read from right to left including Hebrew, Arabic Urdu, and others. Big and Little endians simply answer this question: from which end do I start reading a value?

Consider, for example, the following decimal string:

    1 2 3 4

This value in Big Endian format is written the same as above: 1 2 3 4.

How can you remember this? If you were to write the decimal columns over each number, you would write "Thousands" for the leftmost column, "Hundreds" for the second column, "Tens" for the third column, and "Ones" (or "Units") for the rightmost column. Hence, the first number is the "big" end of the number, or Big Endian, because the 1 in the string is in the Thousands column.

NOTE The more technical reason for this numeric ordering actually has to do with the most or least significant byte, but that's harder to remember!

Little Endian

This is the opposite of Big Endian. In Little Endian, the value 1 2 3 4 is recorded as 4 3 2 1. In other words, if you were to write the decimal columns, they would be in reverse: "Ones" (or "Units") for the leftmost column, "Tens" for the second column, "Hundreds" for the third column, and "Thousands" for the rightmost column. Because the first digit recorded is from the Ones (or Units) column, you can remember this as the "little" value—hence, Little Endian.

Internal Byte Order

Internal Byte Order is a little more complex than Big and Little Endianness.

Using the 4-byte hex string A91D1966 as an example, Internal Byte Order does several things:

- Its splits the string into its individual bytes: A9, 1D, 19, and 66.
- The individual bytes are read in Big Endian order (left to right) as normal.
- The bytes are then reversed, making the string Little Endian but with each individual byte remaining Big Endian, as follows: 66, 19, 1D, A9.

This is illustrated in Figure 3-10.

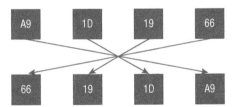

Figure 3-10: Visualizing Internal byte order.

It's not terribly complicated, but it does mess with your head a bit.

EXERCISES

1. How would you write the value 827326 in Big Endian?
2. How would you write the value 123456 in Big Endian?
3. How would you write the value ad9847DF in Little Endian?
4. How would you write the value kettle in Little Endian?
5. How would you write the value 1A2BC3D4 in Internal Byte Order?
6. How would you write the value 789ABCDE in Internal Byte Order?

Answers:

1. 827326

2. 123456

3. FD7489da

4. elttek

5. D4C32B1A

6. DEBC9A78

The Bitcoin header uses both Little Endian and Internal Byte Order. Take a look at Figure 3-11.

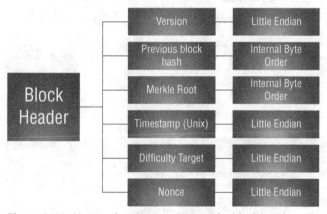

Figure 3-11: How each entity is written in the block header.

Applying This to the Downloaded Hex

In your hex editor, you should have the 160 hex characters that make up the header of the block (this is block 358230 on the Bitcoin blockchain). Take a look at the first 4 bytes or 8 hex characters. This is the version number and Figure 3-12 shows what this looks like in Little Endian format.

This is otherwise known as version 2 of Bitcoin. However, what if you want to find something more interesting like the date and time the block was hashed? You simply need to do some counting, which your hex editor can help you with. You know that there are 4 bytes (8 characters) for the version, 32 bytes (64 characters) for the previous block value, and another 32 bytes (64 characters) for the Merkle root value.

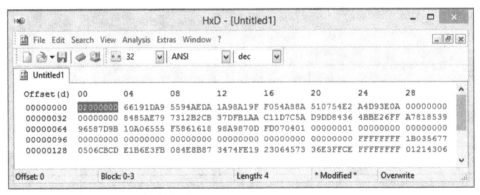

Figure 3-12: The version in Little Endian.

To find the date/time, count the next 32 bytes, which gives you the value of the previous block hash in Internal Byte Order format, as shown in Figure 3-13.

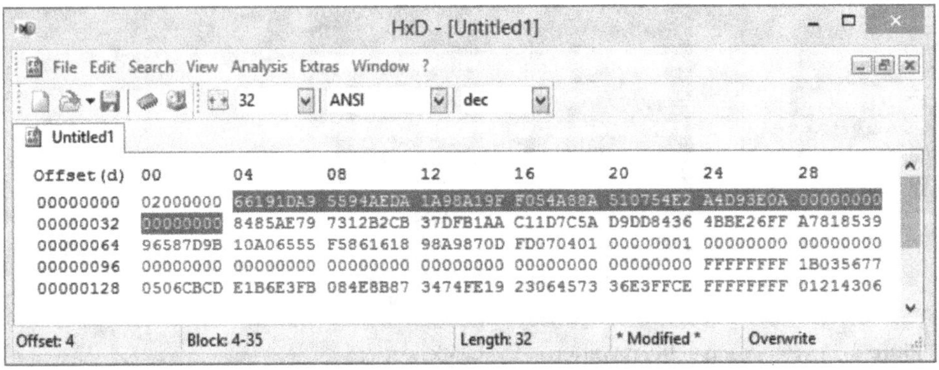

Figure 3-13: Previous block hash in Internal Byte Order.

Then you count the next 32 bytes, which provides the value of the Merkle root as shown in Figure 3-14.

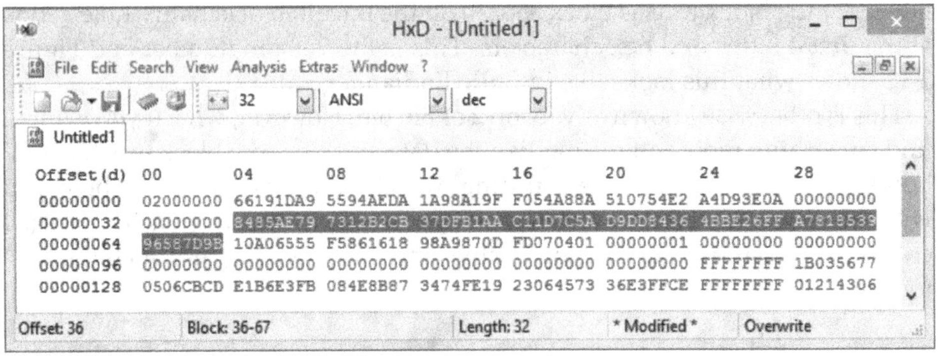

Figure 3-14: Merkle root in Internal Byte Order.

The next 4 bytes are the timestamp, as highlighted in Figure 3-15.

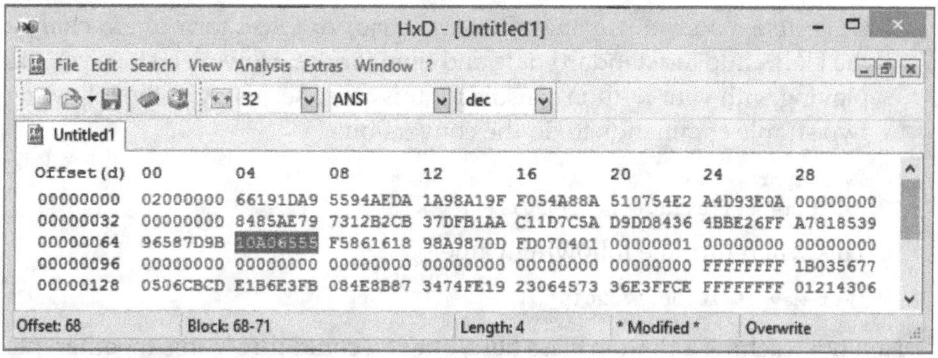

Figure 3-15: Timestamp in Little Endian.

The timestamp is both in hex and in Little Endian format. To turn this into a value that's of use to a human, you need to do some conversion. The hex you have found is

```
10A06555
```

This has to be reversed from Little Endian, so you have a value of

```
55560A01
```

You now need to convert this into a decimal value. Lots of convertors are available online, such as at `http://bit.ly/1ExkXDM`. However, since you now have Python installed on your computer, you can use a very simple Python command to do it for you. Just follow these steps:

1. Open a Windows command shell and type the following:

   ```
   Python
   ```

   If you get an error, it's probably a path issue as I mentioned earlier. You can resolve this by adding the install path to the System Environment Variables. Or, you can simply change directory to the python folder, which is usually in the root of C. Just type the following:

   ```
   cd c:\python27 (where 27 is the python version)
   python
   ```

   You should now be presented with something like this:

   ```
   Python 2.7.13 (v2.7.13:a06454b1afa1, Dec 17 2016, 20:53:40) [MSC
   v.1500 64 bit (AMD64)] on win32
   Type "help", "copyright", "credits" or "license" for more
   information.
   >>>
   ```

2. At the >>> prompt, type the following, which forces a conversion from base 16 to a decimal integer:

   ```
   >>> int("55560A01", 16)
   ```

The value 55560A01 is the hex timestamp value, and the command provides a decimal result of 1431702017. This is the UNIX time value.

3. Of course, you can use an online convertor or Excel formula to change the UNIX into the standard data and time format. However, since you are playing with your Python console for this exercise, just type the following two simple commands to do the conversion:

```
>>> import time
>>> time.ctime(int("1431702017"))
```

This will return the following value:

```
'Fri May 15 16:00:17 2015'
```

I am not teaching a Python class here, but you could throw this together into a very simply little Python script. Open Notepad++, type in the following code, and save it as unix_conv.py:

```
import time

rawtime = str(raw_input("Whats the value from the hex?"))

#The next line flips the hex from little to big endian

flip = rawtime[::-1]

u_time = int(flip, 16)

final = time.ctime(int(u_time))

print final
```

Run the script as follows:

```
python unix_conv.py
```

It will ask for the value in the hex. (Of course, you could save the hex dump and get Python to count it out for you, but I'll leave that up to you.) It then flips it to Big Endian, converts it to decimal (as you did at the console in the preceding exercise), and then does the time conversion.

This simple technique of counting 68 bytes to find the timestamp is a good way of demonstrating how easy it is to extract these values from the raw blockchain data.

Number of Transactions

You can use the same technique to enumerate the number of transactions that are in the block. This number is right after the end of the block header and is stored in Internal Byte Order format.

Directly after the header ends (remember it's 80 bytes or 160 characters long), you'll find a marker FD. The 2 bytes immediately after FD are the number of transactions in the block. However, because they are in Internal Byte Order, you need to do some moving around to be able to decode the value. Follow these steps:

1. Browse back to the raw block you were looking at previously: `http://bit.ly/2xcEmP5`.

2. To make your life easier, copy and paste a few lines of hex that you ascertain by eye is about 200 or so characters. This will ensure that you have the 160 characters of header and the following bytes that you need for the number of transactions.

3. Use HxD or your chosen hex editor to count the 160 characters to the end of the block. (Remember that you need to have the View ⇨ Offset Base menu option set to Decimal.)

   Figure 3-16 shows the count, and Figure 3-17 shows the value that starts with the FD marker.

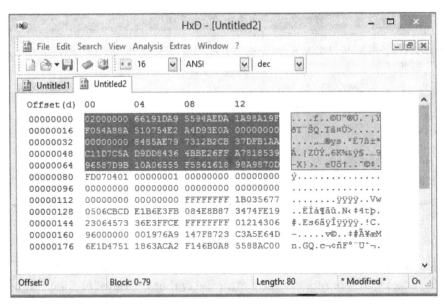

Figure 3-16: Counting 80 bytes.

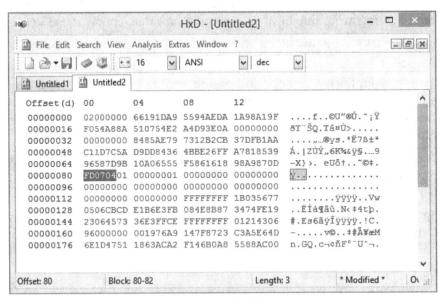

Figure 3-17: Number of transactions bytes prefixed FD.

You now have the following value:

```
0704
```

4. To interpret this value correctly, leave the value of each byte in order but reverse the bytes as follows:

```
0407
```

5. Use the `int` Python command to change this value into its decimal equivalent, as follows:

```
>>> int("0407", 16)
```

This gives you a value of `1031`, or 1031 transactions in this block.

EXERCISES

Take a look at the following raw blocks and find and decode the number of transactions in the block:

1. `http://bit.ly/2xt1p7z`

2. `http://bit.ly/2w3UtOz`

Answers:

1. `1086`

2. `1836`

Block Height

When conducting an investigation, the investigator will often stumble across a block number, which is also referred to as the *block height*. Going back to our LEGO® analogy, this is the number of blocks above block zero.

The first block was block zero, otherwise known as the *genesis block*. If a block has a number or height of 481750, then it is the 481751st block including the zero block.

In the Introduction, I mentioned that the genesis block was created by the Bitcoin founder Satoshi Nakamoto. You can see the raw block at `http://bit .ly/2wAXXeJ`.

Copy the entire hex code into your hex editor. If you're using HxD, remember to turn on View ⇨ Visible Columns ⇨ Hex And Text. In the text column, you will be able to read the hidden message that Satoshi left in the genesis block (see Figure 3-18).

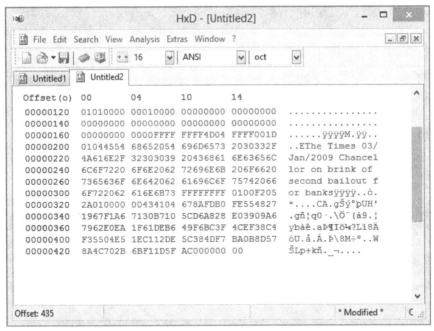

Figure 3-18: The genesis block with text visible.

You can find numerous sites to browse block information for all of the major cryptocurrencies. Some of my favorites include:

- www.blockexplorer.com
- www.blockchain.info
- www.blockcypher.com

We will use these sites and others extensively in the investigation portion of the book, but for now, just take a moment to browse to these sites and perhaps compare how they display the information for block 481961.

Forks

Forks in a blockchain are often considered to be very complex, but in reality, this concept is not very difficult to understand. Think of it as a fork in a road with a decision to be made: Should I go left or right?

Several different types of forks relate to a blockchain and we have discussed a type of orphan fork previously. Orphan forks created by mining synchronization issues happen all the time when a block is mined virtually simultaneously by more than one miner. Let's say that miners all over the world are looking for the proof-of-work solution for block 214002. Two miners find the hash solution at almost the same time. Using the Peer-to-Peer protocol of the blockchain system, these two miners start to tell their peers that they have the solution. Imagine part of the world being told that miner A has the solution, while other nodes around the globe are being told that miner B has the solution. For a time, this means there is a fork: essentially two versions of 214002 on different parts of the network. How is this resolved?

> **NOTE** Bitcoin and Ethereum handle this slightly differently. With Bitcoin, only one miner will receive the block rewards, whereas Ethereum has something called the Ghost protocol that rewards blocks, called *uncle blocks*, that do not end up in the primary block chain.

Within a few minutes, the next block will need to be mined. It is extremely unlikely that a second block would be found by two miners simultaneously, so the branch of the fork that finds the solution to the next block is the block that remains, while the other fork is orphaned. See Figure 3-19.

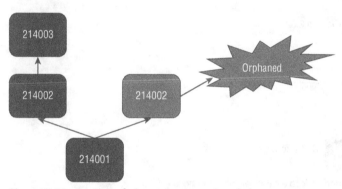

Figure 3-19: A mining fork causing an orphan fork to appear.

The quicker that blocks are set to be mined, the more likelihood there is that blocks will be found at virtually the same time. For example, Bitcoin is 10 minutes, Fastcoin is 30 seconds, and Ethereum is 15 seconds.

The next type of fork is the *hard fork*; this is where miners accept recommended changes to the underlying software and protocols that are not compatible with the historical blockchain. Perhaps the most well-known hard fork is Bitcoin Cash, which increased the maximum block size limit from 1 MB to 8 MB, allowing around four times the number of transactions per day—an increase from approximately 250,000 to 1 million. Another example is the hard fork from Ethereum to Ethereum Classic. The name choice can be a little bit misleading—Ethereum is actually the fork, and Classic is the original. Without the gory details, a hacker managed to extract $50 million in Ether, and a new fork was made to get out of the hole and refund those who had lost money.

A *soft fork* is a software upgrade that is backward compatible with the previous version. Software changes are made and accepted by the mining community, but the change does not cause an underlying adjustment that isn't compatible with past mined blocks.

You will remember that when we looked at the "version" field in the raw hex of a block, it provided a software version number. When a recommendation is made for a significant upgrade that will cause either a hard or soft fork, miners simply have to change their version number in mined blocks to the new version number or leave it as it is. This creates a sort of vote and will either confirm or reject a proposal. For example, the 2015 soft fork that brought in BIP66 had 95% of the miners' hashing power in agreement to change their block version to version 3.

A soft fork has three outcomes:

▪ The miners all agree, and the fork isn't really a fork, just a software change (see Figure 3-20).

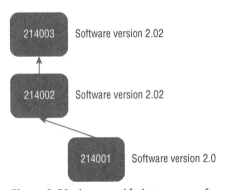

Figure 3-20: An agreed fork to a new software version.

▪ A majority of miners agree, the new fork sticks, and the old fork slowly dies (see Figure 3-21).

▪ A majority of miners disagree, and the new fork dies (see Figure 3-22).

As you can see, forks are really quite simple. When I'm teaching a class on this subject, I often use the illustration of a literal fork in a road. Imagine that you are in a long stretch of traffic and approach a fork. The sign says that there is a better view if you travel to the left, but traveling to the right is a little quicker. Also, depending on how many vehicles use each road, one road will stay open and the other road will be closed.

If the majority of travelers use the quicker road, that becomes the dominant fork, and the other road falls into disuse. This is similar to a hard or soft fork. In some circumstances, a significant number of cars use both roads, so then two approved routes exist. This is like a new hard fork such as Bitcoin Cash.

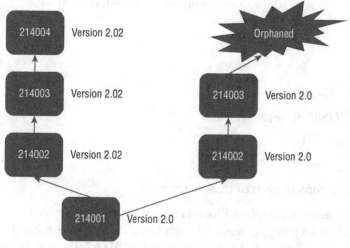

Figure 3-21: The majority of miners agree, and the old fork fades away.

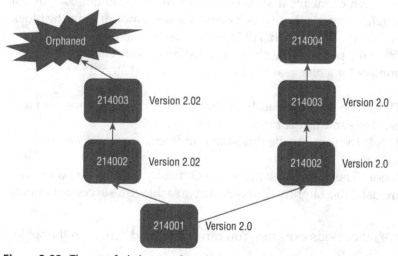

Figure 3-22: The new fork does not have support and dies.

The Ethereum Block

The Ethereum block is different in structure to the Bitcoin block but you will recognize a number of variables from the Bitcoin block.

Ethereum uses the following equation-based notation for each variable in a block and block header:

- Block = B
- Header = H or B_h
- Transactions = B_t

The variables in the block header are very similar to the Bitcoin variables:

- parenthash = H_p
- ommersHash = H_o
- beneficiary = H_e
- number = H_i (like height)
- timestamp = H_g (UNIX time)
- mixhash = H_m (difficulty)
- nonce = H_n

Here are brief descriptions of each of these variables:

Parenthash   This is the same as Previous Block Hash and contains the hash of the previous block in the chain. However, Ethereum uses its own hash algorithm called Ethash, which is a SHA derivative called SHA3-256 and SHA3-512.

Ommershash   I previously mentioned that Ethereum blocks are mined every 15 seconds or so, which means that blocks can often be found almost simultaneously. Ethereum rewards these blocks with a lower amount than the block that has carried on the blockchain. A block that has been correctly mined but doesn't carry the place on the chain is called an *ommer*. There could be a number of ommers for a block, and these are hashed and stored in the ommershash.

Beneficiary   This is the Ethereum address that the block rewards are paid to.

Number   This is the same as the block height in Bitcoin.

Timestamp   This is the same as the timestamp in Bitcoin and is stored in UNIX time format.

Mixhash and Nonce   These are the same as the Difficulty Target and Nonce in Bitcoin but are used in a slightly different way to achieve a successful mining of a block.

A number of other fields exist too. You can find a good article on the subject at http://bit.ly/2fDL213.

Block explorers are available specifically for Ethereum, especially etherscan.io, which is my personal favorite. If you want to take a look at an interesting block, browse to etherscan.io and search for block 3930000. In the comments section is a picture of the Ethereum founder Vitalik Buterin holding a piece of paper with the block height and hash written on it. This is an ingenious "proof-of-life" idea that is similar to holding up a newspaper with the date on it.

It's not easy to get the raw data for Ethereum; however, Blockcypher.com has an API to enable users to get at data via a format called JSON.

API stands for application programming interface. It provides a method to get at the raw data on a database and is used extensively by programmers in many different areas. For example, you can download and use Twitter software; however, if you want to get at the raw data (perhaps to embed Tweets on a website), you can make use of the Twitter API. An API for a blockchain enables you to get at raw block and transaction data.

JSON stands for JavaScript Object Notation. It uses human-readable language to notate data. You can find an excellent tutorial at `http://bit .ly/2yWcuzB`.

You can access data either via a programming language or just from a browser. Although some browsers will try to format the API data, I recommend using Firefox. Using the Add-On Manager, search for JSONView and install it. Then open a Firefox window and type the following:

```
https://api.blockcypher.com/v1/eth/main/blocks/4202088
```

This address asks the API to return information on the Ethereum (eth) block number 4202088. Your browser will return data that looks something like this:

```
{
  "hash":
"0f408977378082b52d10510e4cdb10250d1294a92b80aeb4913c68122420ed9d",
  "height": 4202088,
  "chain": "ETH.main",
  "total": 119556993654581291234,
  "fees": 9926819550000000,
  "size": 3885,
  "ver": 0,
  "time": "2017-08-25T10:45:46Z",
  "received_time": "2017-08-25T10:45:46Z",
  "coinbase_addr": "ea674fdde714fd979de3edf0f56aa9716b898ec8",
  "relayed_by": "",
  "nonce": 16547416540787094411,
  "n_tx": 24,
  "prev_block":
"ef6631ea51f5629bcbf501c8718fbea0fc562207aefcf115d8921d0d86fb7790",
  "mrkl_root":
"23913adc9fb63a8a1bef28089a9cba101bda448498bb1c86b5885dfc260dca5e",
  "uncles": [
    "b6018cf273248c5db96eaefb789eaefcb6f9ee18aa3d5c749219b35e12f181f0"
  ],
  "txids": [
    "4f418d3edf4b605a1999d533ebe3bbe8b4f16f81a6bc153a192f8d6ce3502025",
    "56f560955d26edc755bddabd1a4201cb65a2523025af41faf4d40ed2822d82d2",
    "6fe55b96ad4361e4c744a28d92dcc79aef3370d744f47dc5662455a0e31c838c",
    "8cddec8de1f71c3a2a37eaf65fe293d363f69ce34e1c517ac082cb392cb5794e",
```

```
"00bd72d2e08fe6fcb05a04469080cbb7b4b78e89d9b0756b10d5fc0ed563e0f3",
"0c88baf1bb3b187847ff877b9e5e3d5cf89470d9073b845eda5f39f708176d2a",
"8bb83a4f0f1a1e0a652d84cd431905f2a7fe40061447824a30f9615de0da6188",
"a6990c8fe34caf10684f0304d54d0ea70abe245e1d3b64e34b9411f7feb5aa1b",
"c25a648088ff9cb6c0618733a3c1e48da6d8c3df64eae205deff24ed7e55d3a0",
"34d8669152c3c785a89f0934ac8fbdd2be959f11f6ba8b277e658e522f9654e6",
"5cfb3ef6111b4be05d8cbe82f27f7860c48e95810734793b8a380f83e2e5632d",
"70d864edfb7284d328496576d3a5c5e9c18646a661c0d5b654db559da6b5222f",
"9cab5e2c79cd71ec5d625478077aadfb1d89a32f9a69d3bb3788e44be0662be9",
"ad07108012341d5eacaf22cf5a69b79da34b930cabd8ba6e3b775e9b4867791f",
"0003522dd3ffce8444b63407e3d562aa207b7f4670bde90ec5e36d610c41c797",
"147aef0eccc3ba5fcfc93026deadb9abc022b1b364b355c070cdf99556a70d65",
"f2f82dae3109be2822775940b6fcbd4f80e3af46a24fab60cb16b6f223ce1bf9",
"897394d1ff93b70350e8bd6b73d3bad8dd58a62ab6ef1c6fbca26b4454eb3f64",
"fcfc03b54752bf0e086527f6248b3aa931a2cd53e4a54b5b7d99a3bd6603e373",
"406114f56d2914641b0117f896e3f63d35ca6bd35d4d113f080224ef00684e94"
```

This provides data that you can easily search or import into another database. You can use the same API at Blockcypher to access raw data from a number of cryptocurrencies including Bitcoin, Litecoin, and Dogecoin. Here are some examples:

- Bitcoin: `https://api.blockcypher.com/v1/btc/main/blocks/481961`
- Litecoin: `https://api.blockcypher.com/v1/ltc/main/blocks/1264707`
- Dogecoin: `https://api.blockcypher.com/v1/doge/main/blocks/1856723`

Simply replace the block number/height at the end and it will recover the raw data. Being able to get to the raw data can be very useful to an investigator, and we will be using APIs to get at information during the investigation phase of this book.

If you are using Linux, you can use the `curl` command to pull the data back from the API into a script or terminal. For example, the following code will create a file called `test.json` that contains data from the API:

```
curl -o test.json https://api.blockcypher.com/v1/btc/main/blocks/481961
```

You can also download a numerical series using the `curl` command. Let's say that you want to download every block from 481960 to 481970. You would simply add `-o` before the URL and then put the range in square brackets like this:

```
curl -o test.json -O https://api.blockcypher.com/v1/btc/main/blocks/
[481960-481970]
```

This will work through each URL in turn and write the data to the `test .json` file.

You can also use Python to extract the data, which I will discuss in more detail later in this book.

Summary

In this chapter, you learned how blocks are structured. You used crafted URLs to extract the raw data and then used techniques to find the hex to decode dates and transaction counts. You have learned about different encoding patterns and how you can use different tools to decode them. You have also looked at the differences between Bitcoin and Ethereum headers.

Being able to get at the raw uninterpreted information is vital for an investigator to be able to check data displayed by websites and other software. In this chapter, you should have started to understand how you can get that from a blockchain.

Transactions

Crimes committed on the blockchain can be complex. Many investigations will be about purchases made or funds moved via a cryptocurrency, so it is vital that the analyst understands precisely how transactions are prepared, transmitted, processed, and stored. With this knowledge, an investigator can effectively "follow the money" and explain the process to others when asked or challenged. We will discuss what a transaction is and how it is constructed as well as understanding the different types of transactions on the Bitcoin and Ethereum blockchains.

The Concept behind a Transaction

Transactions on a blockchain like Bitcoin are interesting and require a change in thinking from normal transactions. Traditional money transactions all have one thing in common: the movement of currency from one owner of that currency to another owner. What do I mean by this? Consider the following cash transaction: you go the hairdresser and have your hair cut, and then you reach into your wallet and extract $20. In handing the bills to the hairdresser, you physically move the currency to a new owner.

The same is essentially true with an electronic transaction. Let's say you choose to pay your hairdresser with a bank card. The transaction is fundamentally the same, except you don't see the money move. Behind the scenes, the money is "taken" or debited from your account, and "given" or credited to your hairdresser's account.

In both of these examples, the transaction is controlled and underwritten by a central authority. In the UK (where I live), a Sterling bill carries the statement, "I promise to pay the bearer on demand the sum of . . ." followed by the value of the note. The "I" in the statement is the Bank of England. The bank's website states:

The words "I promise to pay the bearer on demand the sum of five [ten/ twenty/fifty] pounds" date from long ago when our notes represented deposits of gold. At that time, a member of the public could exchange one of our banknotes for gold to the same value. For example, a £5 note could be exchanged for five gold coins, called sovereigns. But the value of the pound has not been linked to gold for many years, so the meaning of the promise to pay has changed. Exchange into gold is no longer possible and Bank of England notes can only be exchanged for other Bank of England notes of the same face value. Public trust in the pound is now maintained by the operation of monetary policy, the objective of which is price stability.

The currency used to be based on gold held by the government—in fact, you could swap your bill for real gold. However, that is no longer the case—the currency is "maintained by the operation of monetary policy," which basically means whatever the government wants it to mean. Regardless, the currency is centrally controlled by the UK government and is termed "fiat" money, which comes from the Latin word for "let it be done." This also means that if you want to get your hair cut in Paris, you can't just give the hairdresser a £5 note—a currency exchange has to manage a transaction from Sterling to Euros, and then you can give the hairdresser his or her payment in a form that their bank will accept. This is expensive as money is always lost in a currency transaction in fees and exchange rates, which is one of the reasons Europe phased in the Euro to try to deal with this problem.

With cryptocurrency, there is no such problem because there is no central authority to deal with. The distributed ledger (discussed in Chapter 1) means that there is no overriding control, and changes to the blockchain are only carried out by a consensus of users.

NOTE Other services such as Ripple (Ripple.com) facilitate the transfer of fiat currencies using blockchain technology; however, the currencies being transferred are still inherently government-controlled. Some countries, such as Russia and Dubai, are discussing introducing cryptocurrencies with some of the benefits of the blockchain and ease of payments, but these would have some central bank control.

The Mechanics of a Transaction

A Bitcoin address is fundamentally a public key; however, the address is a little more complex than that. It's formatted as a Base58 Check value. I will discuss Base58 Check in detail later in this chapter. It is vital for an investigator to understand that a Bitcoin or Ethereum or Litecoin address is not a wallet. The address is recorded on the blockchain with a value or no value at all—in fact, you can assign almost anything to an address, including a block of text (as we'll discuss in the "Detecting and Reading Micromessages" section of Chapter 12). An address can assign its value to another address, creating a transaction of that value. The receiving address may already have a value, and the increase is added to it.

Let's assume that an address named 1FA2 has a value of 2 bitcoin. It carries out a transaction by transferring its value to 1EA3, which already contains 1 bitcoin. This address now has a value of 3 bitcoin. It can then transfer its value to another address: 1AF2. This address was previously empty, so it now has a new value of 3 bitcoin. This is illustrated in Figure 4-1.

Figure 4-1: Transfer of value from address to address.

These transactions are recorded in an area called the mempool, which is the holding area for transactions before they are included in a block that is then mined and closed (see Figure 4-2).

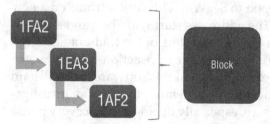

Figure 4-2: Transactions form part of a block that is then mined.

So, how does this work in practice? Who owns an address? To understand this, we just need to go back to our Public/Private Key encryption model.

An address is a public key with a value attached. If you own the private key that can transact an address, you own the address and hence own the value. For an investigator, this is a key point. If you have your suspect's private key you have control, or ownership, of all the public key addresses derived from it. This is vital if you want to seize assets. I recently witnessed a police force bemoaning the fact that they would need their suspect's computer in order to seize the cryptocurrency assets he had control of. This is simply not the case—you just need his private key. This could perhaps be acquired by other means, such as a covert entry, social engineering attack, or some other method. The entire machine did not need to be seized. We will be examining methods to achieve this in Chapter 9, "Analysis of Recovered Addresses and Wallets."

A bitcoin address encoded to Base58 looks something like this:

```
1Ej4Jm8J83tKG4wUAbikNF3rQoGckH4Emp
```

Obviously, having 58 characters available in the Units column before it needs to become a two-, three-, or four-character value means that it requires fewer characters than writing the address in hexadecimal, making it easier to write down or copy. However, in my experience, it can still be a pain to copy this type of address correctly.

Base58 is essentially a pruned version of Base64 in that it has the 0, O, I, and 1 removed to try to limit copy errors. However, L, l, and o are still used. The address also includes 4 bytes of SHA256 error-check code so it can detect copying errors automatically. In addition, Base58 Check also reduces attacks where an address can be created by an attacker that looks very similar to a *real* address. By using characters like I and l an attacker may be able to fool a user into paying to the wrong address.

You can find a good encoder/decoder at `https://www.browserling.com/tools/base58-encode`. [Removed text as inaccurate.]

During the writing of this book a "soft fork" was introduced to Bitcoin called Segregated Witness, usually shortened to SegWit. This fork introduced a new addressing system called Bech32. The addresses start with 'bc1' and are typically 42 characters long rather than the 34 characters of the traditional Bitcoin address starting with '1'. SegWit promises lower transaction fees and some other technical benefits. As it is too early to know if this software fork will gain a following, I have decided not to cover it in any detail. However, an investigator needs to be aware of 'bc1' addresses, especially during the discovery phase of an investigation.

Creating a Bitcoin address to publish or trade is really rather easy. You first need to create your private key (or choose it if you already have one), and then do a bit of math, as follows:

1. Choose a random 256-bit number and record it in a secure place. This can be any number, and you don't need to worry about whether someone else has it (there are more choices than atoms in the universe).

2. With your 256-bit private key, generate a number using the elliptic curve that Bitcoin uses: the ECDSA curve.

3. Run that value through SHA256 hash.

4. Run that value through RIPEMD160, another hashing algorithm.

5. Convert it to Base58.

6. Add a checksum.

7. Add a prefix.

NOTE   A prefix for a standard address, called Pay-to-Hash or Pay-to-Public-Key-Hash, is always 1. A prefix for a Pay-to-Script-Hash address is always 3.

You can make about 2 billion public keys from a private key, so you are not likely to run out. The generally accepted method to complicate tracking of your transactions is to use a new public key for every transaction. Although many do this, especially where an address is published publicly, the reality is that new addresses are often not used for each transaction. When a person does use a new address for each transaction, this can make the analyst's life much harder when trying to track funds.

Three primary types of Bitcoin transactions exist:

P2PKH (Pay-to-Public-Key-Hash)   This is what you might consider a standard transaction in Bitcoin, with one public key address transacting value to another address. The vast majority of transactions on the Bitcoin blockchain are P2PKH.

Multisignature   With multisignature, more than one private key is required for the transaction to spend the value of an address. This can be useful when several company directors are required to approve a payment, for example. A multisignature address will begin with a 3.

P2SH (Pay-to-Script-Hash)   Multisignature is an example of a P2SH transaction. The address paid to will begin with a 3 but will have requirements set that must be fulfilled before the value can be transacted again. For example, the script could require multiple keys such as in a multisignature transaction or need a password or any requirement one can build into the script.

When you spend a coin on a blockchain, you do not send it to a specific destination as in the case of a traditional fiat currency transaction. Instead, every full-node user of the blockchain needs to be notified that a transaction has taken place. To connect to, and notify, every full-node user would be time consuming and inefficient so to simplify the process you just need to tell a small selection of nodes that your Bitcoin client is connected to. Those nodes, in turn, tell the nodes they are connected to, and so on.

For example, if Alice wants to send 2 bitcoin to Jane, her client prepares the transaction which, if she is a full node user, is verified and then transmits to her peers. By each peer then communicating the trade to their peers, the entire network can be notified very quickly (see Figure 4-3).

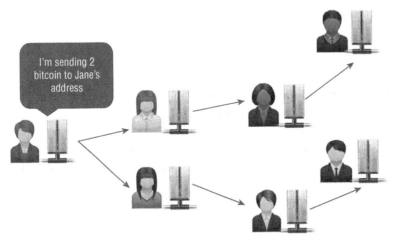

Figure 4-3: Transmission of a transaction from peer to peer.

If you installed and set up Bitcoin Core as directed in Chapter 1, you can write a command to ask the network what peers you are connected to, and it will respond with the IP addresses. To do this, open Bitcoin Core and select Debug Window from the Help menu, and then click the Peers tab. This will show you the IP addresses of the other Bitcoin full node users that you are connected to, as illustrated in Figure 4-4.

NodeId	Node/Service	User Agent
0	213.113.58.243:8333	/Satoshi:0.15.0/
1	178.162.6.187:8333	/Satoshi:0.14.2/
2	94.242.252.57:8333	/Satoshi:0.15.0/
3	125.227.159.115:8333	/Satoshi:0.14.2/
5	88.99.190.119:8333	
6	54.251.178.246:8333	

Figure 4-4: IP addresses of peers in a Bitcoin client.

But how does Jane know that she has received a payment from Alice? By looking at the blockchain and analyzing the addresses she has the private key to own, Jane is able to discern that a payment has been made to her. Her wallet will usually do this for her by aggregating all the addresses Jane has access to and providing a total balance.

I have mentioned a few times that Jane can control, transact, or own an address, but how does the blockchain do this in reality? What does Jane need to prove to the network in order to gain access to a payment?

When Alice created the transaction, her Bitcoin client locked the transaction with something called either an "encumbrance" or a "locking script." Every transaction includes a script that dictates what is required to own the output of a transaction and is a simple stack-based script that requires a series of commands to be carried out, which, if done correctly, will provide access to the address in the transaction. In the simplest case, this is the need to have the private key to match the public key. You will often see data in a transaction that may include commands such as OP_DUP or OP_CHECKSIG. This is the series of commands that make up the encumbrance. (We will look at this script in more detail later in the chapter.)

A transaction can be in either one of two states:

- Spent state—This is where the value of an address in a transaction has been moved on to another address.

- Unspent state—This is where the value in an address has not been spent. An unspent transaction is known as a UTXO, or Unspent Transaction Output. To determine your pseudo-balance, you add up all the UTXOs in all the addresses that you have the private key to unlock.

A critical element of an address is that you can't spend part of it. If you have an address with 5 bitcoin in it, and you want to buy something for 1 bitcoin, you must transact the entire 5 bitcoin in the transaction and receive the remainder back to you as change.

Take a look at the example in Figure 4-5.

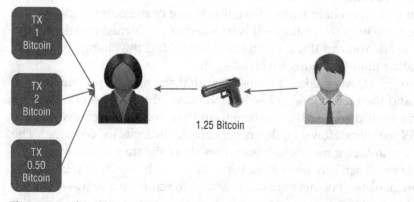

1.25 Bitcoin

Figure 4-5: Alice is buying a gun and has three transactions to choose from.

In the example, Alice wants to buy a gun on the dark web from Bob. The weapon costs 1.25 bitcoin. Alice has a series of three different addresses with values from previous transactions. These are currently UTXOs. Her addresses have 1 bitcoin, 2 bitcoin, and 0.5 bitcoin in them. To buy the gun for 1.25 bitcoin, Alice can aggregate the 1 and the 0.5 bitcoin and send those two addresses to Bob and then claim back 0.25 in change. She has other options too, as shown in Figure 4-6.

		Inputs and Outputs	
10fa6377a8f1928b6954685bb019826f361950cefdc37745605c7d4338310183			
1KtGghajuBUefEzCExTZM4rOVL6C1BbApX ($ 536.20 - Output)		19VRa4qwFRMvn687w3xkJyBmmZLYZvnnkc - (Unspent)	$ 1,656.26
1PtJ5mYqNP53FFR34E9R8ZteGgMvJoguae ($ 1,546.86 - Output)		15ayXucHjUc1BPkmU2aTyCbdQN1oc2DeWN - (Spent)	$ 417.01
		5 Confirmations	$ 2,073.28

Summary		**Inputs and Outputs**	
Size	373 (bytes)	Total Input	$ 2,083.06
Weight	1492	Total Output	$ 2,073.28
Received Time	2017-08-29 09:31:48	Fees	$ 9.78
Lock Time	Block: 482458	Fee per byte	601.609 sat/B
Included In Blocks	482459 (2017-08-29 09:38:02 + 6 minutes)	Fee per weight unit	150.402 sat/WU
Confirmations	5 Confirmations	Estimated BTC Transacted	$ 1,656.26
Visualize	View Tree Chart	Scripts	Hide scripts & coinbase

Figure 4-6: View of a transaction on the blockchain.

Figure 4-6 shows this transaction in a different way and introduces two important terms: outputs and inputs. I often find students getting confused with these terms. The two addresses transacted to Bob are inputs from Alice. The complexity comes from the fact that an input to a transaction is the output from a previous transaction. You can think of this as Alice putting her coins into a container. Bob receives the total of 1.5 bitcoin as *outputs* to the transaction, so you can think of this as Bob taking the cash he has received out of the container. In a normal transaction, Bob would give the required change back to Alice, but in a blockchain transaction, this is one of the outputs. Bob really has nothing to do with the change—it is handled and returned to Alice by the blockchain itself. You can think of this as Alice taking the change out of the container rather than Bob being involved at all.

To be more exact, Alice takes a transaction that she has the private key for, unlocks it, and then locks it with Bob's public key, which is essentially Bob's Bitcoin address and some other information that Bob must resolve to take ownership of the coins. However, Bob never actually unlocks the container. The fact that he *can* unlock it means he has ownership of the transaction and owns the coins. He won't actually unlock the container until he needs to transact the value to someone else. Bob never needs to accept the coins in any way—simply the fact that he is the only one who can unlock the container means he is the rightful owner.

Consider the analogy of a safety deposit box with two keys. Alice can unlock the box but then lock it with Bob's key. However, that key can't be used to open it again because only Bob has the right key. He doesn't need to unlock the box until he needs to pass ownership to someone else, at which time he too will relock the box with someone else's key.

Take a look at the real-world Bitcoin blockchain example in Figure 4-7. The top string is the transaction ID, and the inputs and outputs are the bitcoin addresses being used. Don't be confused by the output label to the right of the inputs—this just links back to the outputs of the previous transaction that this value came from.

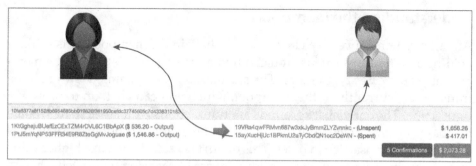

Figure 4-7: Alice transferring Bitcoin to Bob.

In Figure 4-7, you can see that Alice wants to purchase goods from Bob for $1656.26. However, Alice only has two addresses that are UTXOs: one containing $536.20, and the other containing $1546.86. Neither of these is sufficient to pay the bill by itself, so both addresses are used as inputs to the transaction. The inputs to the transaction comprise the appropriate amount going to an address owned by Bob and the change going to a new address owned by Alice. (Later in this chapter, I will discuss how you can use this to infer ownership of addresses during an investigation.)

Now let's add up the amounts:

Outputs:

536.20 + 1546.86 = 2083.06

Inputs:

1656.26 + 417.01 (change) = 2073.27

It appears that there's about $10 missing. This represents the fee that the network has charged for the transaction. The fee then goes into the proverbial pot to be collected by whichever miner successfully mines the block that contains this transaction.

If you go to `http://bit.ly/2vnW30J` and look at this transaction on the blockchain in more detail, you will see that the fees that are being charged are detailed underneath the charge that was applied per byte, which in this case are 601.609 satoshis per byte. A satoshi is a sub-unit of bitcoins like a cent or a penny but represents 0.00000001 BTC (a hundredth of a millionth of a bitcoin). When I took a snapshot of this transaction, there were five confirmations, or five blocks that had been mined; however, you will see many more confirmations when you look at this transaction in real time. In fact, if you want a little investigation practice, you could work out approximately when (within 10 minutes) I took the snapshot that's shown in Figure 4-7.

Understanding the Mempool

Any transaction not yet in a closed block is held in the mempool. This is like a holding area for transactions. You can find a really good viewer for the mempool at `http://bit.ly/2y8dtPe`. The site maintains a dynamic view of all the transactions currently in the mempool, which you can click on to browse a transaction. The darker backgrounds are transactions with lower than average fees based on an average from the last hour. The line at the bottom of each cell is the size of the transaction in bytes. This doesn't necessarily mean a higher value transaction, but a large number of addresses are likely being transacted—hence, a larger number of bytes in the transaction. See Figure 4-8.

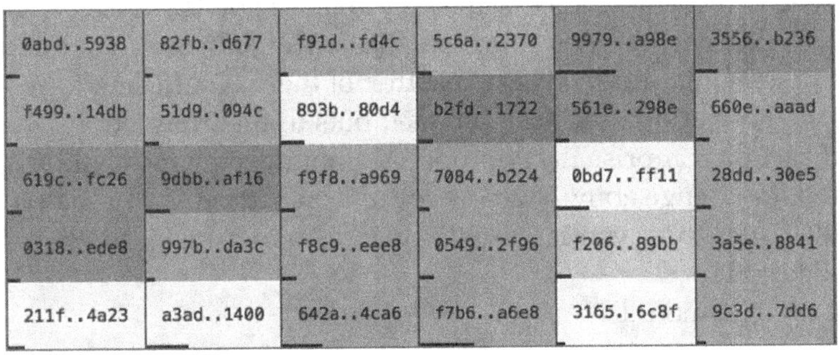

0abd..5938	82fb..d677	f91d..fd4c	5c6a..2370	9979..a98e	3556..b236
f499..14db	51d9..094c	893b..80d4	b2fd..1722	561e..298e	660e..aaad
619c..fc26	9dbb..af16	f9f8..a969	7084..b224	0bd7..ff11	28dd..30e5
0318..ede8	997b..da3c	f8c9..eee8	0549..2f96	f206..89bb	3a5e..8841
211f..4a23	a3ad..1400	642a..4ca6	f7b6..a6e8	3165..6c8f	9c3d..7dd6

Figure 4-8: Snapshot of the mempool.

If a transaction has been sent with a very low or zero fee being offered, it can be ignored from the next block, and perhaps the next block and so on. Eventually it will be picked up but it is dangerous for an investigator to conclude that the time a transaction was placed on the blockchain is within 10 minutes of the block time. In reality, it can be many hours later before a low-fee transaction is included. This is shown in Figure 4-9.

The figure shows us several transactions in a single block but the received time of the second transaction is around 30 minutes older than the others. This is reflected in the recorded time the transaction was received from the network (05:39UTC), but we can see the reason when we look at the transaction more carefully and note the low fee being offered to mine it. The other two transactions in Figure 4-9 offer a transaction value of between 130 and 170 satoshis per byte; however, the center transaction offers just 4.38 satoshis per byte. This is the reason that the transaction was delayed and likely missed a couple of blocks before it was included and mined.

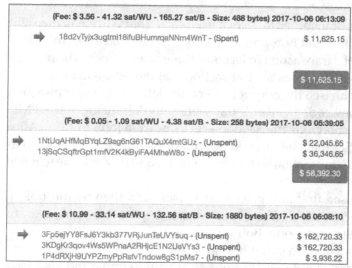

Figure 4-9: Note the low fee in the second transaction.

If you use any standard blockchain explorer such as blockchain.info, you will see an unmined transaction with a red label that says "Unconfirmed Transaction," as depicted in Figure 4-10. This simply means that it is in the mempool and will change to green and one confirmation once the block is mined.

Figure 4-10: Unconfirmed transaction.

Understanding the ScriptSig and ScriptPubKey

I mentioned previously the example of the safety deposit box. Alice must "unlock" the box before she can relock it with Bob's key. To achieve this on the blockchain,

Alice must prove to the blockchain that she is the rightful owner of a transaction. To do this, her transaction script includes something called the ScriptSig. This proves she is the owner and unlocks the "box" so that it can then relocked with a new key and hence moved to a new owner. To "move" the ownership, her transaction script must also lock the box again with Bob's public key; this is called the ScriptPubKey.

The ScriptSig is also called the unlocking script because it unlocks the transaction for Alice. The ScriptPubKey is called the locking script because it relocks it with Bob's key.

The two scripts work together to form a guarantee that Alice has the right to transact the value and that Bob, and only Bob, will now have control of it.

It's easier to think of a transaction in terms of three transactions. The transaction from Alice to Bob references the transaction that moved ownership of the coins to Alice from John (see the output links on the left side of the transaction in Figure 4-6). The raw code in Alice's transaction to Bob includes the TXID (transaction ID) of the previous transaction—let's say, from John to Alice. Alice must prove in ScriptSig that she can take control of the transaction from John and she then locks the transaction so that Bob will need to do the same to move the coins onward.

ScriptSig is processed first and placed on a stack, and then ScriptPubKey uses the value and carries out a series of processes including Bob's public key to create the locking value. Now only Bob's subsequent ScriptSig will agree with the value in the transaction, enabling him to control it.

The calculations carried out in ScriptPubKey are quite simple and are based on an old programming language called Forth. An instruction is put on the stack, resulting in a value, and then a new process can be carried out, and so on. Here are some examples:

- OP_DUP duplicates the value on the stack.

- OP_CHECKSIG checks the signature on the stack.

- OP_HASH160 hashes the value on the stack.

NOTE A *stack* is a software construct where instructions are carried out one at a time, and the result carried over before being processed by the next transaction. Think of a pack of playing cards with each card having a software instruction written on it. Take the card from the top of the pack, process it, and then take the next card on the stack, and so on.

The example given really describes a P2PKH or Pay-To-Public-Key-Hash transaction. Although it can have multiple inputs and outputs it only requires one signature. A multisignature or P2SH, Pay-To-Script-Hash is slightly different in that, for example, it may have multiple signatures required to unlock or lock the transaction.

Transactions are a pretty complex process and hard to understand, but it's vital for an investigator to comprehend what happens in a transaction and not the explanation that is often given in lectures and on websites, which is so often, in my experience, subtly wrong. In basic terms, money does not change hands, just potential control over a value.

Interpreting Raw Transactions

It is possible to extract the raw hex of a transaction from the blockchain in a similar way to getting the raw hex of a block. We can use blockchain.info and request the data in hex using `format=hex`. You construct the URL as follows with TXID being the full transaction ID:

```
blockchain.info/rawtx/<TXID>?format=hex
```

```
https://blockchain.info/rawtx/61635d927796c87164fa919ac21367fd7b67afc57a
b40b4984130a18f33fd7a3?format=hex
```

This simple example transaction gives us the following result:

```
020000000108ea335579f6ee3a4e463192dfbefcbfc24b4d892fe
7815ef5e15a993561cf86060000006b483045022100cff7025f08
7cf3615120f82946a4d7cef09cdd745d90dc086f78437a3d8189b
b02206050b45d6e758def8ab358edda74c644d2c4c54bcb47ab30
6bb395cddd0603ad01210307c6dabe1509bddcbdb984b10b9a092
bd0c4323edb2cfab90cb6d2654e5a24aafefffffff026a48030100
0000001976a91401990fc0ff0b73e0b00073b5aac229e7778a41b
b88ac548ff900000000001976a914e66df7b370eb31be3316e64cf
13534b4e12d830f88ac80770700
```

Transactions are very difficult to deconstruct by hand because they can have multiple inputs and outputs, but a number of fields are quite easy to find.

Software Version Used in the Transaction—Little Endian The result here is version 2:

```
020000000108ea335579f6ee3a4e463192dfbefcbfc24b4d8
```

Number of Inputs to a Transaction—Big-Endian The result is just 1 input:

```
020000000108ea335579f6ee3a4e463192dfbefcbfc24b4d8
```

Hash of Previous Transaction It's interesting that although all the blockchain viewers show the input values and output values, the input values do not exist in the actual transaction hex, just the link to the previous transaction where the amount will exist in the outputs. This is in Internal Byte Order and translates to

```
86cf6135995ae1f55e81e72f894d4bc2bffcbedf9231464
e3aeef6795533ea08:
```

```
020000000108ea335579f6ee3a4e463192dfbefcbfc24b4d892fe
7815ef5e15a993561cf86
```

Output Index Number   The next value is the output index number from the previous transaction. In this example, it is 6, meaning it was the sixth output of the previous transaction recorded in Little Endian format:

```
020000000108ea335579f6ee3a4e463192dfbefcbfc24b4d892fe7815ef5e1
5a993561cf86060000006b4
```

Output Values   The next value that we can ascertain is the total value of the 1st output from the transaction. This value is recorded in Internal Byte Order and decodes to the value in satoshis. In our example, the value is 16992362 satoshis. How do we locate and calculate this value? These values often stand out because of the many zeros that usually exist in the value. The value is 16 hex digits or 8 bytes long and you can start at the final zero and work back, in this example from 00 to 6a. Hence, 6a48030100000000 in Internal Byte Order translates to 16992362 satoshis. The zeros will never be used up as the value would be more than all the bitcoins that can ever be mined.

```
020000000108ea335579f6ee3a4e463192dfbefcbfc24b4d892fe781
5ef5e15a993561cf86060000006b483045022100cff7025f087cf361
5120f82946a4d7cef09cdd745d90dc086f78437a3d8189bb02206050
b45d6e758def8ab358edda74c644d2c4c54bcb47ab306bb395cddd06
03ad01210307c6dabe1509bddcbdb984b10b9a092bd0c4323edb2cfa
b90cb6d2654e5a24aafefffffff026a48030100000001976a9140199
0fc0ff0b73e0b00073b5aac229e7778a41bb88ac548ff900000000001
976a914e66df7b370eb31be3316e64cf13534b4e12d830f88ac80770700
```

There is a second output value in this transaction. Once again, if we look at the raw data, we will find another 16-hex-digit value including a string of zeros. The Internal Byte Order string is 548ff90000000000. If we convert this value to decimal, we get a total value of the second output of 16355156 satoshis:

```
020000000108ea335579f6ee3a4e463192dfbefcbfc24b4d892fe7815e
f5e15a993561cf86060000006b483045022100cff7025f087cf3615120
f82946a4d7cef09cdd745d90dc086f78437a3d8189bb02206050b45d6e
758def8ab358edda74c644d2c4c54bcb47ab306bb395cddd0603ad0121
0307c6dabe1509bddcbdb984b10b9a092bd0c4323edb2cfab90cb6d265
4e5a24aafefffffff026a480301000000001976a91401990fc0ff0b73e0
b00073b5aac229e7778a41bb88ac548ff900000000001976a914e66df7b
370eb31be3316e64cf13534b4e12d830f88ac80770700
```

nLockTime   This value sets when the transaction should be triggered. It can either be a UNIX time value or a block height. In this instance, the block height is 489344. The value is encoded in Internal Byte Order as follows:

```
020000000108ea335579f6ee3a4e463192dfbefcbfc24b4d892fe781
5ef5e15a993561cf86060000006b483045022100cff7025f087cf361
5120f82946a4d7cef09cdd745d90dc086f78437a3d8189bb02206050
b45d6e758def8ab358edda74c644d2c4c54bcb47ab306bb395cddd06
03ad01210307c6dabe1509bddcbdb984b10b9a092bd0c4323edb2cfa
```

```
b90cb6d2654e5a24aafeffffff026a480301000000001976a91401990
fc0ff0b73e0b00073b5aac229e7778a41bb88ac548ff9000000000019
76a914e66df7b370eb31be3316e64cf13534b4e12d830f88ac80770700
```

Extracting JSON Data

Although it is useful for an investigator to be able to deconstruct a transaction from hex, an excellent hex decoder exists. It returns the values in JSON (JavaScript Object Notation) format.

Find a transaction ID on `blockchain.info` and get the hex from:

```
Blockchain.info/rawtx/<TXID>?format=hex
```

Then paste the hex into:

```
live.blockcypher.com/btc/decodetx/
```

The output will look something like what's shown in Figure 4-11.

```
Decoded Transaction

{
    "addresses": [
        "1JWut9SmijfHtC128Hr1qpp6E4ky1neR5i",
        "1GctuvXwDGgpnoknyK5vRekGjne4G3zsbF",
        "1LDN7DKmqBSjk9Zax8kTTWD6UTWWg2tgqT"
    ],
    "block_height": -1,
    "block_index": -1,
    "confirmations": 0,
    "double_spend": false,
    "fees": 38194,
    "hash": "07fd2cccb1752a867465431c887cbd4b628eee753194f355a241677444edccf1",
    "inputs": [
        {
            "addresses": [
                "1LDN7DKmqBSjk9Zax8kTTWD6UTWWg2tgqT"
            ],
            "age": 486426,
            "output_index": 1,
            "output_value": 2498330674,
            "prev_hash": "f6f85686c957964c4b628fb963156ea42d16149b16cf42d70e3b5
103248e1e62e4910c4fa4a445d869faa7bd862646b9d47525a7b5144709c1ca8712",
            "script": "47304402205c641db6b8ffd95a18f00f9cd9f7c1233fb7a989549ab4
",
            "script_type": "pay-to-pubkey-hash",
            "sequence": 4294967295
        }
```

Figure 4-11: Transaction decoded to JSON.

We are able to directly access the JSON output of a transaction by using the following URL:

```
https://blockchain.info/rawtx/<TXID>?format-json
```

For example:

```
https://blockchain.info/rawtx/61635d927796c87164fa919ac21367fd7b67afc57a
b40b4984130a18f33fd7a3?format=json
```

This provides us with a semi-raw view and enables us to import the data into databases or other analyst software that supports JSON.

Analyzing Address History

In addition to being able to extract data from a transaction, we are able to ask any of the blockchain websites to provide us with a history of an address. This will show all the transactions that the address has been either an output or an input for and provide information such as the current balance. This is as simple as browsing to a site such as `blockchain.info` and entering an address. For example, browse to `blockchain.info` and try this with the address:

```
1istendqWJ1mKvrdRUQZDL2F3tVDDyKdj
```

We can also access the raw hex by using `blockchain.info/rawaddr` as follows:

```
blockchain.info/rawaddr/1istendqWJ1mKvrdRUQZDL2F3tVDDyKdj
```

This will give us the entire history of the address in JSON format.

Blockchain.info gives us a number of options to be able to just extract the data we want from the blockchain. For example, perhaps we just want to see the collated coin balance for an address. For this, we use the URL call `blockchain.info/balance?active=<address>`. For example:

```
https://blockchain.info/balance?active=1istendqWJ1mKvrdRUQZDL2F3tVDDyKdj
```

```
{"1istendqWJ1mKvrdRUQZDL2F3tVDDyKdj": {
  "final_balance": 6726564,
  "n_tx": 273,
  "total_received": 119311998
}}
```

This output provides a short snapshot of the transaction history of this address. We see that is has been involved in 273 transactions, has received a total of 119311998 satoshis, and has a current balance of 6726564 satoshis. It is easy to build this type of look up into a Linux shell script or Python program to quickly extract the raw data we need rather than trying to copy and paste from the main GUI screen.

We can also gather the data on any unspent transactions where, for example, our sample address `1istendq` was involved. For this, we use the URL call `blockchain.info/unspent?active=<address>`. For example:

```
https://blockchain.info/unspent?active=1istendqWJ1mKvrdRUQZDL2F3tVDDyKdj
```

```
{

  "unspent_outputs":[

    {
      "tx_hash":"12b670d6bd844cc99f86fd288b692359e214573e88bd0b7a1b36885
0a3fa1c8a",
      "tx_hash_big_endian":"8a1cfaa35088361b7a0bbd883e5714e25923698b28fd
869fc94c84bdd670b612",
      "tx_index":179615209,
      "tx_output_n": 1,
      "script":"76a91407eb8924e74fbdb01be58072d503f704aba70ba288ac",
      "value": 163100,
      "value_hex": "027d1c",
      "confirmations":56766
```

You will note for our sample address a significant number of unspent transactions exist but each transaction is a distinct node, so it's fairly easy to read. We can easily see the value, the TXID, and the number of confirmations (blocks mined) since the block with this transaction in it. Again, this makes the data easy to analyze and report.

Creating Vanity Addresses

Did you notice the start of the address in our last example was `1istendq`? The start of the address is no coincidence—it belongs to the owner of a website called www.bitlisten.com. Go and see it (or listen to it), and you'll discover that it turns Bitcoin transactions that are happening live into musical tones with the pitch based on the transaction value. It's rather ethereal and calming.

However, these types of addresses are called vanity addresses and can be calculated to have any prefix as long as the address begins with 1. Although any address can technically be calculated, the longer the string the more processor cycles are going to be needed to work it out. A lot of private keys need to be generated to try to produce a public key with the desired value in the prefix.

Vanity addresses are useful to the investigator because they tend to be reused, they are often published on a website or forum looking for payment or donations for something, and they can also be spoofed quite easily. An attacker can take the vanity part of the address such as this one, 1isten... and calculate a new public address with a different ending value but with the same vanity part. If you can then hack the real user's site and change the address, it will look the same to casual observers because they will focus on the vanity part.

If you would like to create your own vanity address, there is a great website that will do it for you. At the time of writing, it is free for up to four letters—more than that, and you need to pay a fee. I tried this with my usual name `nickfx` and it wanted to charge me 0.015 bitcoin. When you have chosen your vanity value, it will eventually e-mail you with the results including the public vanity key and the private key to import into your wallet (see Figure 4-12). Browse to `vanity.coin.dance` and give it a try.

Figure 4-12: Result of generating an address beginning with 1nick.

If you would prefer not to pay for a longer vanity address, you can generate your own using the tool `vanitygen64`. You can download it from `http://bit.ly/2yMbPDH`.

It's a very straightforward tool to use. Just open a command shell in the folder where the vanitygen64 executable is and type:

```
Vanitygen64 1<prefix_you_want>
```

Here's an example of a prefix you might use:

```
Vanitygen64 1tobs
```

This will attempt to brute-force a public key with the prefix `1tobs`. Four characters will be pretty quick; five characters will take a while, but if you are patient, it will find one eventually; and six characters starts to get serious. See Figure 4-13.

```
                              vanitygen-0>vanitygen64.exe 1tobs
Difficulty: 264104224
Pattern: 1tobs
Address: 1tobsgSbaCooGCcnHiw5AT4Tavq3B3YJY
Privkey: 5JwQiZVK48z
```

Figure 4-13: Using Vanitygen64 to create a vanity address.

Interpreting Ethereum Transactions

Transactions in Ethereum are, at a basic level, quite similar to Bitcoin in that the underlying blockchain technology works in essentially the same way. If you browse to `www.etherscan.io` and click on a transaction, you will see some fields of information that look the same and others that are quite distinct (see Figure 4-14).

Transaction Information	
TxHash:	0xdf9661c2c24fdacd6c2ed0f8ccdf72b9ccef690a4bbda50b38654ff74ec3b361
Block Height:	4371269 (6 block confirmations)
TimeStamp:	1 min ago (Oct-16-2017 01:03:28 PM +UTC)
From:	0x0a860fbdbb2a9acb0fe1d7c7da1b35c2cf1be751
To:	Contract 0x8b1f49491477e0fb46a29fef53f1ea320d13c349 ⊘
	⌐ 1 ERC20 (MicroMoney) TOKEN Transfer From 0x0a860fbdbb2a9acb0fe1... to → 0xf04b4d5d1ae946f58e06...
Value:	0 Ether ($0.00)
Gas Limit:	200000
Gas Used By Txn:	125106
Gas Price:	0.000000003 Ether (3 Gwei)

Figure 4-14: View of an Ethereum transaction.

One of the specific differences is that of "Gas." Whereas the Bitcoin fee is based on the size of a transaction in kb, Ethereum works differently. It uses a measurement called gas to calculate the cost of a transaction based on the computation work required to process it. If you browse to `bit.ly/2ys5mNw`, you will see that the gas used by the transaction was 125106. The Gas Price is 3 Gwei (0.000000003 Ether). It is notable in this transaction that the Value is 0 ether. No ether was transacted; instead, a transaction took place to transfer an ERC 20 MicroMoney Token. (You will learn more about tokens later.)

The transaction fee is the gas used multiplied by the gas price called Gwei. The fee is charged in ether to the one initiating the transaction. If you browse to www.ethgasstation.info you can see live details on the current and historical price of gas. There is also a table that recommends the gas you should pay depending on how quickly you would like your transaction processed. In the example in Figure 4-15, you can see that a gas price of 0.6 would mean a wait of 15.7 minutes for your transaction to be included in a block, whereas a gas price of 20 would insure block inclusion in just 2 minutes.

Recommended Gas Prices
(based on current network conditions)

Speed	Gas Price (gwei)	Predicted Wait (minutes)
SafeLow (<20m)	0.6	15.7
Standard (<5m)	4	3.2
Fast (<2m)	20	2

Figure 4-15: View of gas price.

Etherscan.io also has an API available for us to be able to acquire raw JSON data from the Ethereum blockchain. If you browse to etherscan.io/apis, you will see examples of what can be achieved.

To get the balance of an address:

```
https://api.etherscan.io/api?module=account&action=balance&address=<addr
ess>
```

To get the balance of multiple addresses:

```
https://api.etherscan.io/api?module=account&action=balancemulti&address=
<addresses divided by commas>
```

To get a list of transactions for an address:

```
http://api.etherscan.io/api?module=account&action=txlist&address=<addr
ess>
```

Summary

In this chapter, you have learned how a transaction works and how you can deconstruct a raw transaction from hex and acquire the data in JSON. You have seen how the unlocking and locking scripts work to shift ownership from one address to another and how the scripting language helps with that process.

CHAPTER

5

Mining

"Mining is the process of hashing the block header repeatedly, changing one parameter, until the resulting hash matches a specific target."

—**Andreas M. Antonopoulos**, *Mastering Bitcoin: Unlocking Digital Cryptocurrencies*

In Chapter 1, "What Is a Cryptocurrency?," you learned about the tribespeople of Yap and their huge stone coins called Rai coins that are mined on islands hundreds of miles away across the Pacific. The work involved to obtain a stone coin has always been a significant undertaking, so the expense and work involved gives a Rai coin its accepted value.

When we played with our NickCoin spreadsheet, we used the simple Python script to take the hash of a number of transactions and then, by adding incrementing values and hashing them with SHA256, we would search for a value starting with a certain number of zeros. When a solution was found, this could be used to close the block. Finding the solution required a significant amount of processing power, so the solution is a proof of an investment of work—in fact, not just work, but real time and money. When we played with the NickCoin spreadsheet, the winner of the hashing game won a few NickCoin. This is exactly the same as the real world: when a miner finds the solution to a block, he or she currently receives 12.5 bitcoin and the transaction fees that were taken for each transaction in the block.

The process is not dissimilar to trying to unlock a padlock that uses a combination. You need to try every combination in turn until you find the solution; however, once the solution is known, opening the lock becomes really easy, essentially back to our one-way algorithms.

The obvious questions are: "Is it really hard work? Does it really cost anything?" When you explain mining to non-technical people, they cannot see the work element. It seems that the new coin comes from nothing, so they do not see computer operations as "work" in the traditional sense. However, as you will see, the costs to find a block solution are significant and even the reward of "free" coins hardly covers the investment.

Virtually no cryptocurrencies are left that enable you to mine with just a CPU or single GPU. ZCash, Monero, and one or two other less known coins are the closest to being feasible but if you really want to have a try at it just out of curiosity, numerous sites exist that will talk you through the process.

Most cryptocoins now require specialist hardware to be able to mine with any type of speed, such as vast numbers of high-end graphics cards or ASICs, otherwise known as Application Specific Integrated Circuits. Often, people mistake ASICs as being a cryptocurrency-specific system, when in fact, ASICs have been around for four decades and are essentially just chips that have been designed for a specific task. ASICs for Bitcoin and other currencies are designed to be able to calculate and check hashes very, very fast indeed—that's all they can do.

There is a large hobbyist following around building efficient miners with open-air "crates" available to be purchased to be able to mount multiple graphics cards. Many companies will sell you mining rigs and will tell you how much the rig will make you each month—these are almost always exaggerating or, at worst, lying. A current mining rig for sale on Gumtree for $3300 promises to make the user $250 to $300 per month. Even if that were the case, it would still take a year or more to break even, and that's before factoring in the cost of the electricity. These rigs are very power-hungry and get very hot indeed—most run large cooling fans but often need room cooling to run efficiently. The costs can spiral quickly.

It has been reported that Chinese Bitcoin mining companies are moving to rural areas with hydroelectric power plants nearby providing cheap power to run and cool their warehouses of thousands of mining rigs. Sadly, the amateur hobbyist doesn't really have a chance!

When you ran the Python miner example, you probably would have been checking anything from a few hundred to around 100,000 hashes per second depending on the speed of your computer. My Mac, which is configured with Windows VM, a single processor, and only 1 GB of RAM, is only capable of around 50 hashes per second, whereas my 2017 32 GB RAM iMac is able to do about 90,000 hashes per second. For about $1200, you can buy an Antminer S9. This can carry out 14TH/s; that's 14 trillion hashes per second! And you still need an awful lot of them to make any money with Bitcoin.

The Proof-of-Work Concept

Proof-of-work is the concept of finding the solution to a hashing problem. The more computing power you have, the more likelihood there is that you will win the competition to find a blocks solution and be rewarded the new Bitcoin. However, the Bitcoin system works such that every 210,000 blocks mined, the reward will be cut in half. This means that on June 14, 2020, the reward will drop to 6.25 coins, then another 210,000 coins later, it will half again, until all the 21,000,000 coins that can ever be produced will be in circulation. At that point, miners will only receive transaction fees, which will not likely be sufficient to keep them in business, and the value of transaction fees will fall as miners try to accept every possible transaction on the network. There is a concern that this could eventually make Bitcoin unworkable as it could be unaffordable to run miners or even leave the network with few miners, making a 51-percent attack more possible. Alternatively, Bitcoin could stabilize, with a continuing rise in hard-currency value, then fees could be reasonably static but their value in fiat currencies could make the continuation of mining for fees alone profitable. Because of this, some cryptocurrencies such as Ethereum are looking to move to a system called *proof-of-stake*.

In Bitcoin, blocks are set to mine about every 10 minutes no matter how fast the computing power mining them becomes. The network calculates what the difficulty should be for the calculation to ensure that 10 minutes pass between blocks, using a formula similar to the following:

```
New difficulty = Old Difficulty * (Actual time of last 2016 blocks /
20160 minutes)
```

This ensures that the difficulty remains such that blocks will not be mined too quickly, or conversely, too slowly.

Once mined, the block is validated and added to the blockchain. Validation is critical to ensure that it is not a faked or duplicated block. The validation of a block includes the following:

- Block data is valid.

- Header hash is less than difficulty target.

- Timestamp is correct.

- Block size within limits.

- First (only) transaction is a coinbase (new coin) generation transaction.

Ethereum does things differently. Currently, only 15 seconds pass between each block, although at the time of writing, Ethereum developers are considering a hard fork to increase block times to 45 seconds and dropping the reward from five ether to three ether. In 2018, they are also looking to implement proof-of-stake to replace proof-of-work.

The Proof-of-Stake Concept

With proof-of-stake, you have no vastly complex calculations to do—you simply have to prove your "stake" or coin-ownership in the currency. For example, with Ethereum, if you owned and could prove you own 1 percent of all the Ethereum coin, then you could mine an average of about 1 percent of the transactions. This method forces miners to have a literal stake in the success of the coin. It also opens mining back up to the person at home. Even if they only own 0.000000001 percent of Ethereum, that will still enable them to potentially mine and receive reward, especially as part of a pool (which you will learn about in a moment). The reward is just transaction fees—no new coins are created.

In a proof-of-stake system, miners are called *validators*. Let's say that you have five validators competing to mine a block: one has 40 percent, one has 30 percent, one has 20 percent, and one has 5 percent. Each validator has a chance to mine the block commensurate with the stake they have. If you are paying attention, you will realize that this will make the rich richer. However, this also means that you are less likely to negatively attack the network or try to fork it as you risk devaluing or losing your increasingly valuable stake.

Proof-of-stake is also more environmentally friendly:

> **"While proof of work requires miners to effectively burn computational power on useless calculations to secure the network, proof of stake effectively simulates the burning, so no real-world energy or resources are ever actually wasted."**
>
> *—Vitalik Buterin*

It is believed that Ethereum will move to a proof-of-stake some time in 2018 in an upgrade called Casper.

Mining Pools

As described at the start of this chapter, mining has become a very complex and expensive business. One of the largest miners in the United States recently told me that their current mining expense was costing at least $1000 per bitcoin. Of course, that is good when a single bitcoin is worth $4000, but when it drops to below $1000 as it did in early 2017, that's not so good for business. To help flatten out the investment, a number of mining pools are available for almost every cryptocurrency. The simple idea is that you collaborate with many other miners around the world, adding your mining power to the whole and then sharing the proceeds. Some mining pools have become very powerful indeed. For example, in Figure 5-1, which was produced by `blockchain.info`, you can see the percentage of blocks mined by each mining pool in a four-day period in late 2017. At the time of this writing, just four pools—AntPool, F2Pool, BTC, and BTC.TOP—make up over half the network power at the time. In fact, AntPool was mining one in every five blocks.

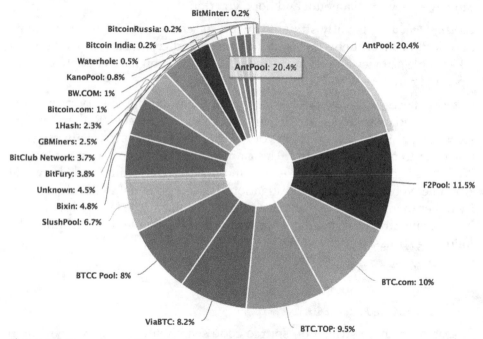

Figure 5-1: Percentage split of Bitcoin mined by mining pools.

NOTE You can chart the latest mining pools graph by visiting `blockchain.info/pools`.

It is very easy to sign up with a mining pool—you simply download mining software and run it with the mining pool as the target and authenticate with a user name and password. The pools are essentially free to use, but they all charge a percentage of the coin that you are awarded for your efforts, which can lead to scams and mining fraud.

Mining Fraud

Like streets paved with gold, everyone loves the idea of running something on their computer and generating free money. Of course, when something seems too good to be true, it probably is. A large number of frauds are based around mining companies. Here are some examples:

Commission Scam   Companies can make the percentages and charges for you mining with them very expensive, so although you may click the Terms and Conditions box in good faith, a mining pool can simply use your mining power and then give all manner of reasons why you haven't earned any coin. Or they can pay a very small amount and hope you don't notice.

Exchange Fraud   It is fairly straightforward to set yourself up as an exchange in order to convert between regular currency and cryptocurrencies. You can take people's money and cryptocurrency, and when you have enough, you can close and run.

Software Miners   We have looked at the fact that mining is very processor-intensive and costs money to run the machine and keep it cool. Rather cleverly, some companies have been using your visit to their website to briefly use your processor to mine some hashes. This came to the fore at the end of September 2017, when code to mine coins was found on CBS's Showtime and Showtime Anytime websites. Further investigation showed potential malevolent activity rather than CBS trying to make a few extra dollars. The JavaScript injected into the site carried the payment address and some unique code including the following strings:

```
coinhive.anonymous('
```

and

```
coin-hive.com/lib/coinhive.min.js
```

A search on these strings on source code search site `www.publicwww.com` revealed almost 14,000 sites that contained the same code at the time of writing (see Figure 5-2).

Although not illegal per se, it's certainly underhanded if sites are adding this code on purpose. You could even argue that it's stealing processor cycles.

Pirate Bay admitted the same idea, but they were honest about it, suggesting that it could offset or reduce advertising on the site. This is quite a good idea if customers don't mind—perhaps a site visitor could opt in or out of this service.

You can find a good article about software mining at `http://bit.ly/2oBqBG7`.

Private Key Phishing   Although not strictly mining fraud, several software tools are available for free download that purport to do coin mining. In the setup process, it asks you to enter your *private* key for payment! Those who are not well-informed are easily taken in by this.

Stealing Power   For years, criminals have been siphoning power from neighbors or straight from the grid to provide the lighting and heating for growing marijuana. The same process of stealing power could be very useful to a cryptocurrency miner because it would remove a significant proportion of the cost of mining.

Misleading Promises   Many websites, known colloquially as *faucets*, promise free bitcoin for either spending time on a website or visiting advertisements. My favorite example, which I will not include in the book as I am concerned about possible malware on the site, promises 200 satoshis per 5 minutes. That sounds good until you realize that 200 satoshis represents just over 1 cent, which means it would require you to spend more than 8 hours on the site to make $1. Not illegal—just misleading promises!

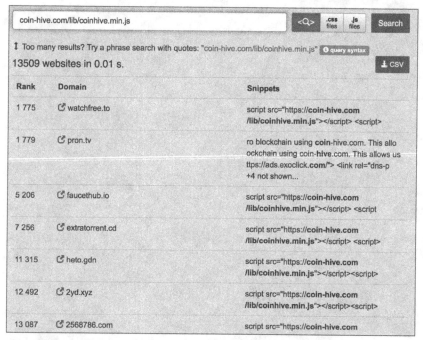

Figure 5-2: Some sites where the coin-hive software miner was found.

Summary

Mining is a fairly straightforward process that usually uses specialist equipment to solve hashing problems. It is unlikely that investigators will stumble across a crime that involves mining specifically, but they could get involved in investigating fraudulent mining software, power stealing, or other crimes. Most of these crimes are really just standard fraud, theft, and the like, but it is still useful to understand the underlying technology.

CHAPTER

6

Wallets

"Sometimes in the quest for enlightenment the only thing that gets lighter is your wallet."

—Steve Maraboli

The Internet says: "A cryptocurrency wallet is a secure digital wallet used to store, send, and receive digital currency like Bitcoin." I won't tell you where that quote comes from, because I wouldn't want to embarrass them, but it's wrong. In fact, it's technically wrong in virtually every way—a wallet doesn't store your bitcoin, and because it doesn't store them, it can't send or receive them! I'm being a little picky here—I know exactly what they mean by the statement—but the reality is important: the wallet simply maintains a list of private and public keys that it can resolve. By either watching a local copy of the blockchain or communicating with a copy belonging to another full-node user, the wallet simply builds a balance from the transactions it can control.

A forensic lab contacted me some months back and asked if I could "recover a suspect's bitcoin from a hard drive." I told the analyst that his suspect's computer never had any bitcoin stored on it in the first place. He sounded confused and told me that the suspect had admitted to storing ill-gotten gains in bitcoin on his computer. I sensed that fun could be had, so I told my new friend that I already had his suspect's bitcoin on my computer. Silence. I broke the silence by asking him if he would like me to e-mail those bitcoin to him. Silence continued. I think he was trying to decide if I was joking, serious, or somehow already involved in the case. It was getting a bit embarrassing now, so I asked if he had the Bitcoin addresses used by the suspect. He read me the address that had been published by the suspect on the dark web. About 10 seconds later, I gave him the bitcoin balance on the address. The poor man falteringly asked how I could possibly know that. Of course, I then took the time out to teach him how Bitcoin works.

At the time, I was already thinking of building a course on cryptocurrency for investigators, and it convinced me that any class (or indeed this book) should include some appropriate but significant technical detail on how exactly a cryptocurrency works.

A little later, I visited the lab and gave some of the investigators an overview of how a blockchain works, and we built a simple tool to carve public and private keys from a drive. I was planning to share the tool with you in a later chapter, but then a friend of mine built a better one, so I will put that in the book instead when I get to that topic.

I think I might just say it again for repetition: a wallet does not store any coins, but as I mentioned, it can reference any transactions on the blockchain that it can resolve with stored private keys. As you learned in the previous chapter, using a private key, the wallet can generate a transaction by referencing a transaction a person has a private key to unlock and the address he wants to relock the transaction with. So, although we often talk about a wallet sending and receiving bitcoin, this is just for ease of syntax—in reality, the wallet is just telling the blockchain to unlock and lock a transaction. Alternatively, the wallet can examine what transactions exist on the blockchain that is already locked with a Bitcoin address that the wallet controls and create a balance.

In addition, a wallet may store a local list of transactions it's been involved in as well as user preferences and the constantly updated balance.

In this chapter, I will focus on Bitcoin wallets. The wallets for other currencies work in very similar ways, and if you'd like, you can do a little research on your own to discover the differences.

Wallet Types

For each cryptocurrency, numerous types of wallets exist that can work on desktops, mobiles, and tablets. Some of these wallets connect to the blockchain remotely, while others maintain a complete blockchain locally (known as a full node).

Software Wallets

Three wallet types exist:

- Full Node Wallet—This is where the entire blockchain is downloaded locally. Transactions can be processed and verified locally and then transmitted to its peers

- Thin Node Wallet—This client connects to another full node for transaction processing.

- Online Wallet—This is a wallet that only exists on an online wallet site; the transaction data is usually not synced to a local client.

If you browse to `http://bit.ly/1gfYNgg`, you will see a number of downloadable choices of wallets including Bitcoin Core, Electrum, Bitcoin Knots, Arcbit, and many others. They all have their own variety of features and abilities, so they need to be chosen carefully.

If you downloaded and ran Bitcoin Core in Chapter 1, "What Is a Cryptocurrency?," then you will have a full node running and ready. However, tools like Green Address allow multi-signature transactions, Bither has hot and cold modes (which will be covered in a moment), and Electrum does not enable a full node but only works online by connecting to a remote node. They all have their own pros and cons.

Many of the clients have versions that will run on a mobile device, primarily Android or IOS. Ethereum has fewer choices, but a number of wallets are still available including Jaxx, Coinbase, MyEtherWallet, and Coinpayments.

Hardware Wallets

Hardware wallets are physical devices that store your private key and other data such as your account balance. Some primary examples are the Ledger Nano S, the Trezor Wallet, and Keepkey. These three examples are shown in Figure 6-1.

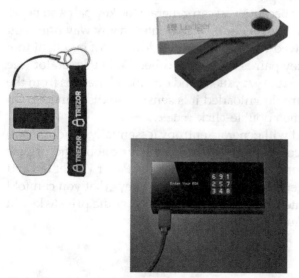

Figure 6-1: Examples of hardware wallets.

These tools are generally very secure, so if one of them is seized, it will usually require the suspect's cooperation to unlock it. However, each of these tools has recovery capabilities in case you lose your PIN or mislay the device. By understanding the recovery steps, an investigator may be able to gain access to the coins without needing to recover the device or PIN.

Cold Wallets or Cold Storage

As you just learned, a wallet has nothing to do with the storage of actual coins, and storing or even backing up a wallet is just a matter of keeping a record of the private key. This means that you could, if you wished, simply write your private key on a sticky note and put it in your drawer. This is a good example of a cold wallet—a private key on a piece of paper. However, cold storage really defines any key kept offline, and this could be on a USB key, a paper note, or a hardware wallet as defined in the previous section.

Although a key may be stored offline and would need to be imported into a wallet to be able to transfer funds out, the offline wallet can still receive coins from senders. As you learned, this is because it never actually receives the coins but just references the address on the blockchain. So, an address and its private key or a backup such as a mnemonic seed stored on a piece of paper in the safe can still get richer while being completely offline.

It is very easy to set up a paper wallet. In its simplest form, you can just write your private key on a piece of paper and put it somewhere safe. In fact, you might want to put it in a fireproof safe.

You can also generate a public/private key address pair without it ever being online. This is extremely secure because you can generate the key pair and never have the private key appear in a wallet or on a computer in any way until you need to move any funds received to the public key address. An excellent tool to generate a public/private key pair is a free tool called WalletGenerator (see Figure 6-2). Browse to `http://bit.ly/2yIHeWu` and download the files from the GitHub page. Once the files are downloaded it is sensible to disconnect from the Internet, then locate and then double-click `index.html`.

Moving your mouse around will generate entropy (essentially, randomness) and when the colored bar is complete, it will display your public and private keys along with their corresponding QR codes. Click the Paper Wallet tab and then Print to PDF. This will generate an output of your keys that you can fold and store wherever appropriate. You are welcome to look at the private key in Figure 6-3, but alas you will find it empty.

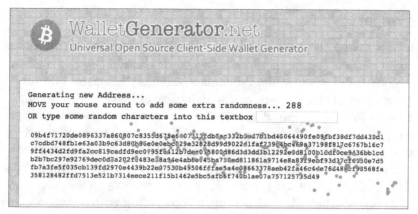

Figure 6-2: Moving your mouse around the WalletGenerator window creates entropy.

Figure 6-3: A generated public/private key pair ready to print.

Why Is Recognizing Wallets Important?

For the investigator, recognizing wallets is essential to be able to investigate the movement of a suspect's funds within cryptocurrencies and potentially seize assets. The potential insecurities of each method of storage can also work into the hands of the investigator, enabling private keys to be found and seized and hence gain control of funds.

Software Wallets

When analysts are working through disk images, they tend to follow a similar pattern of investigation depending on the case. Forensic software will generally attempt to reconstruct the file system metadata such as the Master File Table in Windows and provide the investigator with a view of live and deleted files, as well as a list of installed applications. Recognizing when a cryptocurrency management tool is installed could be very helpful during an investigation and may open up areas of money movement and laundering that had not been known about before. Digital forensic first responders should be trained to know the names of key cryptocurrency wallet software tools so that they can be recognized and reported. This is the same when dealing with mobile phone dumps—it is vital that thin client apps are recognized so that cryptocurrency assets are not missed.

Many software wallets depend on the security of the operating system to keep the keys safe, meaning that if you have managed to image the device or have secured the operating system password, you may have an easier time gaining access to the wallet and hence the assets.

In Chapter 10, "Following the Money," we will look at examples of how you can export a wallet or private keys and use them on your own workstation to investigate or seize assets.

Hardware Wallets

Would your house search teams recognize a Trezor hardware wallet? Would you? Perhaps just as importantly, would your house search teams recognize the printed recovery card that provides all the information you need to gain access to the account?

In Trezor, when you set up your device and choose a PIN, you are also prompted to record a number of supplied words onto the recovery card. If the Trezor is lost or the suspect refuses to reveal his PIN, you can acquire a new Trezor and then set up and configure it with the original keys by entering the words on the recovery card. Instructions like this are provided by the manufacturer for each hardware device, which can be exploited by an analyst to recover the suspect's keys. The instructions can usually be found on the website of the manufacturer.

Paper Wallets

The fact that these wallets are on paper means that they are probably tucked away somewhere and easy to miss. However, if a suspect is thought to have a reasonable sum stored on a blockchain, then a paper wallet will most likely be stored very safely. You would need to check a safe, if one exists, and any locked filing cabinets. Perhaps you would even need to look for evidence of a safety deposit box at the bank. A house search team should be trained to recognize and seize paper with long strings written on it. This will be discussed in more detail in Chapter 8, "Detecting the Use of Cryptocurrency."

The Wallet Import Format (WIF)

A WIF key is just your private key in a format that's easier to copy and retype. However, once it's gone through its transition from private key to WIF key, it is only shorter by 13 characters: 51 instead of 64. The WIF is in Base58, which means that it's harder to mistake characters such as 1 or o. It also has built-in error checking, which means that an erroneous WIF key should simply not work rather than a mistake being made copying and a new private key being used without the user's knowledge.

All the wallets I have tested that allow the importing of private keys only support the importing of WIF formatted keys (with the exception of back up files and mnemonic seeds).

Generating a WIF key from a private key manually is quite simple and can be achieved by following these steps:

1. Start with your 64-character private key:

   DB77FBE5B48C46B5A071387CF080F6D6065BA1DE8301135F8ED7D0B67973B63F

2. Add 0x80 to the front of the key:

   80DB77FBE5B48C46B5A071387CF080F6D6065BA1DE8301135F8ED7D0B67973B63F

3. SHA256 the new key from step 2:

   77BF93B1EECE4240EBD9CDE6FAF762AEF2D79F9E811286AA72EF41BDDA80CCAC

4. Run SHA256 over the key from step 3:

   F4FCFFFA78E05A34D9FEC3F95B09967D361A724AF961A34E05BF442EE06170EB

5. Take the first 4 bytes from step 3. This is your checksum:

   F4FCFFFA78E05A34D9FEC3F95B09967D361A724AF961A34E05BF442EE06170EB

6. Add the checksum to the end of the key from step 2:

   80DB77FBE5B48C46B5A071387CF080F6D6065BA1DE8301135F8ED7
   D0B67973B63F**F4FCFFFA**

7. Base58-encode the result from step 6:

   5KUwcbfmiHeDn3U1NnGLLrCSbHB9SrfW8ZEBsw9GcWjGSuvVV5s

You now have your private key in WIF format. That all sounds very long-winded to simply create a new shorter value. Why not just Base58-encode the original private key? The answer is the checksum. If you miss-key this, the checksum will not match, and the key will not be valid. Let's take a look at how the checksum works. Follow these steps:

1. Start with your WIF-formatted key:

   `5KUwcbfmiHeDn3U1NnGLLrCSbHB9SrfW8ZEBsw9GcWjGSuvVV5s`

2. Decode from Base58 back to the hex formatted bytes:

   `80DB77FBE5B48C46B5A071387CF080F6D6065BA1DE830113`
   `5F8ED7D0B67973B63FF4FCFFFA`

3. Remember that the last 4 bytes are the checksum: F4FCFFFA. Drop them from the end of the string:

   `80DB77FBE5B48C46B5A071387CF080F6D6065BA1DE8301135F8ED7D0B67973B63F`

4. SHA256 the result from step 3:

   `77BF93B1EECE4240EBD9CDE6FAF762AEF2D79F9E811286AA72EF41BDDA80CCAC`

5. SHA256 the result from step 4:

   `F4FCFFFA78E05A34D9FEC3F95B09967D361A724AF961A34E05BF442EE06170EB`

Note the first 4 bytes of the result of step 4 is `F4FCFFFA`. This should match the last 4 bytes from step 2. If you look back at step 2, you will see the last 4 bytes are indeed `F4FCFFFA`. You can also check that the result of step 2 (converting from the Base58 WIF to hex) starts with `0x80`. If these all match, then the key is valid and can be used.

You can do this process online at `http://gobittest.appspot.com/PrivateKey`. Please remember that entering your private key online is very risky, because the website owner could record the key and gain control of all your funds.

It could be useful to check to see if a recovered private key is legitimate before importing it and trying to locate assets on the cryptocurrency. Carrying out this reverse check would at least tell you if the key is a real private key.

How Wallets Store Keys

Wallets store keys in a number of ways (although some are now old technology and rarely used). These methods define the way that public keys are created from either a single or many private keys. As an investigator, it is important to understand how keys are derived because it can help to track complex wallets, especially those that are used by organizations or individuals with complex transaction needs. These methods break down into the following three primary categories:

Nondeterministic   Otherwise known as Type-0, nondeterministic keys are stored in a simple list of public/private key pairs. This is also known as JBOK (Just a Bunch of Keys). This method means that you have a lot of keys to manage, especially if you follow the recommended process of using a new key for each transaction. This also means that there is a lot of data to back up and keep safe.

Deterministic   Deterministic wallets are also known as Type-1 or "seeded" wallets. All of the private keys are derived from a single seed that's based on a random number. This method is significantly better because you only need to store and back up the seed to be able to recover all the generated private keys. This makes the wallet much easier to manage.

Hierarchical Deterministic   Otherwise known as "HD wallets," this is the most up-to-date wallet protocol in use and was implemented in Bitcoin Core in 2016. As with standard deterministic wallets, all the private keys are derived from a single seed, but keys in an HD wallet can generate their own private and public keys in a hierarchical tree structure. Once again, the seed can be backed up, and the entire structure of the tree can be recovered from the backed-up seed.

The seed is often represented by a series of 12 to 24 words. The process is fairly straightforward and is known as a BIP39 (a mnemonic named after the Bitcoin Improvement Proposal 29). Here's how it works:

1. Take the seed (random 256-bit sequence).

2. SHA256 the seed.

3. Add a checksum.

4. Divide the result into 11-bit sections.

5. Use each 11-bit section to reference the index of a dictionary of 2048 words.

To see an example of this, browse to `http://bit.ly/21pOWAr`. Here you can generate a new seed with its associated mnemonic words (see Figure 6-4). Select the number of words and click the Generate button.

BIP39 Mnemonic	prison chuckle tornado employ orange invest endorse across pipe ask retreat tennis athlete student license
BIP39 Passphrase (optional)	
BIP39 Seed	b0139da31884c6694c1c4d834f81e216336daa7e4f4b78af00e41f654334e7c5f7f5b1f942ebd72abb19d8845ed107c7bbc3ccc68fbe0232be7d6888b f87d6bb
Coin	BTC - Bitcoin
BIP32 Root Key	xprv9s21ZrQH143K3pCH1XElTwWJAZE7iBTgcq7XPTTf5APMYsqb2msp2AhacDPhtpuTFMvoWdd87QroUBgoKmkPByL56h7NYA1cn24B35fAWK9

Figure 6-4: The seed words that can be used to back up my private key.

These words can be used to re-create the seed and hence all the derived keys. You will also notice that under the Coin drop-down menu, a large number of cryptocurrencies are supported—in fact, any that support hierarchical deterministic wallets. Word lists such as this are used to back up many wallet types, so it is vital that search teams recognize them. (Chapter 8 discusses this in more detail.)

If you scroll down, you will see a list of all the derived keys including the private key, public key, and Bitcoin address (as shown in Figure 6-5).

Derived Addresses

Note these addresses are derived from the BIP32 Extended Key

Path	Toggle	Address	Toggle	Public Key	Toggle	Private Key	Toggle
m/44'/0'/0'/0/0		15Bhw4kbEatab93nKnTKg8qa8sVTG3dwyp		0216961bb142d2e1d07e4c10f6a83b880cd6b24184fac49336b4b7c4c10bd8e365		Kxv92hJ4at2HQfntV1UgVdZ4zRacniB4Rro1rQVsgXSqcsFQzST	
m/44'/0'/0'/0/1		1Dupbxu3yY9AEfamhPViL9EW4C6FbLaaJC		02bf2fe7b80e0693ceb5baa20995880430422769620c3ea3ff5f4de2355f5a2363		L5JXVQ8RM858414pm7cUaCRqdTkXAuMY2gbqoqudPMe4yCTV42uB	
m/44'/0'/0'/0/2		1Hhyvj X6vyPjcuq6vBk1wxHvXUAgAGLE6o		028151ff024a26acb6866ac7c2443daf3398lbaa9aa36815c5ff4a3c21b8b6732d		L4aJR9vXxBEphIynqeYzewRK54Kq8pWEj3K1zLT6wxfYkvosmUn7	
m/44'/0'/0'/0/3		18MfR8oDw0bGqJoDnNR4vYtVeoJnqeE53u		0314120fd5457 1693b7b87 06e4016d50295acd2alb4a13aacc5e9422ble9db3cc4		L34Abk25MJjOR4RbE5JTGF9wEVJdDdHJBG7jf3ecf8q8fvBjQ4LR	
m/44'/0'/0'/0/4		138B42Y5L2AqEYUEdHvLG8kizTK6Lq9EP9		0375f371b4346fe8815880db37d450850a3ab393e9a35c16a949578363b65442ec		Ky2SA3JMz7Kx5y5U7qvveZM8S6VubFjdmSRtakdF2513mvGxHxwk	
m/44'/0'/0'/0/5		1PyY7CDmoe6r4skdu4hJaWA5tA94QQoLP9		02f72615ab4a9b576fb499ableaed3a07344e342c43aabb4d11b5a1c69f45da12c		KxdEdPzLu1skyEzLqyYamxBV8EyUovBo5pwdjMEtK4HmGcDRj2f5	
m/44'/0'/0'/0/6		1Q2g5LfQ8cVqm2H1zuuewTj1Jwvtpd8cbC		028a8c669ba4ef1ddbd27c86fd95b3263ae0cb087e9bbeeaae7ec3aa588af71f30		L1rsXvpsexaywuekvPScJhEcfS5B3xnkoU8Q4N57qcSOvqjeKCcA	
m/44'/0'/0'/0/7		1CThioG73bMtXuRDurnKodao58rXK1ayiG		03ec607097bff44b6fad4da8acea9343fffseac709afdalb5d7c07670a7a7ef626		L5eUgoMpwZavZ9hab6cBLW1zj2TWEUzrrGrVJva8kxa5dEQMPvan	
m/44'/0'/0'/0/8		15tyxDBKDHV74rU2Wngb8ahw4CKqT39r8L		027d5db6147 16oe5bef764718d04f2b6aa627908ab9985dbe1326f286667954lef		KxinDeuqbkQvSKXuezumy4ET6WhAT ho4NibgWBmx5RMTvqqffPoh	
m/44'/0'/0'/0/9		1P85jCzGzKb293csGA46gnWbe8XX8wBY4t		03ce2d9ad76f88feod8e560166c404518792215eb1151e55f7oc2fda132800e506		KzsC4iQRj2VZmBGbz9WZyjRV9YaVjQ85xVln45YVVUuwGpMJ3TkA	
m/44'/0'/0'/0/10		1NAz5Jy1tuahiLTH1JRdzaWlA9znXy6ocY		02fa2e7fb3a28o5e79d3593780420586d88a1ef3911ff3e5646d3517210ed23169		L2FkbBnYD1jb8D8b5aAQ6ueAk6bVW9wFaxSpzkiTmpcAw9LXUSqK	
m/44'/0'/0'/0/11		14e89PYtDxTe5jw6W3v2842hkPm875Soq P		03a05e08df41d19256ff2of6622b1644258d5781318e89ce264420f34ca174bd3e		L2nwrUny8FPwCHiXMvPvlyaTbTy6JELB23rZy54sm4BiZBKCEoKQ	
m/44'/0'/0'/0/12		1FcSDNTmMz11HbSxw8X68VR826NH1Rnf6eW		03acb80cb60a0d794f6623fb6675aac5d0538d42e41231e416bfa9930455d5adfe		Kxh9kMELBdCru2gPrjLMBa9Xm1yCCfmrC3c2y4Sfq1VWCEpx2SoV	
m/44'/0'/0'/0/13		1KmbzG2swQJNLoJWsn19tK58HauoWUSW7o		02efdcfc6f7f1823deeda68e8aae8b935f52174b26a870743c7d61bb99d7cc0107		L1QXrsjVTPd6EkXKVV4R7YfnyZLTPdeyjcYDsiAnzj4fkVgQZrQY	
m/44'/0'/0'/0/14		1JbnFa8fUsWdLQSe2asrgmGATEVw6pKSmR		0381b6fb0ff96e31ffe3274091e94a328e83cd5863f06c5c4c36e33blb612cd936		KwZXFo1pP4AjAQUhrk99JH9kUX3JdRPFCuKgf3zM1yxP6Ecv98fG	
m/44'/0'/0'/0/15		1DrxDjFjb7VbmGR8f3PSSSIfYGxCXrT2vZ		034b235727b15e747d3b4cd476b57c30d7f0a8dbe4a8f7aaca205bf66elee6a84c		L45BtPxNj68awssPlalDPEl2oQJypHNyVueaTgzLi9hjyTn7W3Dk	
m/44'/0'/0'/0/16		1PARTq5QDwGx1767arjwiwCbhAebiuHaM5		03f916d956bb6683d29aa4b615a5d3c8bc20a3faa99aa118bf60976b5bd8725169		KwrBqhvbeKzinLfKEw67a6jmY5nyy7SRPLMhWiBJUE217cJ5hD8B	
m/44'/0'/0'/0/17		18R5LcRnqNAqRCJwU5JPoPKX84vuWFWskq		02d4441ca31c4e2caefab75a61eecb715bb3cefaa3a2d3bacd85842e55d2573223		L4tbyjT6UQdXiFNKHYfA5o8PG6RCmLybLA7DDrED8NLkJbz6GMRc	
m/44'/0'/0'/0/18		1PFuUwXg81qywiUBzK1FQzmRJ9V4gyoYWy		03cafb9feaaff5aba2c11ffc28e3dbe4d568be8ac2bda5fcacadead77a46d624b5		L2wRK8hxQdP31m9a7U8oxN86vdotheQptMxCCLTCVcPWJeez9aMF	
m/44'/0'/0'/0/19		1P5s9LFm9mgSUC4HJN2bFyQkKDyfHLEK57		023baaclade89b3a04ad9dc67c9ccc546b60cb693c2326a281b8150e869e2bbe6b		L52Fgcjh tCsftENrfm6tyewD4HhnF89DuGsh353H8GKXqf6355hF	

Figure 6-5: List of public and private key pairs recovered from the seed words.

However, as I mentioned previously, this is not just a bunch of keys, but rather, a structured tree of private and public keys. Figure 6-6 shows how this works. The seed generates a master key known as k_m. This key can generate further keys as children of the master. These carry a number identifier such as $K_{m/0}$, $K_{m/1}$, $K_{m/2}$, and so on. Each of these keys can generate "grandchild" keys, which would be, for example, $K_{m/0/0}$ or $K_{m/1/1}$, and so on. It is this naming method that is used to know where a key exists on the hierarchical tree.

Wallets such as Bitcoin Core currently use a simplified version of a hierarchical tree known as BIP32. However, BIP44 extended this method to provide more information and flexibility in the tree and is currently supported by hardware devices such as the Trezor. It seems likely that BIP44 will become the standard in due course. It is structured like this:

```
m/purpose/coin_type/account/change/address_index
```

where:

- *m* is the master key.
- *purpose* is the BIP implementation (for example, 44 would be BIP44).
- *coin_type* is currently 0 for Bitcoin, 1 for Bitcoin Testnet, and 2 for Litecoin.

- *Account* is an interesting capability that really shows the benefits of the hierarchical system. This enables an organization to set up subaccounts for a variety of reasons. Perhaps account branch 1 could be for purchases, 2 could be for simply receiving monies, and so on.

- *Change* flags the address as an address purely to receive change from a transaction.

- *Address_Index* is a number representing the numbered receiving address for payments. Remember that numbering starts from 0, so the value 3 would be the receiving address 4 on that branch of the tree.

You would hence read the tree like this:

- `m/44'/0'/0'/0/2`

    This can be read as the third receiving public key for the primary bitcoin account.

- `m/44'/0'/2'/1/13`

    This can be read as the change address for the third Bitcoin account.

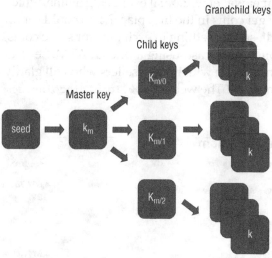

Figure 6-6: Hierarchical key tree.

Setting Up a Covert Wallet

A person may have the need to set up a wallet and assign funds to it covertly. This could be for criminal reasons or if he or she is looking to avoid surveillance by a nation state. I do not want to outline the detailed steps to set up a wallet and operating it covertly, but I think it is worth investigators knowing what they would be looking for. You will need the following three primary things to remain anonymous:

Anonymous Hardware and OS That Cannot Easily Be Infected with Malware or Spyware   An investigator would be interested if during a premises search USB devices were found with operating systems such as TAILS installed on it.

Anonymous Data Transmission   Is the suspect using a virtual private network (VPN) or the TOR network to communicate? As most cryptocurrency data is unencrypted due to its open nature, a suspect may decide to use an encrypted tunnel of some type to obfuscate—for example, communication with a Bitcoin peer. But both TOR and VPN clients leave traces for a digital forensics investigator. Also, acquisition of RAM (computer memory) allows the extraction of data packets, and even if packets are encrypted, the From and To IP addresses are always unencrypted.

Secure Payments to Their Wallet   It is no good setting up covert hardware and network traffic if you simply buy coins from a primary exchange where you have to provide your name, address. and other personal information. We have considered how you can set up a paper wallet without it ever being online, which would work well, but how do you get coins in the first place? You could set up a miner and mine the coins yourself, sell something in exchange for some coins, have some gifted to you, or buy bitcoin for cash using a Bitcoin ATM. Several sites are also available that will connect you with bitcoin sellers who will gladly take your cash—but much care is needed! The website `www.localbitcoins.com` is an example (see Figure 6-7).

Buy bitcoins with cash near United Kingdom			
Seller	Distance	Location	Price/BTC
lylejacob (100+; 98%)	1.1 km	Victoria Station, London SW1V 1JT, UK	4,657.76 GBP
GlobalBitcoinLady (100+; 100%)	0.8 km	London, UK	4,677.16 GBP
GlobalBitcoinLady (100+; 100%)	1.1 km	Victoria Station, London SW1V 1JT, UK	4,677.16 GBP
aclassliving (3000+; 100%)	1.1 km	Victoria Station, London SW1V 1JT, UK	4,678.55 GBP
aclassliving (3000+; 100%)	1.2 km	Mayfair, London W1J, UK	4,678.55 GBP

Figure 6-7: Bitcoin for sale for cash.

These three methods are not foolproof, but they would certainly help a person stay anonymous. Therefore, they are areas an investigator could look for to see evidence of someone trying to hide his or her tracks.

As an investigator, there may be times when you want to set up a type of covert wallet as alluded to previously. If you are working as an online undercover investigator, there may be times when you need to do covert purchases or money transfers; hence, the steps in this section could apply to you. You would also need to consider your "opponent." Is the suspect a person in a bedroom somewhere in the world who would have no way of demanding that a company provide account details of your activities, or is it a nation state that can make a request for information? If it's a nation state, you may want to get your bitcoin via less-direct means than through a standard exchange where their request for information would provide them with the name and address of the police station you work from! Not good tradecraft.

You may also want to set up a wallet to investigate data recovered from a suspect's machine. For example, in Chapter 10, "Following the Money," we will look at how you can use Bitcoin Core to analyze a wallet file recovered from a computer. In this instance, you may not want to use your primary wallet to do any transactions so as not to corrupt anything you might do on the suspect's wallet and, of course, to avoid any corruption of your own wallet.

You may also want to set up a wallet purely to seize assets from a suspect. In this instance, you will need to document everything you do, and you may wish to have a multi-signature address procedure in place so that there can be no suggestion of malpractice on the part of the investigator. We will look at this setup in Chapter 9, "Analysis of Recovered Addresses and Wallets," and in Chapter 14, "Seizing Coins."

Summary

Many types of wallets exist, and investigators would do well to be familiar with the primary types and their various features for cryptocurrencies that they may encounter. It is also important for premises search teams to understand what to look for in case hardware or paper wallets are being used and stored offline.

With Bitcoin addresses, it is also useful to check a private address that may have been recovered to see if it is valid using the checksum method that was outlined earlier in the chapter.

Investigators should also consider their processes and "tradecraft" for setting up wallets to be used covertly or as storage for seized funds.

Contracts and Tokens

This is a short chapter that covers the ability of some cryptocurrencies to encode contracts within a transaction. This feature, especially of contract-based cryptocurrencies such as Ethereum, has led to companies releasing tokens based on the blockchain, which hold the promise of some reward when the business performs well.

An investigator may be faced with blockchain-based contracts that have been involved in some fraud or theft. Initial Coin Offerings (ICOs) may be fraudulent and need investigating.

Contracts

A transaction of money, even on a blockchain, is essentially a contract. For example, if I decide to purchase a lemon drizzle cake (in the café I'm currently sitting in), both sides agree on a swap of a certain value for the drizzle cake. This would be the case with any transaction of goods, services, or generic agreements. Interestingly, a contract can also have a "promise" on one or both sides of the agreement. An example of this would be a marriage contract. Although goods and services are not traded, marriage is essentially a contract with an embedded promise in the vows and marriage certificate.

Bitcoin

Bitcoin and its derivative cryptocurrencies carry the ability to embed small amounts of data, whether code or text, to act as a contract. Bitcoin's ability to have multi-signature transactions means that both parties can sign the transaction, and it's then on the blockchain forever. Of course, this process is not without cost, because a small amount of bitcoin would need to be included in the transaction to cover the miner's fee.

In 2010, Satoshi Nakamoto said that he designed into Bitcoin the ability to carry out multiple contract types including escrow transactions, bonded contracts, third-party arbitration, and multi-signature contracts.

Bitcoin uses the simple stack-based language that was discussed in Chapter 4, "Transactions," but only a very limited number of operations can be done. The standard script for a pay-to-hash transaction is

```
<sig> <pubKey> OP_DUP OP_HASH160 <pubKeyHash> OP_EQUALVERIFY OP_CHECKSIG
```

This takes the public key and duplicates it, hashes it using SHA256 and RIPEMD-160, checks that the inputs are equal, and then checks that the input signature is valid. The OP_CHECKMULTISIG at the end of this script checks that the supplied signatures on the transaction are valid signatures from the specified number of public keys. This enables multiple public keys to be used to "lock" the transaction.

A number of ways exist to create a contract on Bitcoin. One way uses two transactions: the contract and the payment. If each of these transactions requires signing by both parties involved in the contract, then trust can be achieved.

Another type of contract uses a feature of the script operation nLockTime, which can be used to delay a contract from being included in the blockchain until a specific time or block height is reached. If the nLockTime value is less than 500 million, it is interpreted as a block height number, and if it's over 500 million, it is then understood to be a UNIX timestamp. This operation means that the transaction will not lock until the specified height or time is reached. This could be useful for something as simple as a son wanting to send money to his parents on their wedding anniversary. He would just set the UNIX timestamp locktime to the anniversary date, and the transaction will not happen until then.

nLockTime can also be used in contract transactions to ensure that the contract or payment is not encoded on the blockchain until a specific point in time.

Bitcoin has not been used significantly for complex contracts to date, but that could change in the future.

Ethereum

Ethereum is different from a Bitcoin-type blockchain in that each transaction is essentially framed as a contract. Although Ethereum will only allow a transaction from one address to another, a contract can call multiple transactions. Ethereum also has a considerably more complex scripting language called a Turing-Complete, which can be used to design a program that can perform any computation.

With Ethereum, the process of enabling transactions to complete only when certain conditions are met is straightforward. For example, imagine a gambling site based on Ethereum where bets are placed on the blockchain and payment is made in either direction when the conditions for a win or lose are met. Another example might be encoding a transfer of sale for a car or a house. Deeds of ownership could never be lost or destroyed, because the proof of ownership would exist on the blockchain in thousands of places simultaneously. That is assuming, of course, that you do not lose your private key, which would remove your ability to prove ownership of the contract.

Essentially, a blockchain like Ethereum could be used for just about any type of contract. An interesting example of this is the first wedding contract that was made available for Ethereum. The code is available on GitHub (`http://bit .ly/2zgx1BF`) and can be edited it to change key elements such as the names of the betrothed and add any other stipulations. Using an Ethereum transaction, the betrothed couple simply calls the contract and they both sign it with their Ethereum public keys. You can see this in use at the Ethereum contract address `0x5657b8d985be88af0f3d2dc064e2db784071ae1c`. Just enter it into `etherscan .io` and click the Read Smart Contract tab (see Figure 7-1).

Figure 7-1: Marriage contract on Ethereum.

A blockchain such as Ethereum could also work to improve resilience where trust is vital. Consider, for example, a modern car that regularly receives software updates over the Internet. Imagine if a car could be hacked by a nefarious person, perhaps intercepting the over-the-air update and adjusting the code so that the brakes are somehow turned off. How could this attack be intercepted? The software could be hashed each time the car is started, and the value could be checked with the main server. But what if the server was hacked? A blockchain would make this more resilient. If the developers roll out a new software update to the car-based blockchain via random peers, there would not need to be a single update server, because the software would be sent to a random number of cars on the network. If all these cars were nodes on a peer-to-peer system, they could send the software update to each other and then, when a car is started, the car could check the consensus of all other cars on the network to ensure that the majority agreed with the hash of the software version being run. The contract would just need to state something like this:

On car start:

> Does my checksum agree with the consensus on the blockchain (which in this example would be every other of this model car in the world)?

- If yes, allow the car to be driven.
- If no, notify the manufacturer that something is wrong.

This type of contract could work with almost anything that requires updates to help ensure that updates from the factory are not intercepted or hacked in any way.

Tokens and Initial Coin Offerings

Ethereum is being extensively used to launch funding campaigns for new products and services. This involves creating a type of contract called a token. These tokens are offered for sale on the Ethereum network in exchange for ether and represent the hope that the company or service will become successful and then the token can be traded at a higher value than the original investment. This is very similar to a share offering, except the token does not represent any ownership of the company and is not yet regulated by any legislation or body, although many countries are looking to regulate in the same manner as share offerings.

The standard token is called an ERC-20 token. The owners of the company wanting to raise funds will assign themselves a number of tokens, for example 100,000. They will then launch an ICO or an Initial Coin Offering where people can purchase tokens at a set rate. Often a purchaser will have some free service or reduced price product offered as a benefit of purchase.

The problem is that although some solid business plans are available for some of the companies offering ICOs, many—I would suggest a vast majority—are at best tenuous and at worst, fraudulent.

To illustrate, looking at some of the ICOs coming up at the time of writing includes a system based around a blockchain for finding return loads in the shipping industry or to enable non-technical people to create Ethereum contracts. Those are interesting applications of blockchain technology and one can see the potential. However, others include "Funding the ultimate board game with free access for users" or "A platform on the blockchain that reinvents cyber security." What does that even mean? Reading the blurb is equally confusing and doesn't tell me at all how they will redefine anything except how to write a business plan that doesn't actually say anything.

At the extreme end of this are ICOs that are designed to be fraudulent, taking investments for a business idea and then liquidating the money without providing the service. I believe that this will happen often in the coming years without stronger legislation.

To see an example of an ICO, browse to `http://authorship.com/contribute/`. I am not suggesting anything wrong with the validity of this offering, apart from explaining that it's a blockchain-based book publishing system (see Figure 7-2).

Figure 7-2: The Authorship Token sale.

We can use the Ethereum blockchain explorer etherscan.io to search for those who invested in Authorship tokens. Browse to `etherscan.io/tokens` and search for the word "authorship." Here you can see the address of the token contract and records of the transaction of tokens being transacted with buyers (see Figure 7-3).

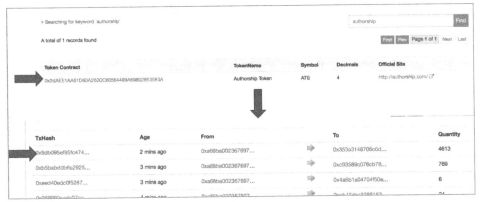

Figure 7-3: List of purchasers of Authorship tokens.

If you click any of the transaction hashes you can see the details of the token transaction. The first thing you will notice is the tag that identifies this as an Authorship token. You will also see that no Ether was transferred, just the contract code that makes up the token (see Figure 7-4).

Figure 7-4: The hash of the contract for the Authorship token.

By clicking the contract address, you are able to see the Contract Source and Read Smart Contract, which enables you to see the token name, the total supply available, and the address of the owner (see Figure 7-5).

As with any blockchain with a reasonable anonymity, it would be very difficult to trace the owner if no other information were provided. This can make it quite straightforward for a fraudster to set up and market a token for the sole purpose of eventually stealing the money. I am not in any way suggesting this is the case for Authorship, but investors need to make sure to do their homework.

Figure 7-5: Details of the Authorship token.

I cannot put it any better than Kevin Roose did in the "Is There a Cryptocurrency Bubble?" article that he wrote for *The New York Times* (http://nyti.ms/2wwww4jr). Here's a brief extract from that article:

> **Imagine that a friend is building a casino and asks you to invest. In exchange, you get chips that can be used at the casino's tables once it's finished. Now imagine that the value of the chips isn't fixed, and will instead fluctuate depending on the popularity of the casino, the number of other gamblers and the regulatory environment for casinos. Oh, and instead of a friend, imagine it's a stranger on the Internet who might be using a fake name, who might not actually know how to build a casino, and whom you probably can't sue for fraud if he steals your money and uses it to buy a Porsche instead. That's an ICO.**

Even though tremendous risk exists, ICOs are continuing to be wildly popular when a company manages to catch investors' eyes. Let's hope the majority of them are not just snake oil.

In September 2017, the U.S. Securities and Exchange Commission charged what is thought to be the first companies perpetrating an ICO fraud (see http://bit.ly/2x3p2mt to read more about this event). Interestingly, the fraud itself was fundamentally that the business owners were misrepresenting the investments they were making and the fact that the coins being offered were not backed by real estate as was advertised. The lesson here for an investigator is that the investigation actually had little to do with cryptocurrencies or blockchains and more to do with traditional lying and misrepresentation—it's just that the technology in the back office was a little different. I mention this because sometimes we get hung up on the technology when, in fact, we are just investigating a crime that's really been around since the dawn of time. Or at least since 300 BC, when a Greek sea merchant named Hegestratos took out a type of insurance policy to transport corn but decided to scuttle his empty boat and run off with the money and the corn. He drowned trying to escape his sinking ship. But even 2000 years ago, the crime was just simple fraud—in many ways, no different from any fraud today. In recent years, I have seen many Internet-based crimes that are not investigated due to a lack of technical knowledge on the part of the investigator. However, sometimes you just need to look at the basics of the actual crime being committed and worry less about the mechanics.

Summary

The long-term future of the blockchain is possibly not just in its role as a currency mechanism, but also as a way to create and store contracts between parties for virtually any reason. Bitcoin can do this already to a limited degree, but by using Ethereum, a person is able to construct and store complex contracts. This ability has led to the rise in ICOs (Initial Coin Offerings) as a way to raise money. As I discussed in this chapter, some of these are legitimate attempts to raise capital and others are, perhaps, fraudulent. An investigator should make an effort to understand the technologies involved but not forget that the crimes are essentially simple and no different from other thefts or frauds.

Carrying Out Investigations

The previous seven chapters have been designed to give you a solid grounding in how cryptocurrencies work. You should now understand the concepts of a distributed ledger, the fundamental math that underpins the blockchain, the way public and private keys interact, and how transactions actually function. We have also looked at both software and hardware wallets, and considered their individual merits as well as the application of blockchain technology to contracts and ICOs.

You can now apply this knowledge to the techniques and tools that you can use to investigate crimes that use cryptocurrencies. For example, purchasing illegal goods or storing illegally acquired funds, or alternatively crimes committed against users of cryptocurrencies, stealing online funds through fishing, fraud, and so on.

In this section, we will look at a wide range of techniques to identify where a suspect is using cryptocurrencies, acquiring addresses and private keys, following the money, visualizing transactions using free tools, and attempting to link an address to a particular user.

It is worth noting that a number of excellent software tools for investigating cryptocurrencies are available to purchase that will help considerably in following the money and identification of a user. Chainalysis (https://www .chainalysis.com/) and Elliptic (https://www.elliptic.co/) are both excellent tools, and I urge you to buy one of them, but please remember that both of these tools are for investigating Bitcoin only (at the time of writing), and they cost a significant amount of money! The techniques I will teach you in the coming chapters will focus on Bitcoin and Ethereum, but the concepts will work with any cryptocurrency. So it is vital that you do not just learn to use one tool and are then stuck when you are faced with investigating other currencies. Techniques used by both tools attempt to almost brute-force an eventual identification of the owner of a particular address. Although I will cover how to do these things manually, they are very difficult and time-consuming if attempted outside of these specialist tools.

CHAPTER 8

Detecting the Use of Cryptocurrencies

I was speaking to a police officer in a European country a few weeks ago, and he was explaining to me why he would not need to read this book. He said they had invested in an expensive cryptocurrency analysis tool, so he would not need to actually understand how cryptocurrencies worked or how to investigate them manually. I asked him if he realized that the tool only analyzed Bitcoin. His reply was, "Are there others?" This was somewhat of a shock to me. When I mentioned a few names, he realized that he had heard of them but wasn't worried because none of them had appeared in cases. I added the word "yet" to the end of his sentence. I reminded him that seven or eight years ago, high-tech crime units were saying something similar about Apple computers: that they didn't need knowledge to investigate those computers because none ever appeared in the lab. Now, of course, a huge number appear as evidence, and those high-tech units are often still behind the curve. Worse, they've probably just bought and been trained on a tool, and do not actually know the fundamentals of OSX investigation without the software tool.

I then asked this police officer if the high-tech crime team always actively looked for the existence of cryptocurrency use on the hard drives and mobile devices they analyzed. He admitted that not only was that not done, he didn't think they would really know what they were looking for. I humbly suggested he read this book.

Before you can start any investigation to follow transactions on a blockchain, you need to locate evidence of cryptocurrency use and then find the addresses or private keys that are being used by a suspect. This is not just the task of a high-tech crime investigator but needs to start right at the initial premises search.

The Premises Search

Several years ago, I stood in the corner of the room of a Middle-Eastern house. The walls were roughly painted, with no pictures hanging on them, and the floor was dusty with a couple of worn Turkish-style rugs strewn across it. It was really hot and pitch dark—the room was only visible with the night vision goggles pressed against my face. In the background, I could hear the sounds of life from outside: neighbors squabbling in the far distance set to the backdrop of sounds animals and insects make in the hour or so before dawn. I knew people were coming, but it was still a shock when the front door clicked and quietly opened. The first four law-enforcement officers that came into the room looked other-worldly—moving smoothly and low, respirators and Kevlar helmets enveloping their heads and, most concerningly, automatic weapons lifted to eye height sweeping left and right as they covered their individual arcs of fire. They silently cleared the room and the room to my left, moving past me like I was invisible. They were being watched by a different instructor, so I wasn't really interested in them—I was there to watch who came next. The next two counterterrorism officers that came into the room were different. Their sidearms were holstered, and they carried a couple of flight cases, which they put down next to a laptop on a desk in the far corner from my observation spot. Their job was to create, if possible, a forensic copy of the memory and hard drive of the laptop. They covered the screen to obscure any light, and the touchpad was tapped. Even with the cover on the laptop screen, the light burned into the screens of the night-vision goggles, and the officers had to self-adjust to the new light source. As the screen came into view, I saw the Enter Password box I knew would appear. One flight case was open on the floor with small tools, hard drives, hardware write-blockers, and other bits of kit. I knew the officers had been trained how to use these things, but would they take the hard or the easy route? They would get extra points if they managed to extract the contents of the computer memory, but in this instance, that would mean cleanly logging in, which would require the password. The room search had already started and was being carried out with speed, yet with care and precision, by a team that had done this task 100 times before. As the U.S. Special Forces say, "Slow is smooth, and smooth is fast."

In the bottom drawer, which was deliberately tricky to open, was a book, and in the front cover of the book was a sticky note. On the sticky note was written a single word in Arabic. It took them less than 5 minutes to find it. One of the officers would now need to enter the word onto the unfamiliar keyboard, plug in a device from one of the flight cases, and wait while the device did the copying job for them. The only female in the group, recognizable only from her slightly smaller stature, spoke a little Arabic, so she stepped up and entered the word. It worked, as I knew it would. They fired up the imaging kit and relaxed slightly, with one of the team looking over at me for the first time. I gave a thumbs-up signal and looked to the instructor to my right. He was watching two other officers who needed to locate a small SD camera card hidden in a break-in the concrete under a rug. He also gave a thumbs-up, and the exercise was over, goggles off, lights came on, and we all headed down the 50-foot tunnel where the training houses were located and out into an unusually bright but cold day in the English countryside.

The search was an interesting one. The officers knew the SD card was there, and they were tasked to image the laptop. They were limited by a defined time on target and had no way of knowing if there was a password anywhere to be found. Their search drill was flawless, and they found what they needed as well as 9 of the 10 bonus items. But would they have found evidence of cryptocurrency use? In this case, if any of the team had found a string of disconnected words or numbers, they would probably have recorded it, and either photographed or seized it depending on the job. The team was so good that they would have seen anything out of the ordinary as interesting even if they didn't know exactly what it was. Would that be the case with your search teams?

A New Category of Search Targets

Police search teams are routinely trained to look for technical equipment or data, whether that is uncovering USB drives, CD-ROMs, or especially finding notes that may contain passwords. In the current technical climate where encryption is being used more often by suspects, finding a password can be very useful indeed. Most people only use three passwords or derivatives of them. If you can find one password, you have around 33 percent of their passphrases.

Search teams also need to be trained to look for evidence of cryptocurrency use both at the premises search and later in the lab when examining computers and mobile devices. This is a new category of search, but it's one that is not complex to train. For many years, search teams have been trained to look for passwords on sticky notes, in notebooks, and written on pieces of paper. Passwords are fairly easy to identify because they are a simple word or phrase written down, often without context. It is even better if a suspect writes down a complex password with numbers and characters, which will then often be clearly identifiable as a passphrase. Finding evidence of cryptocurrency use can be just as straightforward.

Public Addresses

You learned in Chapter 4, "Transactions," that Bitcoin addresses start with the character 1 or 3, are 34 characters long, and are formatted as Base58. For example:

```
1AMdziK76JwP6DzEGyB9ruddBxQhM1oeZE
```

Ethereum addresses start with 0x and are 42 characters long. For example:

```
0x66febdddc377e2ee0b997c72b76d12c4aa2ce9be
```

NOTE Segwit promises several improvements such as cheaper transactions. The addresses are known as Bech32 addresses, are 42 characters long, and have a prefix bc1—for example, bc1qyczmfelvq3emduzwy36rgxjem2fjjg7025n6d6. You can find more information about this at http://bit.ly/2oTzA5q.

These simple rules make it easy for a search team to learn what to look for. After all, why would someone have a seemingly random series of characters recorded that clearly is not a phone number, bank account number, or something that looks like a very peculiar password?

Some of the places where a search team might find an address or private key are in the following list, and you can see the examples in Figure 8-1. These examples are taken from real-world cases where addresses have been found:

- A white board
- Included in a printed e-mail
- Printed on paper in a file
- On a sticky note on the computer monitor
- On a card in a suspect's wallet

Addresses can also be recorded as QR codes (see Figure 8-2). This method is often used because it is easier to send someone an image of a long address than to have to manually type it. If a QR code cannot readily be seized, then a photo can be taken of it that can be scanned later.

Private Keys

You can sometimes find private keys on pre-printed gift cards or other paper-based wallets such as the ones mentioned in the last section. If a paper-based wallet contains the private key, this enables you to take control of the funds. (You'll learn more about this later in Chapter 14, "Seizing Coins.")

Although users may not protect the public key as much, they tend to be more careful when it comes to the private key. Private keys are unlikely to be written on a piece of paper and discarded, but they could still be found in filing cabinets or safes.

Figure 8-1: Examples of seized addresses.

Figure 8-2: Example of a paper wallet with QR code.

Bitcoin private keys can be in a number of formats, and searchers should be aware of them all. They may be in a standard 256-bit hex format and 64 characters long, or more often, they will be in Wallet Import Format (WIF), 51 characters long, and start with the number 5. There is also a mini-private key format where the string is 21 characters long.

Private keys can also be in the form of a string of mnemonic code words often called a seed. These are used by blockchain.info, the Electrum software wallet, and the Trezor hardware key. Again, this should stand out to a searcher as a list of handwritten or typed words that do not relate to each other (see Figure 8-3). If you find such words, you can reverse the seed back into the private key by using the appropriate software tool such as Electrum or by entering them into an online recovery engine, which will then provide the private key. Remember that it is dangerous to enter or recover a private key online as there is the risk it could be stolen. To recover a private key you can enter a seed into the online form at `http://bit.ly/2Bcakgl`.

Figure 8-3: List of unrelated words.

Ethereum private keys are 64 characters long. For example:

`aba7e63318ebe4450911b62d5e79139310ad35545338bb89fcb7183365cc3375`

Ethereum public keys are 42 characters long and start with `0x`. For example:

`0x310B065125DDBACeB4822CA5e4F130025F8c9f07`

These are all fairly easy to train and for searchers to recognize without having to teach detailed technical information. This ensures that potentially vital information is not missed.

Questioning

Although I am not going to give a lesson on questioning a suspect, just as it is important that search teams are told what to look for in relation to cryptocurrency use, it is also important to provide some instruction to those who will question a suspect. Knowing what to ask is important but not as vital as asking at all! Asking if cryptocurrency is used by a suspect should be a question that is regularly included in fact finding. Of course, a suspect may just give a "no comment" interview, as is common here in the UK; however, there are times when asking the right questions can be very useful.

A few years ago, my friend John and I were asked to assist the UK Child Exploitation and Online Protection unit in carrying out a house search. The suspect was using a very secure type of Linux called TAILS, and the unit wanted more specialized help when they went through the door. The first thing John saw when he entered the suspect's bedroom was the computer screen switched on with a login screen displayed. John asked if the suspect had been read his rights and then simply asked him for his password. The suspect just handed it over. Asking the right question can save a lot of time.

Here are some questions you might ask:

- Do you use cryptocurrencies?
- Which do you use (Bitcoin, Litecoin, Ethereum, and so on)?
- How do you store your private keys?
- Do your private keys require passwords, and if so, what are they?
- Where do you buy and sell your cryptocurrencies?
- What are the passwords for those sites?
- How much currency do you have?
- What do you buy with cryptocurrency?

Obviously, there are many more questions you can ask, depending on the circumstances or the investigation type, but enabling the questioning officers with the right questions can be the difference between success and failure.

Searching Online

Information about an address can often be obtained online. It is amazing how often addresses are posted in these places:

- Websites
- Forums
- Software-sharing sites
- Twitter
- Social media

Remember that sites such as forums often prevent search engines from indexing all their posts, so it's necessary to browse to the forum and use its own search system. Although cryptocurrency addresses are sometimes found in messages with one user asking for payment for services, for example, it's incredible how often addresses are in forum signatures (see Figure 8-4).

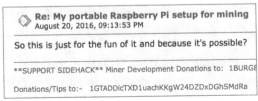

Figure 8-4: Example of address in a forum.

The simplest way of searching online for an address is to just use a search engine such as Google. The problem is that most of the results come from blockchain viewers. For example, a search on the Bitcoin address **1PZ5ebvdt43dvRRgRNgBhsq2PwAKN4X6W** results in what's shown in Figure 8-5.

Figure 8-5: Searching for addresses just returns blockchain viewers.

However, if you adjust your search a little and add the "not" identifier - (a hyphen), you will be able to filter the results somewhat. Try the following Google search:

```
1PZ5ebvdt43dvRRgRNgBhsq2PwAKN4X6W -block
```

This search will remove any results with the word block. The results now look somewhat better, and you should be able to more easily find that the address belongs to the UK's Royal National Lifeboat Institution (RNLI).

You can use the `site` modifier to find results on a specific site, forum, or other online resource that Google indexes. This can be particularly useful when an online resource does not have a search capability of its own. To use this modifier, you just add `site:` and the domain name of the site you want to search. For example:

```
site:bitcointalk.org 1PZ5ebvdt43dvRRgRNgBhsq2PwAKN4X6W
```

This provides search results only from the site domain that you specified (see Figure 8-6).

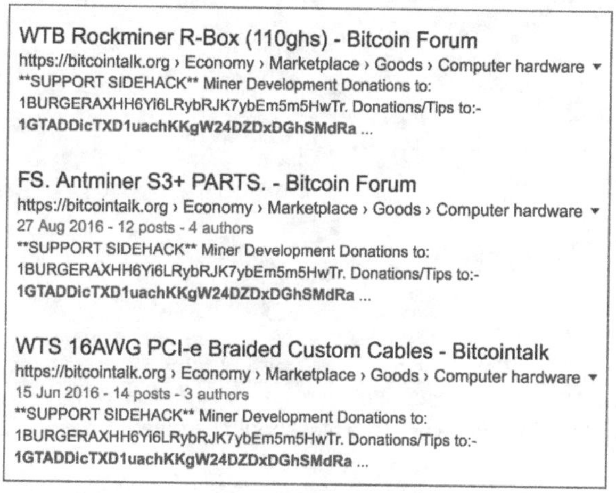

Figure 8-6: Searching a specific site.

Searching using a search engine or even a search system on a website is fine if you know the address that you're looking for, but what if you want to search a website for any address—for example, a Bitcoin address? Google and other search engines do not allow searches that use regular expressions or pattern-based searches, so you cannot ask a search engine to look for any and all addresses in its index for the whole web or for a specific site.

However, there is a way around this—you can download the site you want to search. This may sound extreme, but it is simple to do and provides you with the ability to search in a completely different way. You will need the following two tools:

- Httrack, which you can download from `http://bit.ly/1QbsQdf`
- Agent Ransack, which you can download from `http://bit.ly/2j2PhFi`

Install both of these tools on your system using their default settings.

Running Httrack is very simple. You just fill in the project name and then add the URL or URLs that you want the tool to download. In my example, I am using omninano.org. A number of options exist to change the way that the tool spiders and downloads the website; for example, you can decide to not download images and other media. The first time you run it, simply stick with the defaults (see Figure 8-7 and Figure 8-8).

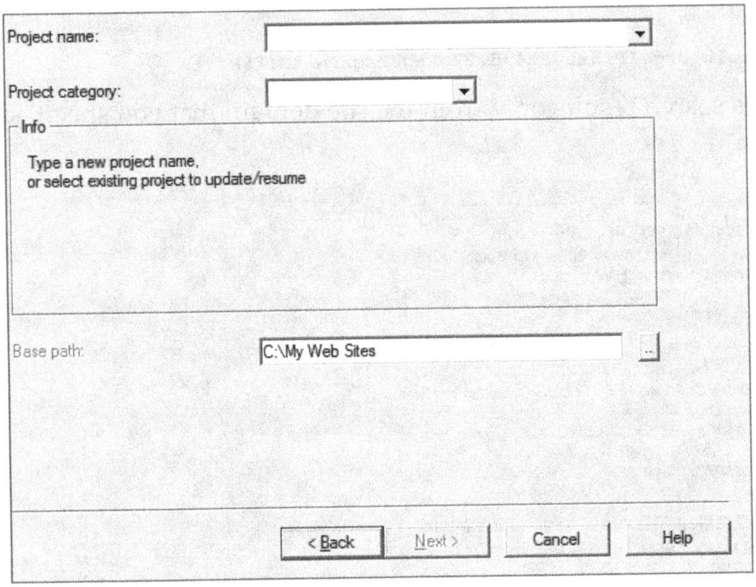

Figure 8-7: Enter the project name and the location where the files should be saved.

Once the site has downloaded, run Agent Ransack. This is a superb software tool that enables you to do powerful text searching within files and recursively search through a series of subfolders. There is an excellent Help facility if you want to learn how to use the tool better.

Within Agent Ransack, perform the following steps:

1. In the File Name field type **.html** or **.htm** (check in the downloaded website files to find the right extension).

2. In the Containing Text field, type the following:

   - `[13] 1-9A-HJ-NP-ZA-km-z] (26,33}<`

   This is the regular expression that will locate Bitcoin addresses for you. (I will not be explaining what the expression means, but please feel free to Google it if you want to learn more.)

3. Using the browse button set the Look In field to the path of the downloaded files from Httrack. By default, this is `c:\My Web Sites\<folder to search>`, which in my example is `omni`.

4. Select the Subfolders option check box.

5. Click the Options tab and set Contents to Regular Expression.

6. Click Start.

Your screen should now look something like Figure 8-9.

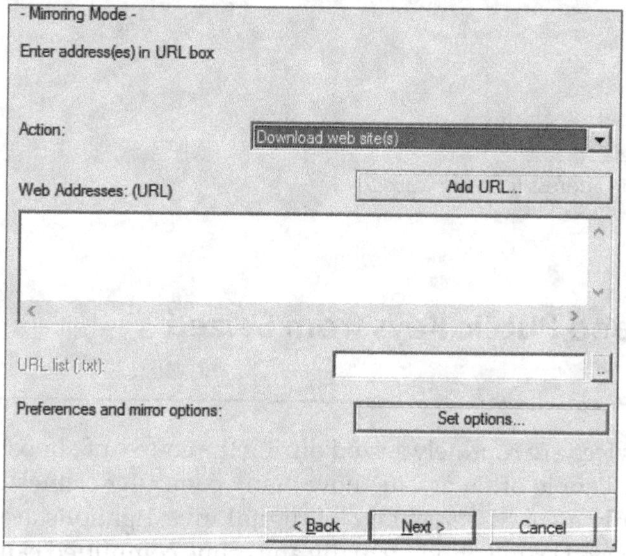

Figure 8-8: Add the URLs to download.

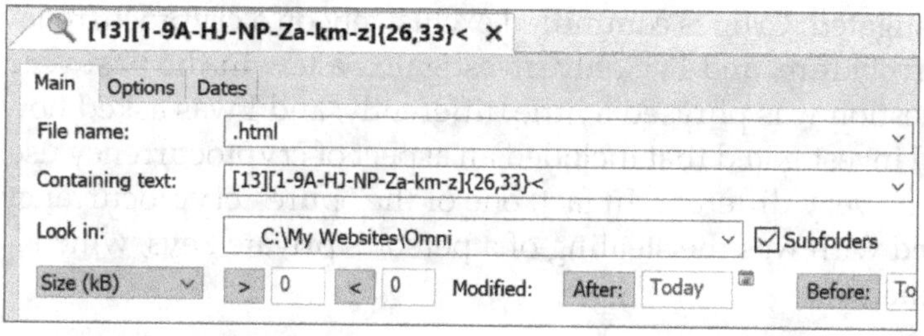

Figure 8-9: Setup of Agent Ransack.

Agent Ransack will now search the entire structure of downloaded web pages, looking for matches to the specified regular expression. If there are any to find, this should locate any Bitcoin addresses (as shown in Figure 8-10 for my example). The regular expression can be adjusted to look for addresses for other cryptocurrencies too.

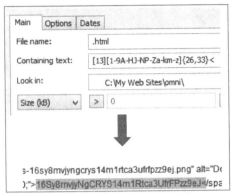

Figure 8-10: Recovery of a Bitcoin address from the website.

Extracting Private and Public Keys from Seized Computers

Computers and mobile devices are routinely seized during the course of almost any type of investigation. People often ask me how many computer crimes I work on. I answer that only a small percentage of digital investigations are actually solely computer-based crimes, and virtually any crime committed can have digital evidence associated with it, whether that be evidence in e-mail or other messaging programs, GPS locations, digital CCTV footage, . . . the list goes on. In the same vein, I have been asked a few times how many cryptocurrency crimes I have investigated. Crimes committed exclusively on a cryptocurrency are currently relatively rare, and I've only investigated a few in the past year. However, if the question was phrased a little differently, and I was asked how many crimes have I investigated that included an aspect of cryptocurrency use, the answer would be very different. In fact, one of the "pure" cryptocurrency cases I was involved with was the stealing of a person's private keys, which is really just a basic theft.

Commercial Tools

When a seized computer arrives in the lab, the first thing that happens is the drives are imaged, or forensically copied. Those images are then loaded into a variety of digital investigation tools such as Guidance Software's EnCase, AccessData's Forensic Toolkit (FTK), X-Ways, or one of the other available forensics tools.

There are also data-carving tools such as the excellent AXIOM tool from Magnet Forensics.

Here is a brief overview of some of these tools:

AXIOM This tool is designed to look for file headers and other values to carve data from forensic images and hard drives. As of version 6.1, AXIOM will natively carve Bitcoin addresses from a Bitcoin wallet, as well as queries on the Bitcoin network from log files created by the Bitcoin client software. You can learn more about this tool at `http://bit.ly/2i3UBHT`.

EnCase In many labs, EnCase is the default digital investigation tool for computer hard drives, although labs are often polarized between EnCase and FTK from AccessData. They are both excellent tools with their own pros and cons. EnCase does not have Bitcoin extraction capabilities built-in; however, an EnScript finder is available that can locate addresses on drive images or other media using the regular expression that you used earlier in this chapter. You can learn more about this tool at `http://bit.ly/2B1XFGI`.

FTK FTK has always been my personal tool of choice, but it does not have the ability to script add-ons like EnCase does. However, you can just use the regular expression searching feature with the expression mentioned previously: [13]`[1-9A-HJ-NP-Za-km-z]{26,33}<`. Although this expression works fairly well on a website as detailed in the previous section, you will find many false positives when searching a hard drive.

Extracting the Wallet File

If possible, it's best to try to find and recover the wallet file. The wallet contains everything you need to investigate Bitcoin usage, private keys, and addresses, records of transactions, and other metadata. If you can get a wallet from a suspect's computer, it's time to celebrate!

Finding the location on a drive of the wallet file for a particular type of cryptocurrency software is usually just a case of googling it, but I'll give you some examples of where the most popular software tools store the wallet file. With most software, you can choose your own installation location (see Figure 8-11), so the default addresses that you can find in the software documentation may not be accurate, but you have the option to search for a wallet file if you can't find it by heading to the default location.

The default wallet locations for the most popular wallet software programs are listed next. The list contains the name of the software, the operating system, the path to the wallet and, if relevant, the name of the wallet in parentheses.

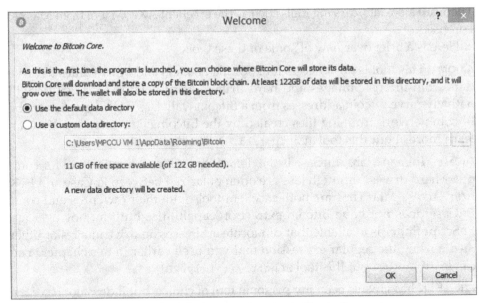

Figure 8-11: You can change the default storage location in Bitcoin Core.

Bitcoin Core

- Windows XP: `C:\Documents and Settings\<username>\Application data\Bitcoin`
- Windows Vista through Windows 10: `C:\Users\<username>\Appdata\Roaming\Bitcoin`
- Linux: `~/.bitcoin/`
- Mac: `~/Library/Application Support/Bitcoin`

Litecoin

- Linux: `/home/<username>/.litecoin.conf`
- Mac: `/Users//<username>/Library/Application Support/litecoin.conf`
- Windows XP: `c:\Documents and Settings\<username>\Application Data\Litecoin\litecoin.conf`
- Windows Vista through Windows 10: `c:\Users\<username>\AppData\Roaming\Litecoin\litecoin.conf`
- Armory: `%appdata%\Armory` (`.wallet`)
- Bitcoin Unlimited/Classic/XT/Core: `%appdata%\Bitcoin` (`wallet.dat`)

- Bither: `%appdata%\Bither` (address.db)
- Blockchain.info: (wallet.aes.json)
- MultiBit HD: `%appdata%\MultiBitHD` (mbhd.wallet.aes)
- Electrum: `%appdata%\Electrum\wallets`
- mSIGNA: `%homedrive%%homepath%` (.vault)

But what if a `wallet.dat` file or similar has been installed to a different location or moved? It is likely that a copy of backup of a `wallet.dat` file would still have the `.dat` extension, so you could simply use your digital forensics tool to search first `wallet.dat` and then just `*.dat`, although that will result in a significant number of false positives.

Perhaps the best method is to search for a "magic value" that always exists inside the `wallet.dat` file. Similar magic values can be found by installing the cryptocurrency software, extracting the wallet, and analyzing it either in a hex editor or simply by extracting all the strings from it. This is really easy to do but requires the `strings.exe` tool written for Windows by SysInternals, which you can download from http://bit.ly/2kbz7wY. The `strings.exe` file will extract all of the ASCII or Unicode strings from any file, by default with three characters or more, although this value can be changed in the command.

If you have a `wallet.dat` file (which you will if you installed Bitcoin Core in Chapter 2, "The Hard Bit"), locate the file and copy it to the same folder that `strings.exe` is in. Open a command shell in the folder where the `wallet.dat` file exists and type the following:

```
strings wallet.dat > walletstrings.txt
```

This will create a new file with a long list of human-readable strings. If you scroll down, you will begin to see text that you may remember from Chapter 6, "Wallets" (see Figure 8-12).

Figure 8-12: Hierarchical paths in the recovered text.

These are the Hierarchical Deterministic paths that make up an HD wallet. If you keep scrolling through the list, you will eventually find a Bitcoin address in plain text that looks similar to what's shown in Figure 8-13.

Figure 8-13: Finding an address with its prefix.

This address has an interesting value prefixing it: name"1. This value, which includes the 1 from the start of a Bitcoin address, has always existed in a wallet .dat file (in my experience). So, now you have a "magic value" that should locate a wallet.dat file, no matter what it is called. Simply use your digital forensics tool to search for **name"1**, and you should find the correct file (see Figure 8-14).

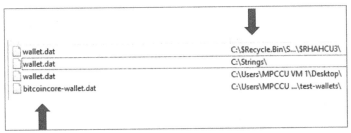

Figure 8-14: Wallets found in the Recycle Bin and renamed.

Notice that four files have been found in this example, including one in the Recycle Bin and one that has been renamed to bitcoincore-wallet.dat. This method is very successful, and you can simply install other wallet-management software and use the same strings technique to locate your own "magic value" to find renamed and hidden wallets.

If you installed Bitcoin Core on your own computer, you can prove this works by using Agent Ransack. Get Agent Ransack to search all of c:\ for the text name"1 (see Figure 8-15).

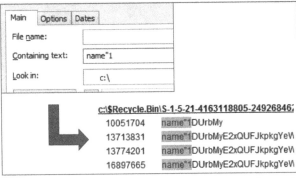

Figure 8-15: Recovered addresses with the magic value prefix.

Automating the Search for Bitcoin Addresses

If you have some programming experience, it is fairly straightforward to write some tools to automate the extract of information from a blockchain. Especially with access to the reasonably straightforward API URLs, simple scripts can be written to automatically grab virtually anything from transactions to balances. I know that a number of police forces have written their own scripts, and most keep them to themselves; however, a researcher named Chris Cohen posted an excellent Python script to GitHub in 2014 called BTCscan. You can download it at `http://bit.ly/2BE6Bbw`. It was accompanied by a very informative article published on the Forensic Focus website in January of 2015. You can find this article at `http://bit.ly/2iykm73`, and I highly suggest that you read it.

In his article, Chris points out that just searching a drive for addresses using the regular expression that you used earlier in this chapter works well, but on a large data set like an entire hard drive, you are likely to get numerous false positives. To counter this, the implementation of Base58 (which, as you may recall, is what Bitcoin addresses are written in) has built-in error checking. By analyzing the checksum of a recovered value, you can confirm whether a recovered value that looks like a Bitcoin address really is. Chris's script does this for you.

The tool is very easy to run and will attempt to recover public and private Bitcoin addresses and/or keys in a variety of formats. The command is built using the primary command and switches in the following list:

- `Btcscan.py`
- `-i`—Use this input command to specify the drive, directory, and/or files to search.
- `-q`—This command signifies Quick mode, which does not search BIP32 HD wallet keys.
- `-u`—This command signifies Unicode mode, only search for Unicoded items.
- `-n`—This command signifies Non-Unicode mode, which only searches for non-Unicoded items.

The tool requires Python 3.5, which you can download from `www.python.org/downloads`. If you have been following along with instructions in the book, you will already have both Python 2 and 3 installed, so you need to tell your computer which version you wish to use. You do this in the command shell by prefixing the `btcscan` command with the command `py -3`.

Open a command shell in the folder where the btcscan program exists. You can then run the software tool against anything from a raw hard drive image to a folder or even a mobile phone dump.

To search an imaged hard disk file, you will need to have a single raw image. For example, if your image is called `HD_01.dd`, then the command would be:

```
py -3 btcscan -i HD_01.dd
```

If you want to search a folder, the command would be:

```
py -3 btcscan -i="C:\folder\"
```

The output creates a comma-delimited file that can easily be imported into a spreadsheet for analysis.

The output is also useful in that it provides an offset of where the address was found in the image file you have searched. This enables you to use your favorite digital forensics tool to go and find the value manually and see it in its context.

Finding Data in a Memory Dump

Computer memory or RAM (random access memory) contains a significant amount of recoverable data. Investigators can mistakenly think that RAM is overwriting itself all the time and there is nothing useful to recover, when in fact, nothing could be further from the truth. There is a significant amount of data to be found, including files, passwords, encryption master-keys, and so on.

Imaging RAM creates significant controversy in the digital forensics world because it means, in most cases, running an executable on the suspect's computer. However, investigators know that "best evidence" means making no changes to the suspect's data sets and that running any software tool will make only minor changes to the drive. With the size of RAM increasing to significant levels in recent years and with tools available that can acquire vast amounts of data from the memory, the small changes made are seen as an appropriate offset to imaging 4, 8, 16, or more gigabytes of evidence. In the past five years, the thinking has changed and most primary police and government digital-forensics departments image RAM as a matter of priority if a computer is on when they search a suspect's premises.

You may wonder why it's worth imaging and searching the RAM when you have the disk. Of course, any addresses loaded into RAM from a wallet file will likely be recoverable from the disk. But what about in the situation where RAM is imaged, the computer is powered down, and the disk is imaged only to discover that the disk is fully disk-encrypted or that the cryptocurrency software is in an encrypted container? An undercover unit may only have access to a computer for a short time—not long enough to image the entire disk but sufficient time to get the memory. In these instances, the RAM may be all you have. Also, a recovery seed may have been generated which could still be recoverable from RAM but was never written to the disk.

Imaging RAM is fairly straightforward. Personally, I am a fan of the RAM imager tool by forensics company Belkasoft, which you can download from `http://bit.ly/2BvPTdr`. Although this tool can be run from the command line, you can simply double-click the executable file (choosing either the 32- or 64-bit build), provide an output path and name, and click Capture! (see Figure 8-16).

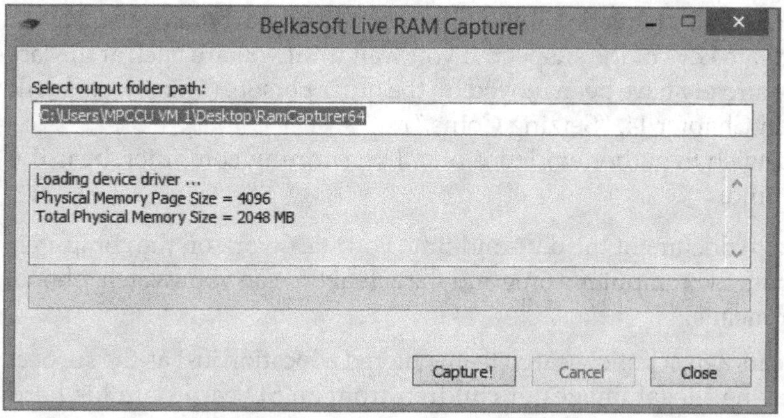

Figure 8-16: Running the Belkasoft RAM capture software.

Running the Belkasoft imager tool will create a `.mem` file that is a raw dump of the memory. Once you have your memory dump, you can do a number of things to look for cryptocurrency artifacts.

One thing you can do is use Chris Cohen's tool BTCscan as discussed previously. It works very well against RAM dumps and is a quick win to see if there is anything extractable. With a command shell open in the folder where BTCscan resides, you can just run the following:

```
py -3 btcscan -i <path_to_RAM_dump>
```

For example:

```
py -3 btcscan -i c:\temp\201811.mem
```

The output will be the same as from a disk, but of course, it will run much more quickly against the smaller data set.

Alternatively, you can simply use Agent Ransack to either search the memory dump for the regular expression `[13][1-9A-HJ-NP-Za-km-z]{26,33}<` that you used previously or just search for the `name"1` string.

Working on a Live Computer

Most police first-responders now accept that if a computer is running when they enter the premises, it is best evidence to, at the very least, acquire the memory. However, there may be circumstances where you would want to extract more data from the live computer before it was imaged or powered down—for example, if the drive is encrypted and battery power is limited with no obvious power source or you do not have the means at your disposal to image the drive while the computer is live. It may be worth considering seizing cryptocurrency assets from the live computer if at all possible, because a third party may also have a copy of the private keys of the suspect. If you wait until you are back at the lab, the assets may already have been moved by the other person. (This process will be discussed in Chapter 14, "Seizing Coins.")

Should you wish to gather evidence on a live running computer, bear the following in mind:

- It is vital to document the date and time you start work on the computer, noting both the computer's time and the actual time on your watch, phone, or other means.

  A few years ago, a police search team entered a location just as the suspect was copying illegal images of children from an SD card onto his hard drive. The suspect was detained, and the investigator sat down to image the memory. Although this was the right thing to do, he failed to notice that the system time was off by 1 hour. If you simply correlated the times in the police notebooks with the times of the activity on the computer, it appeared that the police entered the premises and then they proceeded to copy illegal images onto the computer. This does not look good in court!

- Limit the changes made to the computer, and know what changes are made when you insert a USB key or run a particular tool.

- Document what you did with the times and likely changes made.

One thing you might be looking for on a live computer is whether any cryptocurrency tools were installed or running. If so, it would be good to extract the wallet file. Let's consider a few ways of achieving that.

Acquiring the Wallet File

Many first-responder toolkits can be adjusted to acquire specific data types or filenames; however, this can also be achieved successfully with a simple batch file. My favorite text tool is Notepad++, which you may have installed back in Chapter 2. Let's use it to write a very simple script to find and copy out any `wallet.dat` file that it can find on the system. This works best from an external drive, so I suggest that you find a USB key, portable hard drive, or something similar to run the batch file from. Then follow these steps:

1. Open Notepad++ and type the following into a document:

   ```
   xcopy "%systemdrive%\walle*.dat" /s
   ```

2. Save the document as **walletfind.bat** onto your USB drive.

3. Browse to the batch file and run it.

   The `xcopy` command has been around for many years and can be found on virtually all versions of Windows. The command will search the entire system drive (which is usually c:) and look for anything with a filename pattern `walle*.dat`, and the `/s` parameter will search all subdirectories. Any results will be written back to your USB key in the folder structure that it found on the disk.

As you can see in Figure 8-17, I ran the command straight from a command shell. It recovered two `wallet.dat` files, which it wrote to the root of where I ran the command from. In the case of the batch file saved to the USB key, this will save the results straight to the key.

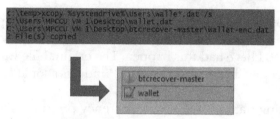

Figure 8-17: Finding and extracting the wallet file.

It can also be useful to know if any cryptocurrency programs are installed on the computer. For this, I use a tool that is built into Windows 7, 8, and 10. The easiest way to run the command is to add it to the `walletfind.bat` script that you have just written. Follow these steps:

1. Add this line to your script:

```
WMIC product get name, version > installedapps.txt
```

2. Save the batch file to your USB key and run it.

   This will create a text file called `installedapps.txt`. If you open the text file, you will see a large list of installed applications (see Figure 8-18).

```
Agent Ransack x64
VMware Player
Dell SupportAssist Remediation
Intel(R) Management Engine Components
Python 2.7.13
Dell Customer Connect
Microsoft Visual C++ 2008 Redistributable
```

Figure 8-18: Subset of the many applications found.

The problem here is that the WMIC command only lists installed applications and would miss any programs that ran from an executable file without installing. For this reason, it can be a good idea to add a second `xcopy` line to the batch file that will copy all the executable files on the system to your USB key. This will be a lengthy list, but at least you won't miss anything. Just add the following line to your `walletfind.bat` batch file:

```
xcopy "%systemdrive%\*.exe" /s
```

This works well and gives you a fairly quick way of ascertaining what is installed on the system without poking around Windows Explorer windows and changing all the Last Accessed Dates, which is not a good thing when working on a suspect's system! With the extracted lists of all installed applications and executable files on your USB key, you can browse the list for known cryptocurrency wallet applications.

Exporting Data from the Bitcoin Daemon

Copying a wallet from an operating system can have problems. For example, if the `wallet.dat` file was being written to when you copy it, there is always the chance of corruption. In fact, I have had this happen. The original file was not corrupted, but the version copied to my USB key was. Windows should handle this, but you never know.

Another way of extracting data from a cryptocurrency program such as Bitcoin Core is to run commands from its console interface. If you want to try this, you will need to have Bitcoin Core installed, which was detailed back in Chapter 1, "What Is a Cryptocurrency?"

To use this data-extraction method on a system with Bitcoin Core installed, follow these steps:

1. Open a command shell and change to the following folder:

   ```
   C:\ C:\Program Files\Bitcoin\daemon
   ```

2. Type the following line in the command shell:

   ```
   bitcoind
   ```

   It is likely that Windows will pop up a Security Alert window. If that happens, click the Allow Access button.

3. Minimize (do not close) the command shell.

4. Open a second command shell and browse to:

   ```
   C:\ C:\Program Files\Bitcoin\daemon
   ```

5. To cleanly dump the wallet from Bitcoin Core, run the following command from this second command shell:

   ```
   bitcoin-cli backupwallet <pathtoUSB>
   ```

   For example:

   ```
   bitcoin-cli backupwallet e:\
   ```

   This will dump the wallet file out to your USB key as illustrated in Figure 8-19.

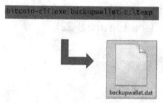

```
bitcoin-cli.exe backupwallet c:\temp
```

Figure 8-19: Using Bitcoin Core to back up a wallet.

There are some other very useful commands that you can run while the computer is live to obtain information that will be extremely difficult to get once the drive is imaged and you are searching via a digital forensics tool. For example, you can run the following command:

```
bitcoin-cli walletinfo
```

This command will write out some very useful information about the wallet including the current balance, the unconfirmed balance (transactions not yet confirmed), and the number of transactions the wallet has done (see Figure 8-20).

```
"walletversion": 130000,
"balance": 0.00000000,
"unconfirmed_balance": 0.00000000,
"immature_balance": 0.00000000,
"txcount": 0,
"keypoololdest": 1504865101,
"keypoolsize": 100,
"paytxfee": 0.00000000,
"hdmasterkeyid": "5883fc2eac5c79048adf25f567653fcd5434ee22"
```

Figure 8-20: Output from the walletinfo command.

It is possible to output this information to a text file by adding > and an output path. For example:

```
bitcoin-cli walletinfo > walletinfo.txt
```

You may wish to extract information on the network usage. The following command will provide information on the number of bytes sent and received (see Figure 8-21):

```
bitcoin-cli getnettotals
```

```
"totalbytesrecv": 1190120162,
"totalbytessent": 10832496,
"timemillis": 1504866947587,
"uploadtarget": {
  "timeframe": 86400,
  "target": 0,
  "target_reached": false,
  "serve_historical_blocks": true,
  "bytes_left_in_cycle": 0,
  "time_left_in_cycle": 0
}
```

Figure 8-21: Output from getnettotals.

You can also use the following command to get information on the type of signaling that is being used to send and receive data (see Figure 8-22):

```
bitcoin-cli getnetworkinfo
```

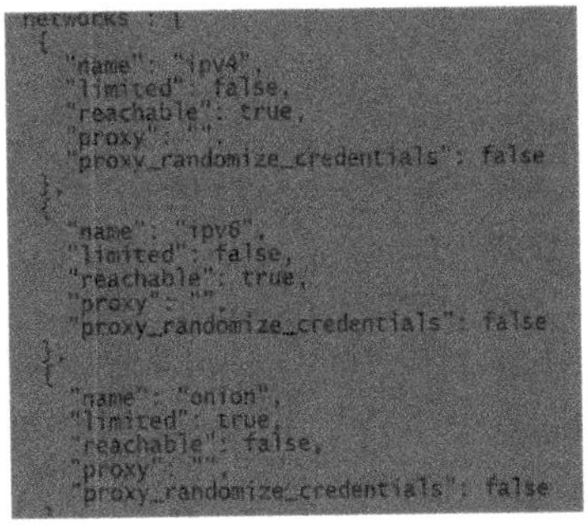

Figure 8-22: Output of getnetworkinfo.

You can use this command to find out whether the Bitcoin Core client is configured to use the TOR Onion network.

Try using the following command to see information on the peers that the Bitcoin Core node is currently connected to (see Figure 8-23):

```
bitcoin-cli getpeerinfo
```

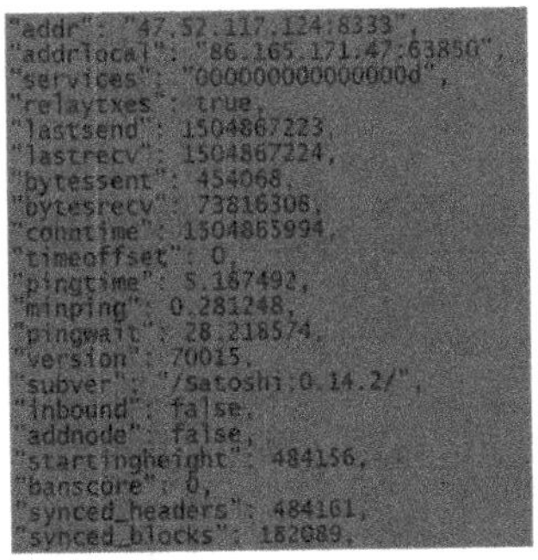

Figure 8-23: Output of getpeerinfo.

This command will enable you to see the IP address of the peer as well as data such as the time offset from UTC, the amount of data sent, and received and the ping time.

The following daemon command is one of my favorites because it lists all the transactions that the node has done (see Figure 8-24):

```
bitcoin-cli listtransactions
```

This shows all the addresses that the suspect has transacted with, which is vital information for an investigator. You can also see the local addresses the suspect has used, so you'll have a huge head start in tracking payments.

This can be a large list, so I recommend that you always use > after the command to output the results to a text file.

```
"account": "1",
"address": "mxnn5V6GPaaqXTYWzsaqhc125zS5Rwv9BW",
"category": "receive",
"amount": 1.79576774,
"label": "1",
"vout": 0,
"confirmations": 15473,
"blockhash": "0000000027bccb62ce99ee7b0a8aadef9087ab8371784b8111f8bcde68b5e975",
"blockindex": 3,
"blocktime": 1505473868,
"txid": "88d66c8823f003898b0c89e2bec74395297cf58bed0a1e9687b5dac5cff9f96c",
"walletconflicts": [
],
"time": 1505473868,
"timereceived": 1505499501,
"bip125-replaceable": "no"
```

Figure 8-24: Output of listtransactions.

You can also see all the unspent transactions by running the following command:

```
bitcoin-cli list unspent
```

The commands I've introduced to you in this section are invaluable to extract actionable data from Bitcoin Core. However, they are quite complex to remember, so I suggest that you write them into a batch script by following these steps:

1. Open a new Notepad++ document and type the following:

```
cd "%systemdrive%\program files\bitcoin\daemon"
bitcoind -d
```

2. Save this document to your hard drive with the name **start_server.bat**.

3. Open a new Notepad++ document and type the following:

```
cd "%systemdrive%\program files\bitcoin\daemon"
bitcoin-cli getwalletinfo > c:\temp\walletinfo.txt
bitcoin-cli getnettotals > c:\temp\nettotals.txt
bitcoin-cli getnetworkinfo > c:\temp\networkinfo.txt
bitcoin-cli getpeerinfo > c:\temp\peerinfo.txt
bitcoin-cli listtransactions "*" 1000 > c:\temp\transactions.txt
bitcoin-cli listunspent > c:\temp\unspent.txt
```

4. Save this file to your hard drive as **getdata.bat**.

5. Create a folder at c:\temp for the results.

6. Browse to your USB key and first double-click the start_server.bat file and then double-click the getdata.bat file.

Your USB key should now contain a list of files with significant data from the Bitcoin Core node. This is an excellent way of quickly gathering data that is invaluable to an investigator but will be difficult to extract later from a disk image.

Extracting Wallet Data from Live Linux and OSX Systems

I won't spend significant time detailing the methods you can use to search for and extract data from Linux and OSX systems, because they are very similar to Windows. For example, all of the `bitcoin-cli` commands in Bitcoin Core work exactly the same in Linux as they do in Windows. When you install Bitcoin Core for Linux, the daemon is also installed into the system path. This means that you can simply open a terminal and type the following command to start the server:

```
bitcoind -daemon
```

Another terminal will then allow you to run all the `cli` commands. These commands are the same as in Windows, including `getnetworkinfo`, `getnet-totals`, and `gettransactions`.

By default, Bitcoin is installed on Linux here:

```
~/.bitcoin/
```

And it is installed on OSX here:

```
~Library/Application Support/Bitcoin
```

There is also an easy way to search for the wallet file in both Linux and OSX. You can use this method to find the wallet file as well as to copy it out of the OS to a connected drive. The command is simply:

```
find / -name wallet.dat
```

To copy the file out, you either need to know the path to your connected USB device or have a shell script, similar to a batch file, on the key that you run. The command looks like this:

```
find / -name wallet.dat -exec cp {} <path_to_USB> \;
```

It may be that you have to run the command as an Administrator user to have success. In that case, you'll need to prefix the command with `sudo` and provide the associated password.

Although I will not cover writing shell scripts in any detail, they are very similar to the batch scripts. One difference is that you must start the script with the path to a terminal such as the following:

```
#!/bin/sh
```

And you exit your script with something like this:

```
exit 0
```

So, for example, you can run the `bitcoin-cli` commands in Linux as follows:

1. Open a text editor in your Linux operating system and type the following:

```
#!/bin/sh
bitcoin-cli getwalletinfo > walletinfo.txt
bitcoin-cli getnettotals > nettotals.txt
```

```
bitcoin-cli getnetworkinfo > networkinfo.txt
bitcoin-cli getpeerinfo > peerinfo.txt
bitcoin-cli listtransactions * 1000 > transactions.txt
bitcoin-cli listunspent > unspent.txt
exit 0
```

2. Save the file as **bitcoin-cli.sh**.

3. This next step needs to be done with the file on a Linux OS because you need to make the file executable. This is straightforward—you just need to open a terminal in the same folder as your .sh file and type the following:

```
chmod +x bitcoin-cli.sh
```

4. Copy the .sh file to a USB key, plug it into a Linux system that has Bitcoin Core installed on it, and double-click the shell script you created.

   This will run the commands and write the output to the USB key just as it does in Windows.

Summary

In this chapter, you have learned how to find and then acquire cryptocurrency keys in a variety of situations. You have considered how to approach premises searches, what to look for, how to find known addresses online, and how to search for addresses in downloaded websites. You also looked at how to find addresses on acquired hard drives and computer memory as well as how you can work on a live running computer and find and extract addresses in that environment.

I have not spent time considering the legal obligations that may exist in your country pertaining to working on live computers or imaging systems. Please research the legal ramifications of anything you do while acquiring data to ensure that your methodology does not put the case, or you, at risk.

Also, the ideas suggested in this chapter are in no way the final word on the subject. Other concepts, tools, and processes certainly exist, but I believe that the ones I presented are fairly simple to implement and will work effectively.

Analysis of Recovered Addresses and Wallets

In this chapter, you will learn about the information you can glean from a cryptocurrency address that was recovered using the techniques covered in Chapter 8, "Detecting the Use of Cryptocurrencies." This chapter explores what can be learned using online resources as well as how you can locally open and analyze a wallet you have recovered from a computer.

Finding Information on a Recovered Address

Once you locate an address, you can use it to find a considerable amount of information about its history and can infer other data by looking at the metadata associated with the address. This section looks at the information you can learn about an address before you start "following the money." A lot of data can be found by simply browsing to one of the primary blockchain viewers for the currency that the address refers to. For example, consider the following Bitcoin address:

```
1istendqWJ1mKvrdRUQZDL2F3tVDDyKdj
```

Rather than having to copy it all, you can browse to it via `http://bit .ly/2weGnf5`, which will take you to the transaction history of the address on blockchain.info. Of course, it is likely that this address may have had further activity since this chapter was written, so don't expect to see exactly the same data as I describe.

A good digital investigator learns to look at data from two perspectives: a literal interpretation, and for what the data can infer. A good example of this is analyzing Twitter data. As an investigator, you may extract 500 tweets from an account of a person of interest; however, you can look at the data in several ways. It may be that you are interested in the contents of the tweets, the words, the media, even the included hyperlinks. This would be looking literally at the data. However, you can also look at the data to see what else it can infer. There are numerous examples of this, including analyzing the times that tweets are made to infer the likely time zone that the person lives in. Alternatively, you may extract any geolocation information and cluster the tweets to locate a person's home or work address, or even where they go on vacation. A similar approach to the evidence can be made to cryptocurrency data.

For the Bitcoin address example in the previous paragraph, you can see the literal data shown in Figure 9-1.

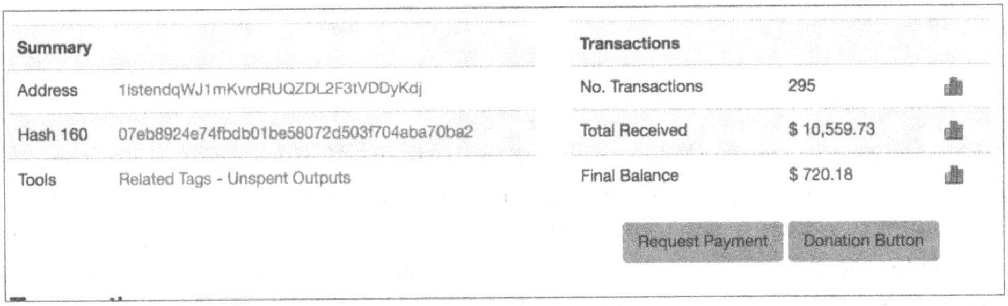

Summary		Transactions		
Address	1istendqWJ1mKvrdRUQZDL2F3tVDDyKdj	No. Transactions	295	
Hash 160	07eb8924e74fbdb01be58072d503f704aba70ba2	Total Received	$ 10,559.73	
Tools	Related Tags - Unspent Outputs	Final Balance	$ 720.18	
		Request Payment	Donation Button	

Figure 9-1: Metadata about a Bitcoin address.

You learn that at the time of writing the account has been involved in 295 transactions and has received over $10,000 of bitcoin at the current dollar exchange rate. Be careful when you're looking at data in the dollar or other primary currency view. In early 2018, $10,000 represents a little over 1 bitcoin, so if the user was transacting bitcoin three years before, this would represent about 13 bitcoin. Although it can be very useful to see the value as a "real-world" value, it is worth bearing in the mind the huge increase in value and fluctuations that existed, especially from late 2016 where the price began to increase exponentially with some notable dips. In the blockchain.info site, you can switch from a displayed dollar amount to a true Bitcoin amount by clicking one of the transaction values as shown in Figure 9-2. This will change all the displayed values as bitcoins.

You can also click the small graph icon next to the Final Balance figure to generate a graph of the balance over time. The graph provides the ability to change the duration from 30 days to All Time and to export the data as a CSV file. You can see the All Time graph in Figure 9-3.

Figure 9-2: Changing the dollar value to bitcoin.

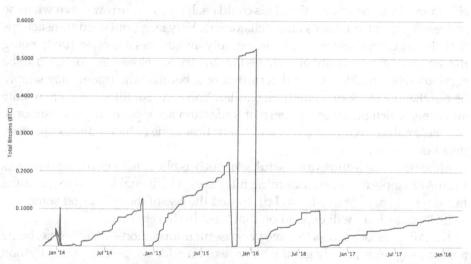

Figure 9-3: Graph of the address balance over time.

You can see that the balance has regularly risen since 2014, with the address regularly emptied before rising again. This graph can be very helpful in understanding the history of an address and the values that have flowed through it. If, for example, this was the published Bitcoin address of a dark web trader, you can discern how successful the trader is being and infer the likely turnover of the trader over time.

You can also filter the trades by using the filter button to view all trades, just sent funds, just received funds, as well as confirmed and unconfirmed trades only. Remember that trades are not confirmed until after they have been mined into a block. Perhaps the most useful option here is the ability to export the history of the address. This enables you to open all the trades in Excel or similar, which also enables you to view the data as you wish and filter it as required (see Figure 9-4).

Figure 9-4: Exporting the raw data about the address.

You have a number of ways of filtering data once it's in Excel including being able to sort by transaction value. This could enable you to narrow down what the addresses are of the trader's larger customers. Very large, outward transactions that almost completely or completely empty an address are often funds being moved to another account also owned by the trader. However, you need to be cautious when making these determinations, because the trader may simply be purchasing stock or something similar. You can also filter the data by date and time, which provides a pattern of trades and an opportunity for temporal, or time, analysis to infer a pattern of life or time zone (which I discuss in more detail later in this chapter).

Although these features are useful, sites such as blockchain.info provide access to an API (application programming interface), which enables you to get at the raw data. In Part I of this book, I discussed the use of the API to get some raw or JSON data, but I will expand on that topic in this chapter.

The API provides access to some very useful information—for example, being able to programmatically get the balance of an address, perhaps via a Python script or using WGET in Linux. This is very easy to do. At a browser, simply type the following, replacing $address with the address you want the balance for:

```
https://blockchain.info/balance?active=$address
```

For example:

```
https://blockchain.info/balance?active=3P91G6V8CurGLRtJgQmdNvkZ49s7GNMEcT
```

The result is returned in JSON format for easy processing, as shown in Figure 9-5.

```
https://blockchain.info/balance?active=3P91G6V8CurGLRtJgQmdNvkZ49s7GNMEcT

{"3P91G6V8CurGLRtJgQmdNvkZ49s7GNMEcT": {
    "final_balance": 166487420,
    "n_tx": 70,
    "total_received": 391186324
}}
```

Figure 9-5: Raw JSON of an address balance.

You can look up multiple addresses simultaneously by separating each address with the pipe symbol (|). This could be very useful if you had a list of addresses, perhaps in a text file. Alternatively, a simple Python script could query them all and return all the results rather than looking up each address in turn. The address can be in Base58 or the xPub format used by some sites such as blockchain.info.

The following Python script will ask you for the path to a text file that just needs Bitcoin addresses in a list. The text file needs to be formatted with a Bitcoin address on each line like this:

```
1431rgwV55CdwwJm4MsHxxStQVFFA3LFo4
13SKd2FMkM88UPxEMUEvSPP3sz138fHeeb
1CM8X9Y6Y68ae4SumSVLmQDd3svyKyHj9c
```

Add your addresses of interest to a text file and save it as something like addresses.txt. Next, type the following script into Notepad++, save it as something like bitcoin_balance.py, and run it by opening a command shell in the folder where you saved it and typing the following (or copy the script from this book's website www.investigatingcryptocurrencies.com):

```
python bitcoin_balance.py
```

It will then ask for the path to the address file. Type in the path, and it will create a new text file called balance.txt. This will have the balance in JSON format for all the addresses in the original text file. Give it a try (please note that the indents must be maintained and should be a Tab key per indent, or 4 spaces):

```
#!/usr/bin/env python


import os.path
import urllib2
import json

datain = raw_input("Enter the path to your 'address' file:")


if os.path.exists(datain):

    data = open(datain, "r")

    outfile = open("balances.txt", 'w')

    print "Extracting balances, please wait....."

    for line in data:

        bal = "https://blockchain.info/balance?active=%s" % line

        balance = urllib2.urlopen(bal)
```

```
        data2 = json.loads(balance.read())

        outfile.write(str(data2) + "\n")

    outfile.close()

    data.close()

else:

    sorry = "Sorry, not a valid path, please re-run the program"

    print sorry
```

Using the same technique, you can look up all of the transactions that an address has been involved with. The address can be formatted in Base58 or Hash160 and has a number of useful options. For this, you use the `rawaddr` command like this:

```
https://blockchain.info/rawaddr/$bitcoinaddress
```

For example:

```
https://blockchain.info/rawaddr/3P91G6V8CurGLRtJgQmdNvkZ49s7GNMEcT
```

There is also an option to just show a certain number of transactions by adding an `&limit` value to the API call. For example:

```
&limit=50
```

The default is 50, and at the time of writing, it is also the current maximum, but this could be used to just return the first few transactions. However, if you want more than the 50 maximum, you can specify an offset that will skip the required number of transactions and then provide the 50 (or the `&limit`), which will list transactions from that point. To do this, you add the following option:

```
&offset=100
```

The output provides each transaction with a number of useful fields including whether the transaction has been spent, the total value, and the number of inputs that the transaction has (see Figure 9-6).

If you have any programming ability, you can write small scripts to automate these commands for you. As an example, there's an API call for listing all of the unspent outputs. By writing some simple Python script, you can request a Bitcoin address from the user and then list out all of the unspent outputs. I then create another file with the balance, but please feel free to tinker with this all you like.

To run the following script, you will need a Python dependency called Requests installed. If you installed Python earlier in the book, browse to `c:\python27\scripts`. Hold down the Shift key while you right-click, and select Open Command Window here. Then type the following:

```
pip install requests
```

```
  https://blockchain.info/rawaddr/3P91G6V8CurGLRtJgQmdNvkZ49s7GNMEcT

    {
      "ver":1,
      "inputs":[
        {
          "sequence":4294967295,
          "witness":null,
          "prev_out":{
            "spent":true,
            "tx_index":243468872,
            "type":0,
            "addr":"14X6gFBso5Pw8HAinqZA2EHW6s4LNqhtze",
            "value":10000,
            "n":3,
            "script":"76a91426999846006d0cdd9a66062224de2fcbf26f288c88ac"
          },
          "script":"4730440220015a1050c5544d627204186edfa7f401eabfda2fc65a84af15fed047f09d
75c20fecb8dcafb4e86b"
        },
        {
          "sequence":4294967295,
          "witness":null,
          "prev_out":{
            "spent":true,
            "tx_index":270464968,
            "type":0,
            "addr":"15JqPKTHqowLSER1FJN3VjnMQZvWibaqsr",
            "value":7917500,
            "n":0,
            "script":"76a9142f3ff6cde37239ec072d99815f1c8e9dad594d5688ac"
          },
```

Figure 9-6: Raw transactions from an address.

Copy the code from the book's website (www.investigatingcryptocurrencies.com) into a new Notepad++ file and save it as unspent_n.py (or something similar).

Next, open a command shell in the folder location where you saved the file and type the following:

```
python unspent_n.py
```

The program will ask for a Bitcoin address and will then output two files: unspent_<address> and balance_<address>. The unspent_<address> file has its data delimited with spaces, so it can be imported into Excel or another spreadsheet program and listed into its columns. It includes the transaction ID, the transaction number, and the value of the transaction in satoshis (see Figure 9-7).

```
TX_ID TX_Number Amount

9c02f51b87461d8bd58b00399a70f941f3ad942de57417c898314dfeae0295af 0 182000 Satoshis
d1d17c1404c07d86bd7a6cb835a0b828248c25f4f9c3706fdeeb8daa39e479ae 0 40000 Satoshis
f495c4c556be923d124855788b449ee5d46c3aff76ab6b5530f97b6c4d8257b3 0 72910 Satoshis
cae9fa15e8b6108c98473a72117832b120745c45a8bdda4d28ad868e5f5c10bb 0 75937 Satoshis
7751c3e3999220bf522f358c4435bccd21ee9d2a5325135d79a1082341ae62c5 0 299590 Satoshis
e220d8c6e6c960f348883bb63d5db2de94e7c956fa60df47ad76104d0d36dbd8 0 9454385 Satoshis
1c87aff08f74ed9d7270a1a607b5e647b08f849ef150764ab56b7c8634f3fac2 0 131003 Satoshis
```

Figure 9-7: Output from the unspent_n script.

Give it a try:

```
import json
import requests


address = str(raw_input("Enter the bitcoin address? "))


myfile = open('unspent_%s.txt' % address, 'w')


resp = requests.get('https://blockchain.info/unspent?active=%s'
% address)


utxo_set = json.loads(resp.text)["unspent_outputs"]


myfile.write('TX_ID TX_Number Amount' + '\n' + '\n')


for utxo in utxo_set:
        myfile.write("%s %d %ld Satoshis" % (utxo['tx_hash'],
utxo['tx_output_n'], utxo['value']) + '\n')


myfile.write('\n' + '\n')


myfile = open('balance_%s.txt' % address, 'w')



balance = requests.get('https://blockchain.info/balance?active=%s'
% address)


for line in balance:
        myfile.write(line + '\n')
```

Extracting Raw Data from Ethereum

All cryptocurrencies have their blockchain viewers, and in my experience, all also have an API that you can use to extract the raw data. For example, you can achieve the same with Ethereum by browsing to etherscan.io. The process is a little different because you have to set up a free account to have access to the API. This is easy to do. You can find a direct link to it at `http://bit.ly/2CbelfJ`. You will need to follow the prompts to create an account and log in. Once you have done that, click API-KEYs ➪ Create API Key, and your API key will appear in a list as shown in Figure 9-8. Copy this key to a text file on your computer, and you won't have to log in every time to remind yourself of the key.

You can now use the key to run API calls to the Ethereum blockchain. For example, you can easily grab the ether balance for an address by opening a browser and typing the following in the address bar:

```
https://api.etherscan.io/api?module=account&action=balance&address=
0x08D86Af2D914C938676b851A02534Ca68A2B32ab&tag=latest&apikey=<YourAPIKey>
```

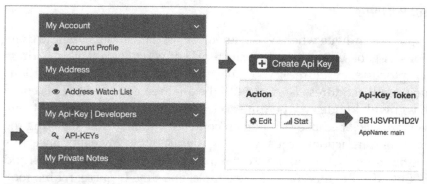

Figure 9-8: Etherscan.io API keys.

This command will return the ether value of the address. You can check that it is correct by looking at the browser-based display for this address, and you can see in Figure 9-9 that the value is correct.

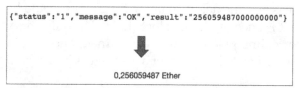

Figure 9-9: Checking the Ethereum value of an address.

Whereas the smallest subdivision of Bitcoin is the Satoshi, Ethereum's smallest denominator is the Wei. One Ether equals 1000000000000000000 Wei.

Once again, you can use Python scripts to extract balances for multiple addresses by adjusting the script used for Bitcoin previously. Just remember to include your API key in your URL call.

Searching for Information on a Specific Address

In Chapter 8, we looked at ways to search for cryptocurrency addresses online. We also looked briefly at searching for a specific address by using a search engine and some specific operators to remove certain results. You can also look at the pattern of an address. Some companies, both legitimate and illegitimate, sometimes use so-called "vanity" addresses. These have the first few characters calculated to relate to the company's product or name. This was discussed briefly in Chapter 4, "Transactions." If you locate a vanity address, searching on the prefix may help you to find the company or person that it relates to. For example, an address that begins with 1CSIT may help you to isolate my company CSITech here in the UK. Also, vanity addresses are often advertised, usually online, so a search engine search or search on a forum may uncover the address and its owner.

Temporal Patterns

Clustering is a technique where you gather a set of data and use that to draw conclusions. A good example is time clustering. If you have a Bitcoin address (or any cryptocurrency address), you can extract all the times that transactions are made from that address (sort of, but I'll explain in a moment). This could provide you with an idea of the time zone that a person is operating from. I use the word *could* because that person could be automatically delaying the deployment of transactions or just working nights, but in my experience, this technique has been useful and more often than not, accurate (again, I must add "sort of," but I'll get to this soon). For example, one time I was searching for a person within a criminal group that was using Bitcoin to move funds around the world. I knew one person of interest was on the East Coast of the United States and there was also a person in Europe. By looking at the times of Bitcoin trades, I saw a significant pattern of them being carried out within a European time zone. I followed this information, and it ended up being correct.

Why do I keep saying that the transaction times are "sort of" useful? When a user creates a transaction, there is no time field—in fact, a transaction could be prepared offline, weeks before it is encoded to the blockchain. The only entity that has a time field is the block time when a block was mined, encoded in UNIX time format. However, some blockchain viewer sites such as blockchain .info add a field, called "received time," which is set when one of their nodes first sees the transaction. You can be reasonably confident that the transaction propagates to all nodes within a minute or so, but the time can only ever be viewed as approximate, which is enough to infer patterns.

Browse to oxt.me. This is a great blockchain browser that provides information in useful ways. For example, when looking at Pay-to-Script or multisig transactions, you are able to plainly see the addresses that are involved in the script (see Figure 9-10).

However, take a look at Bitcoin address 328iXW6tBW16SpEmoXpAv8tevrpd QpL1CT, and then click the Temporal Patterns tab. This tab provides a graphical view of the times that incoming and, most importantly, outgoing transactions, were made. In Figure 9-11, you can see a very clear pattern that all outgoing transactions were made primarily in a 9 a.m. to 9 p.m. time frame. But what time zone is this?

Time zones in Bitcoin are a little bit complicated. A block timestamp is accepted as valid if it is greater than the median timestamp of the previous 11 blocks, and less than the network-adjusted time plus two hours. The first part is obvious enough—essentially the timestamp can't be too old—but what is the network-adjusted time? It's the median of the timestamps returned by all nodes connected to you. Remember that a Bitcoin node is connected to a number of other nodes that could be anywhere in the world. Does this not confuse the timestamp?

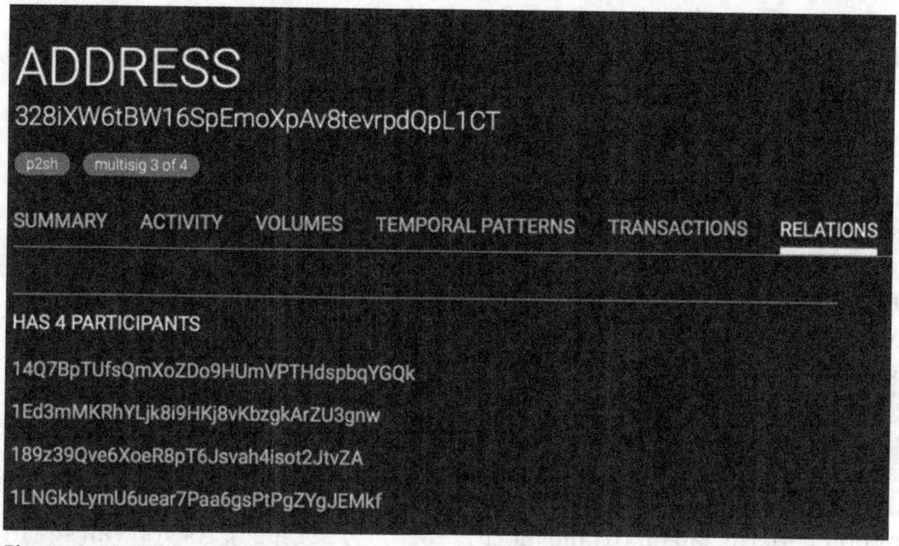

ADDRESS
328iXW6tBW16SpEmoXpAv8tevrpdQpL1CT
p2sh
multisig 3 of 4
SUMMARY
ACTIVITY
VOLUMES
TEMPORAL PATTERNS
TRANSACTIONS
RELATIONS
HAS 4 PARTICIPANTS
14Q7BpTUfsQmXoZDo9HUmVPTHdspbqYGQk
1Ed3mMKRhYLjk8i9HKj8vKbzgkArZU3gnw
189z39Qve6XoeR8pT6Jsvah4isot2JtvZA
1LNGkbLymU6uear7Paa6gsPtPgZYgJEMkf

Figure 9-10: Addresses involved in a multisig transaction.

ADDRESS
328iXW6tBW16SpEmoXpAv8tevrpdQpL1CT
SUMMARY
ACTIVITY
VOLUMES
TEMPORAL PATTERNS
TRANSACTIONS
RELATIONS
SCRIPT
NOTES (0)
INCOMING TXS - DAY OF THE WEEK
INCOMING TXS - HOUR
OUTGOING TXS - DAY OF THE WEEK
OUTGOING TXS - HOUR

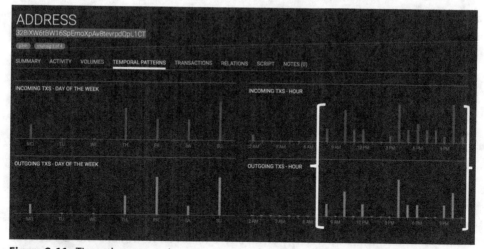

Figure 9-11: Times that transactions were sent or received by this address.

Whenever a node connects to another node, it gets a UTC timestamp from it, and also stores its offset from node-local UTC. The network-adjusted time is the node-local UTC plus the median offset from all connected nodes. Network time is never adjusted more than 70 minutes from the local system time, however.

So, the block time will not be exact but will be within 70 minutes of the local system time. This means that although you cannot be dogmatic by looking at all the transactions and the block time that they were included in, you can infer a time zone and perhaps other data if enough examples are in the set. For example, with very busy traders, you may be able to infer the time they start work and the time they finish. In one case, we were even able to work out how much time the person took for lunch.

Oxt.me uses the block time to record transactions and display the incoming and outgoing transactions graph. Although some transactions can be delayed due to issues with the blockchain itself or related to the fee not being sufficient, once submitted to the network, most of the time transactions are mined within 10 minutes or so. This is not always the case, so taking a single transaction and drawing any conclusion is dangerous, but where you have a large data set, a time zone can often be ascertained.

So, you can use the block time such as the one used by oxt.me, or you can use the receive time of a node such as the time recorded in the blockchain.info database. I tend to use both and see if the collated timings agree.

Take a look at address 1N31P6vM4mJHUZx325qYj6ZFRK8eXHqqfo on the Temporal Patterns tab on oxt.me (`http://bit.ly/2z1e0Cc`). As you can see in Figure 9-12, the block times of the transactions are offset quite clearly between 3 a.m. and 12 p.m.

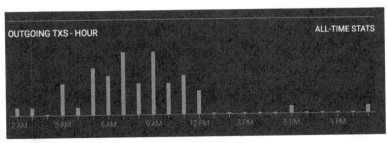

Figure 9-12: Timestamps between 3 a.m. and 12 p.m.

However, as you just learned, block times can be offset by an hour or more from UTC. But if you make an assumption that the majority of people would be sending transactions during normal work hours, then you can make a broad assumption that this address is perhaps five to seven hours behind UTC. This would likely put them in the eastern to center of the American continent. Although this sounds extremely broad, having an idea of the global location of a person is very useful. An idea of where a person is may also infer a language spoken by the user and hence help you discern where a person may hang out on the Internet.

You can use Excel to confirm this by looking at the node received times recorded by blockchain.info. Use the export feature described earlier in blockchain.info (Filter ⇨ Export History) to export the address data. Try it with the address mentioned previously (`http://bit.ly/2AbKx6W`). Then open the data in a single spreadsheet. Sort on the Received/Sent column and delete all the Received transactions.

Next, you need to split the date and time into two fields. You can do this by using Data ⇨ Text to Columns. Select Space as an extra delimiter. This will split Date into the first column and Time into the second column. Format the Time column as "time" and then sort the column. Now you can see the times in order. If you take one of the transaction IDs and search in oxt.me, it will provide the time that the transaction was included in the block.

For example, if you look at the spreadsheet entry in Figure 9-13, you see a received time by blockchain.info of 05:13:36. If you search on the transaction ID in oxt.me, you see a block mined time of 05:21:59. This confirms that the time differences between received and block time broadly agree.

Figure 9-13: Transaction and block times are close enough to agree.

You can also graph all of the entries in Excel to see if they agree with the graphed block times in oxt.me. Delete all columns except the Time and Money Out columns. Select these two columns and use Insert ⇨ Graph, x y Scatter. This will provide a scatter graph showing all the outbound transactions with Time as the x-axis and the value as the y-axis. Although the value is useful, in this situation, you just want to see the clustering of times. As with the block-mined time in oxt.me, you can see that the majority of outbound transactions are between 3 a.m. and 12 p.m. with a few scattered to the sides. This could confirm a suspicion that the owner of the address is offset by approximately five to six hours less than GMT (see Figure 9-14).

If you have a number of addresses that relate to one person, you can correlate them to give a larger set of time data. You can use Excel to do this very easily. Use the export feature described earlier in blockchain.info to export the address data in turn for all the addresses you believe are owned by the person of interest. Then import all the data into a single spreadsheet and proceed as before.

Also, if you are trying to decide if an address does indeed belong to a particular user, checking the temporal patterns may provide you with a little more data. For example, if all the addresses you have suggest a U.S. time zone, but another address suggests an Australasian zone, then you may conclude that the address is erroneous and does not belong to the suspect.

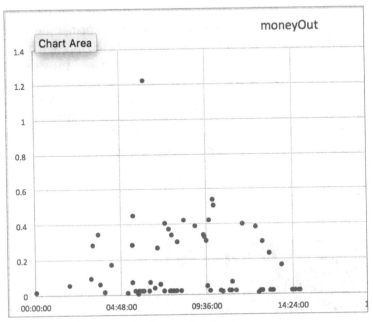

Figure 9-14: Scatter graph of transaction times.

Ethereum Times

Ethereum is similar to Bitcoin in the way that it handles times. Transaction times are not routinely included in the raw data, although it is possible to encode a time into a raw contract. You can extract raw transaction data that includes the time that it was mined—its block time. Because Ethereum blocks are mined so much more quickly than Bitcoin, this provides a clearer picture as to when the transaction hit the memory pool.

You can get a list of transactions for an Ethereum address by running an API call as follows:

```
http://api.etherscan.io/api?module=account&action=txlist&address=<Address
ToSearch>&startblock=0&endblock=99999999&sort=asc&apikey=<YourApiKey>
```

This will return a list of all transactions with the first two fields being the block number that the transaction was mined as part of and then the timestamp of the block in UNIX time:

```
{"blockNumber":"65204","timeStamp":"1439232889",......
```

Because the UNIX time value contains both the time and the data, it can be useful to extract all the dates perhaps using a Python script, convert to standard dating, and use Excel or similar to analyze the groupings of dates, times of day, and so on as described previously.

Analyzing a Recovered Wallet

In Chapter 8, I discussed how you can extract a wallet file from Bitcoin Core. Although other wallet formats exist, I felt it was worthwhile explaining how to extract the data from the `wallet.dat` file because many of the techniques can be applied to other programs.

Once you have the recovered Bitcoin Core wallet file, you can do anything with it that the original users could do. You have full access to their private and public keys and all of their past transactions. Of course, this also means that you now own their bitcoins and can transact them as you wish. This is not dissimilar to having a suspect's bank account numbers and passwords. You are essentially in full control of the assets. It is important to move funds as quickly as possible in case private keys are held by a third party. (This is covered in more detail in Chapter 14, "Seizing Coins.")

As you could be reading this in any country on earth, I don't think that it is right that I comment on the legalities of what you can do when you have access to assets. You may have right of seizure or you may not, and decisions need to be made about how the law is best applied. We will look at methods of asset seizure in Chapter 14.

Setting Up Your Investigation Environment

The first thing you need to do is install a version of Bitcoin Core. You may have already done this back in Chapter 1. Should you wish to install the same version as the suspect, get access to the forensic disk images and browse to `c:\Program Files\Bitcoin\readme.txt`, and it will provide the Bitcoin Core version. You can download older versions of Bitcoin Core from `https://bitcoin.org/en/version-history`. I favor installing a new version of Bitcoin Core each time I work on a new cryptocurrency investigation, and then I can simply point Bitcoin Core to the previously installed blockchain as described in Chapter 1.

I expect that you have already applied the suggestions in Chapter 8 to find the `wallet.dat` file, but in case you need reminding, you will normally find it at `C:\Users\YourUserName\Appdata\Roaming\Bitcoin`.

The first thing you need to do is back up your own wallet file. The best way to do this is to back it up from the Bitcoin command-line interface (Bitcoin-cli):

1. Open a command shell and change to the following folder:

```
C:\Program Files\Bitcoin\daemon
```

2. Type this into the command shell:

   ```
   bitcoind
   ```

3. Minimize (*do not* close) the command shell.

4. Open a second command shell and browse to:

   ```
   C:\Program Files\Bitcoin\daemon
   ```

5. Back up your wallet file by typing the following:

   ```
   bitcoin-cli backupwallet <path>
   ```

   For example:

   ```
   bitcoin-cli backupwallet c:\temp
   ```

6. The next step is to close Bitcoin Core and copy the suspect's wallet file back to the right location:

   ```
   C:\Users\YourUserName\Appdata\Roaming\Bitcoin.
   ```

   It is also possible to start Bitcoin Core with the switch `-wallet <other-wallet.dat>`. For example:

   ```
   Bitcoin-qt -wallet c:\temp\wallet.dat
   ```

   This will start the program with the other wallet that you have specified.

> **NOTE** Although this works, it bothers me because it would be very easy to use the wrong wallet—perhaps from another investigation. I would prefer to have a clean folder and start the software with the right wallet every time before moving that wallet and replacing it with a new one from a new job.

7. Next, dump out the contents of the suspect's wallet. Although you can do this from the command line as before because you are now working on your own computer, you can use the Bitcoin Core console if you wish. With Bitcoin Core open, click Help ➪ Debug Window ➪ Console (see Figure 9-15).

My preference is to work from a command shell and use the bitcoin cli. With bitcoin_cli running in your terminal as previously described, type the following to dump the contents of your suspect's wallet:

```
bitcoin-cli dumpwallet c:\temp\dump1.csv
```

The output is fantastic and extremely useful.

First, the dump file provides you with information that is useful forensically. It provides times and dates when the dump was made so that you have a record of it. Please note that the block height listed here is from your own computer, so don't confuse it with the block height from the suspect.

You then have the xprv or extended private master key, as shown in Figure 9-16.

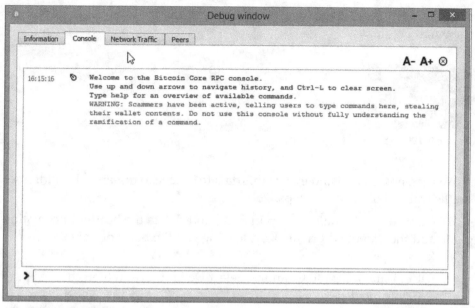

Figure 9-15: The built-in Bitcoin Core console.

```
# extended private masterkey: xprv9s21ZrQH143K31Qk4knT
```

Figure 9-16: The extended private master key.

The private keys are derived from the extended private master key, as shown in Figure 9-17.

```
Kwiq4bKZU3tM7h7vFDFEVAQ3fqizYYAsBYohXDBmASu1
KwVh1BAQLYao7g9gneLk84nHFka7gzTg17hp96gRBeJf
Kyi3oqG3xhZwE9aJ9DcvYQDHcQBxymg2q9HYaftE63nr
L5Mfj5deABjFDvUsX3N94L4eiiKPeE9mzgv2MvrPrdx9
L5SqLJFXdCoFSprVUGCuj9dPQyyjqmzwGrDXkEqHuCm2
L2DMAhTVHVfJghj1f9A9qPAmvKhnpRr3pcWm58FDVdtX
L5bZuN4cEMyFkY6XKvnTs5fbKRDoSkZdmwYTC63JtypG
L5FjGVsnshS17Wkh6qxDuNhqbknVX6J9pzFeqz5Y297Z
```

Figure 9-17: The private keys.

The public keys are derived from the private keys, as shown in Figure 9-18.

```
addr=1JdAefvK7XuRt2KtMLoi23oU6aMRFiFjg
addr=127NMLsYq4qft75vrE7tZAMikvwM48QkxW
addr=134cUpSbHVgR56ZeZPhw8d4ncuaDqd3i38
# addr=14BhLFpEB1BEcroVJKBtV52ajsDpKacmv
```

Figure 9-18: The public keys.

And finally, the HD or hierarchical deterministic paths are displayed as shown in Figure 9-19.

```
hdkeypath=m/0'/0'/21'
hdkeypath=m/0'/0'/46'
hdkeypath=m/0'/0'/66'
hdkeypath=m/0'/0'/57'
hdkeypath=m/0'/0'/62'
hdkeypath=m/0'/0'/92'
```

Figure 9-19: HD paths.

You can now format and export this data to be able to research the addresses in the wallet. Follow these steps:

1. Open the CSV wallet dump in Excel and delete the header information and the Extended Private Key, leaving just the body private and public keys.

2. Select Data ➪ Text to Columns. Select Delimited, and then choose Space and = as the delimiters.

3. Remove all the columns except the public keys. Select the columns with all the public keys in them and use the keyboard shortcut Ctrl+c to copy them. Then select another cell (for example, I often just select a cell underneath the list) and right-click and select Paste ➪ Transpose.

   This will convert the list of public keys into a row as shown in Figure 9-20.

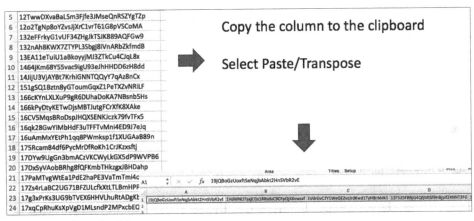

Figure 9-20: Row of public keys.

4. Delete the vertical column of keys and export the resulting row as CSV.

5. Open the resulting CSV in Notepad++ and perform a Search and Replace to replace the commas (,) with pipe symbols (|).

   You end up with a list of all the public keys that were in the suspect's wallet, delimited with a pipe symbol.

6. You can now use the API lookup to get information on all of these addresses. Just type the following in the address bar of a browser, replacing `<PasteinAddresses>` with your pipe-delimited list:

```
blockchain.info/multiaddr?active=<PasteinAddresses>
```

The output from this command is extremely useful. First, it provides collated data from the whole wallet, showing the total number of transactions, the total amount received and sent, as well as the final balance. (In Figure 9-21, these values are zero because they are from a test wallet.)

```
▼ wallet:
    n_tx:               0
    n_tx_filtered:      0
    total_received:     0
    total_sent:         0
    final_balance:      0
```

Figure 9-21: Totals from the whole wallet.

Next, each queried address is listed with the same data, number of transactions, final balance, and so on (see Figure 9-22).

```
▼ 0:
    address:            "1PqroBQh5x1oLrZAueYHLzj5XEWDfYkDEJ"
    n_tx:               0
    total_received:     0
    total_sent:         0
    final_balance:      0
    change_index:       0
    account_index:      0
▼ 1:
    address:            "1768WBcbqWnYKLPZv2nVB51JqcF33dAhEH"
    n_tx:               0
    total_received:     0
    total_sent:         0
    final_balance:      0
    change_index:       0
    account_index:      0
▼ 2:
    address:            "132eFFrkyG1vUF34ZHgJkTSJK889AQFGw9"
    n_tx:               0
    total_received:     0
    total_sent:         0
    final_balance:      0
    change_index:       0
    account_index:      0
▼ 3:
    address:            "1NaeKmDgpU7Buut3gyeuw7ZTk9rZNXtgoh"
    n_tx:               0
    total_received:     0
```

Figure 9-22: Data on each address in the wallet.

This output helps you to identify the addresses that have been used by your suspect, and you can then take those addresses and do further open-source research or ultimately use the blockchain to follow the transactions where the addresses were used. This is the fastest and most efficient way I know to isolate used addresses.

> **EXERCISE**
>
> If you have installed Bitcoin Core, go and dump your own wallet and follow the steps described in this chapter to extract the addresses and analyze what addresses have been used.

Importing a Private Key

It is very possible that you have not been able to acquire a complete wallet from a suspect, but perhaps during a premises search, a private key was found. Or maybe, a file was located on a recovered hard drive with a string that could be a private key. Bitcoin Core enables you to import a recovered private key and hence gain control of the public key addresses. I strongly recommend importing into a new wallet on your forensic machine so as not to have crossover with other investigations. One wallet for each person of interest is much easier to manage and avoid any mistaken crossovers.

With the `bitcoin_cli` daemon running, type the following in a new terminal:

```
bitcoin-cli importprivkey <priv_key_in_WIF_format> Label
```

The private key must be in the WIF format, and the Label can be anything that identifies this particular key.

> **EXERCISE**
>
> Using the WalletGenerator that you downloaded in Chapter 6, do the following:

NOTE If you didn't download the WalletGenerator in Chapter 6, just browse to `http://bit.ly/2yIHeWu` and double-click the `index.html` file. If you are not sure how to use this file, check Chapter 6 for more details.

1. Generate a new public and private key.
2. Import it into Bitcoin Core using the command `importprivkey`.
3. Dump the wallet using the command `dumpwallet` and check the output in the resulting CSV file.

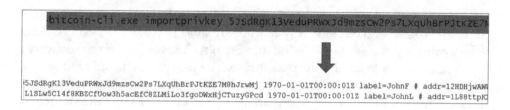

Dealing with an Encrypted Wallet

It is recommended that a wallet be encrypted and protected with a passphrase. If you are planning to own, use, or trade any cryptocurrency, I highly recommend that you protect your wallet with a strong password. Otherwise, the theft of your computer could leave the wallet vulnerable to anyone who attempts to use it. Of course, if you import a suspect's wallet and it asks for a password, you might think that you are at a dead end, but thankfully, there is a tool that may be able to help. It is called BTCRecover and you can download it from `http://bit.ly/2j1u0eI`. If you want to try it, download the zip file and unzip to a folder.

Before I talk about how to use BTCRecover, I need to cover the issues associated with cracking passwords. You learned back in Chapter 2 that passwords are, by definition, difficult to crack, and I referred briefly to methods that you can use to try to reverse a hashed password back to its original phrase. There are only four primary ways of discovering a password from its hash:

Brute Force   Try everything—literally. Start with the letter *a*, and then keep trying different letter, number, and symbol combinations until you get a result. Although this method will always work eventually, it's the word *eventually* that is the problem. This could take many months, years, or even millennia depending on a vast number of factors.

Dictionary Attack   Define a big dictionary, in the language of the user, and try every word in until you (hopefully) have success.

Calculated Tables   Pre-calculated tables such as Rainbow Tables can be used to speed up an attack against certain types of hashes.

Master Key Attack   In most encryption programs such as Bitlocker and Veracrypt, when users enter their password to open an encrypted file container or full-disk encrypted hard drive, the password does not actually decrypt any files but rather is involved in the generation of a master key, such as an AES or DES type key. This is usually stored in memory and is used as the decrypter of any requested files from the encrypted container. If you can access the computer memory, it is possible to extract the master keys and decrypt the files without knowing the passphrase.

The encryption used by Bitcoin Core to secure the `wallet.dat` file is AES-256-CBC and uses a password to master key method mentioned in the Master

Key Attack method described previously. The difficult thing for the investigator is that there is no obvious way to know if a `wallet.dat` file is encrypted. When you copy the `wallet.dat` file into Bitcoin Core and open the software, it will not ask you to enter your passphrase. The passphrase is only requested when you want to do something such as send coins. The quickest way to check if a `wallet.dat` file is encrypted is to open Bitcoin Core with the suspect's `wallet.dat` file in the correct location and click Settings. If the Encrypt Wallet menu option is grayed out, leaving just Change Passphrase available to select, then you know that the wallet is encrypted. Alternatively, you may attempt a `dumpwallet` operation, and if the wallet is password-protected, you will get the following error message:

```
Error: Please enter the wallet passphrase with walletpassphrase first.
(code -13)
```

If you have an encrypted wallet, you are a bit stuck because you won't be able to dump the wallet file. This means you cannot see any addresses, transact using the private keys, or seize any coins.

BTCRecover uses a complex type of dictionary attack that allows you to attempt an attack using just part of a password if you know it, or a dictionary attack using wildcards and word derivatives. If you have fast graphics cards installed in your system, you can use GPU acceleration to massively decrease your search times. It supports an impressive array of clients from a number of cryptocurrencies. Here is a list of supported clients as of this writing (you can find the current list at `http://bit.ly/2j1u0eI`):

- Bitcoin wallet password recovery support for:
  - Armory
  - Bitcoin Unlimited/Classic/XT/Core
  - MultiBit HD and MultiBit Classic
  - Electrum (1.x and 2.x)
  - Hive for OS X
  - BIP-39 passphrases, Bitcoin and Ethereum supported (for example, TREZOR and Ledger passphrases)
  - mSIGNA (CoinVault)
  - Blockchain.info
  - Bitcoin Wallet for Android/BlackBerry spending PINs and encrypted backups
  - KnC Wallet for Android encrypted backups
  - Bither

- Other wallets that are supported by BTCRecover include:
  - Litecoin Core
  - Electrum-LTC
  - Litecoin Wallet for Android encrypted backups
  - Dogecoin Core
  - MultiDoge
  - Dogecoin Wallet for Android encrypted backups
- Bitcoin and Ethereum seed recovery support for:
  - Electrum (1.x and 2.x, plus wallet file loading support)
  - BIP-32/39 compliant wallets (bitcoinj), including:
    - MultiBit HD
    - Bitcoin Wallet for Android/BlackBerry (with seeds previously extracted by decrypt_bitcoinj_seeds)
    - Hive for Android, for iOS, and Hive Web
    - breadwallet for iOS
  - BIP-32/39/44 Bitcoin and Ethereum-compliant wallets, including:
    - Mycelium for Android
    - TREZOR
    - Ledger
    - Jaxx
    - MyEtherWallet
    - Bither
    - Blockchain.info

BTCRecover is a reasonably simple command-line tool to use but has a wide range of features and options, so I will just cover the key ones.

If you know, or think you know, part of the wallet passphrase, you can specify parts of the word or words or use wildcards. There is an extensive help page at http://bit.ly/2AUY3jB, which is essential reading if you want to use BTCRecover to its fullest capacity. Generally, as an investigator, I do not know part of the password. That's not an impossible situation, however, as you may have discovered Windows login passwords, web form passwords, or others during any disk or memory analysis, and it is possible that there is a pattern. It is anecdotally reported that people unconsciously use three passwords as a base and then build derivatives of them. For example, someone might use dog as a password but then use dog1, d0g, and d09 on other websites or password-protected files. This is helpful because if I have part of a password that is used frequently, then I can tell BTCRecover to calculate derivatives of that phrase or phrases and try them. Although you can do this with just a few words, you can also achieve the same with a complete dictionary.

The first thing you need to do is to download or create a dictionary. If you do a web search for **password lists**, you will find a large collection of wordlists to be downloaded that can be used as dictionaries.

You can also create a dictionary by running the Strings program (downloadable from `http://bit.ly/2kbz7wY`) against any file. If you run Strings against a raw disk image or memory dump, you will end up with a file with tens of millions of ASCII strings. This works well if you think that a password may have been recently used and could exist in a disk cache or in a memory register somewhere.

Once you have your dictionary, you can run it against your password-protected `wallet.dat` file. To make life easy, copy your encrypted `wallet.dat` file and your dictionary into the BTCRecover folder then run it by typing the following:

```
python btcrecover.py --wallet wallet.dat --passwordlist <pathtodictionary>
```

For example:

```
python btcrecover.py --wallet wallet.dat --passwordlist c:\temp\rockyou
.txt
```

This will attempt every word or phrase in the dictionary, and if it's a large dictionary and you have a slow computer, this will take a long time. I tested the cracking speeds on several computers, and the results were staggeringly different. A Windows VM with 2 GB of RAM suggested it would take 10.1 days to complete the dictionary. Remember this isn't 10 days for a cracked wallet, just 10 days to get through every word. In comparison, an Apple iMac with 16 GB of RAM said it would take 3.2 days to complete the same job.

Although you can just run a dictionary file, you can also calculate and attempt derivatives of every word in your dictionary. My favorite presets enable derivatives to be calculated without creating a rules file—these can be added to your command line:

- `--typos-swap`

  This swaps two adjacent characters within each word.

- `--typos-repeat`

  This repeats a character in each word.

- `--typos delete`

  This deletes a character in each word.

- `--typos-case`

  This changes the case, from upper to lower and vice versa, of a single character.

You can also specify how many typos are applied to each word. For example, `--typos 2` will apply up to two of each specified typo to each word in the dictionary.

It is also possible to create a typos map, which is a superb capability to specify character replacements. Many people create passwords by using specific character replacements such as switching an *S* for a *5* or an *I* for an exclamation point (!). You can define all these rules by listing them in a file called `typos` `.txt`. Just follow these steps:

1. Open a new Notepad++ document.

2. Add the following lines, separating the two columns by a tab as indicated:

   ```
   oO [tab] 0

   qQ [tab] 9

   sS [tab] 5$
   ```

3. Save the document into your BTCRecover folder as **typos.txt**.

   Every time BTCRecover has a word in the dictionary file that uses either an *o* or an *O*, it will attempt the word with the letter replaced with a zero. Also, both the uppercase letter *Q* and the lowercase *q* will be changed to a *9*.

   The next line is slightly different. Each time BTCRecover encounters either an *s* or an *S*, it will attempt two changes: both a *5* and a *$* symbol.

You can define as many options as you like, but just remember that each word in the dictionary will now have numerous versions to attempt and will therefore take significantly longer. However, this will massively improve your chances of success.

To make use of the `typos.txt` file, just add `--typos-map typos.txt`. For example, with this option included, your command might look like this.

```
python btcrecover.py --wallet wallet.dat --typos-map typos.txt
--passwordlist c:\temp\rockyou.txt --typos 3
```

This command will attempt to crack your wallet using the dictionary rockyou `.txt` while attempting up to three character changes for each word. There's no guarantee that this will work, but if the correct word or the word derivative is tried, the password will be displayed, and you can now log in to your wallet in Bitcoin Core or whatever program you open your wallet in.

NOTE The password-cracking program John the Ripper can also be used to generate wordlists with word derivatives. You can download it from `http://www` `.openwall.com/john/`.

Inferring Other Data

Looking at the transaction values and frequency can be very helpful in an investigation. I mentioned earlier the difference between literal evidence and evidence that can infer data that is, perhaps, not explicit or immediately apparent.

Let's consider an example where we are investigating a store on the dark web. We may have an address recovered from a computer belonging to a suspect and want to infer what we can from it. We have downloaded his site as described in the last chapter, and a search for the address showed that it was used as the default payment address for a particular type of product. Knowing this, we can use the blockchain to infer how successful the suspect was in selling this product type and perhaps the amounts of money made. Interestingly, that last statement is not as easy as it sounds to achieve. How much money did the suspect make? How are we defining an "amount" of money? To illustrate, the suspect described may have been selling online several years ago and was charging 1 bitcoin for his product. At the time, 1 bitcoin may have only been worth a few hundred dollars; however, as we start our investigation, 1 bitcoin is worth $18,000 dollars. To figure out how much the suspect made in a traditional currency sense as well as how much he was really charging for his product, we need to know the bitcoin-to-dollar conversion on the day of each trade.

A good blockchain viewer for this type of analysis is `www.bitinfocharts` `.com`. Browse to the site and search for address **3P91G6V8Cur GLRtJgQmdNvkZ49s7GNMEcT** (or just use `http://bit.ly/2kMaMKz`).

This site provides a very useful view of all the transactions involving an address both as a graph over time and as a table with the amounts color-coded in red for an outward transaction and green for an inward transaction. It also shows the dates in reverse order from the last transaction. From this data, we can first infer how successful this product was by finding out if there were many transactions over a short period or the opposite. However, the most useful thing about this site is the value. The site lists the transacted bitcoin and then provides the dollar value against the dollar trade value when the transaction was made. For example, Figure 9-23 shows that on September 6, 2017 (date not shown), approximately 0.63 bitcoin was received, providing a balance of around 2.95 bitcoin. However, the final column shows that the address balance was now worth $13,446 at a trading price (at the time the transaction was mined) of $4552.63.

| +0.63373902 BTC | 2.95335005 BTC | $13,446 @ $4,552.63 |

Figure 9-23: Bitinfocharts provides the dollar price at the time of the transaction.

Using this calculation, we can track what the dollar value was over time. Also, by using the trading price per bitcoin for each transaction, we can easily calculate the bitcoin dollar value. In this case, we do the calculation 4552*0.63, which gives us a real-world dollar transaction value of $2,867.76. By repeating this across all the transactions, we can figure out the approximate value of each transaction even though the dollar values may be fluctuating wildly.

Summary

In this chapter, we considered how to analyze a recovered address or wallet for information related to it. You learned how to extract data from a wallet file and then use an API to extract information from a blockchain about the suspect's addresses, as well as how to use a tool to crack a wallet that's password-protected. This chapter showed how you can look at data in an explicit way and the way that data can infer conclusions that can help you in an investigation.

But what about the movement of cryptocurrency from one address to another? In the next chapter, you'll learn how to track the money across a blockchain.

Following the Money

In the previous chapter, you learned how to do research on recovered addresses and find both direct and indirect evidence that could help you with your investigation. In this chapter, you'll look at ways by which you can manually follow transactions through the blockchain and how you can do this in a structured manner. You will also look at techniques to attempt to cluster addresses together into a single owner.

Initial Hints and Tips

Throughout the book, I have referenced blockchain viewers such as blockchain .info, oxt.me, blockexplorer.com, and others. These online tools are very straight-forward to use—just search for an address or a transaction, view the details on the screen, and, as I'm sure you have discovered, click other addresses in a transaction to see previous or following transactions. If you have tried doing this, you will have discovered that you get lost, confused, despondent, and generally spun around very quickly indeed! Because of the Base58 and hex naming of address and transactions, following transactions from address to address can be bewildering. When you're working with these tools, I recommend the following:

- Take it slow. Because you can click from transaction to transaction as quickly as the Internet will let you, it is tempting to click away merrily, and this generally results in . . . no results. Each time you click and load a new screen, you need to take time to consider and understand what you are looking at.

- Take good notes. Use a notetaking app or software to map out manually what you find, such as addresses, values, dates, and so on.

- Make use of visualization software. In the next chapter, we will look at both free and commercial software tools that enable you to visually map the relationships between transactions. Although these tools are invaluable, once again there is a risk in mapping many transactions quickly and not stopping to think about what you are seeing.

- Stop clicking. Remember in Chapter 9 I spoke about literal and inferred, or indirect, evidence. What can you see, and what can you conclude before clicking again?

Use the first five or six characters of an address when taking notes. The lengthy addresses of Bitcoin, Ethereum, or any cryptocurrency that uses private keys as its addressing system make it complex for the human eye to process. Using just the first five or six characters makes the string easier for your mind to process and recognize if you see it again. The risk, of course, is that the same string of characters repeats itself with the remaining characters you haven't noted as being different. However, the chances of this happening are really remote. Bitcoin addresses always start with a 1, a 3, or bc1 but with six characters in total there are over 1.3 billion possibilities (ignoring the other characters in the address). So, when I note an address, instead of writing **16B2rHA5znfbHyTEF4g8ddg8aLzErQhmpr**, I would just write **16B2rH**.

Transactions on Blockchain.info

To help you understand the elements of the transaction and how they are displayed, let's take a look at a transaction on blockchain.info. Browse to `http://bit.ly/2f4Kx3q`. This relates to Bitcoin address `17h6CDrXUb4zVUjed kP6ibkpkieDXd116j`. If you take a look at the transaction dated 2017-09-10 at 11:43:35 in Figure 10-1, you'll see a red arrow. This signifies that coin is being sent from the address you searched for.

Figure 10-1: Transaction where the target address is an input.

If you take a look at the transaction from the previous hour in Figure 10-2, you see a green arrow. This relates to coin being sent to the address you searched for.

Figure 10-2: Transaction where the target is an output address.

You can also see the transaction ID, the date, and the fee that was charged. The total value is shown in either bitcoin or dollar value and can be switched by clicking the red or green total value button.

In simple terms, here's what you can learn about Bitcoin address 17h6CD:

- At 10:43 on 2017-09-10, 1MWP6s sent a total of 1.05… bitcoin to two addresses:
    - 1GMJKt received 0.1146 bitcoin.
    - 17h6CD received 0.944… bitcoin.
- Both addresses have since spent the received coins.
- One hour later (at 11:43:35), the target address 17h6CD sent its 0.944… bitcoin to two addresses:
    - 1Hjah3 received 0.5186 bitcoin.
    - 136dCK received 0.42… bitcoin.
- Both addresses have since spent the received coins.

We have just broken down the life of this address. We know where the funds came from and where they went on the blockchain. What is interesting with both these transactions is that one address sent bitcoin to two other addresses. For example, the 17h6CD address sent the funds to two addresses, but can we discern whether either of these addresses actually belongs to the owner of 17h6CD?

You learned previously that you cannot transact part of the value of an address, so if an address contains 1 bitcoin, then we have to spend that entire bitcoin. If we are only paying a vendor 0.7 of a bitcoin, then we can recover 0.3 as change. This means that one of the addresses belongs to the owner of 17h6CD. This technique can help you to build a picture of addresses assigned to a specific owner.

Identifying Change Addresses

We can look at an easier example to learn how to identify addresses belonging to the same person. Browse to http://bit.ly/2y8fzfv, which resolves to transaction 03ba36a19bb7cb3ede88dd4cca78a9bed380524c8995a6a910e98f944ee91053 on blockchain.info. If necessary, click the total value green button to change to bitcoin values rather than the dollar value. If you are unable to follow the link, the input and output values are listed for you.

What do you see? Who owns which addresses?

First, three addresses are sending coin to two addresses. In the vast majority of cases, you can assume that the three input addresses belong to the same person. (I appreciate that the address could belong to a company or otherwise, but I'm using "person" in this example to keep it simple. Other possibilities exist, such as the addresses being passed through a mixer.)

I usually use a pad and pen to note the values, which makes it easier to do the math. The values in this example are as follows:

Input Values

- Input 1: 1FkRsN is 1 bitcoin.
- Input 2: 16SFxo is .0999… bitcoin.
- Input 3: 1C3NQ is .0789… bitcoin.

Output Values

- Output 1: 19Gmgg is .0788… bitcoin.
- Output 2: 1PsKxK is 2 bitcoin.

What can we discern from this? Any of the input values would pay for Output 1, so it would be pointless to include all three inputs to pay for Output 1 if that was the target address we were paying. However, it takes all three input values to pay for Output 2, because no two inputs add up to a sufficient value. From this, we can infer that the payment was to Output 2, 1PsKxK, and it is likely that the change address is Output 1, 19Gmgg. So, the three inputs and 19Gmgg likely belong to the same person.

If we now have 19Gmgg as a change address, by looking at transactions into this address, we can infer further addresses that possibly belong to the same person. Click the hyperlinked 19Gmgg address, and it will load all the transactions that pertain to this address. At the time of writing, we see eight transactions with five of them being coin moving into the address. By applying the same logic as before, we can see that it appears that 19Fmgg is a change address in each instance. This means that we can infer that the same person also is the owner of the following:

- 1A6GHK
- 1AaEih
- 1CMBbd
- 1Gc3RJ

- 1EJYsC
- 19GCG8
- The three addresses indicated previously

You can see examples of this in Figure 10-3. (Remember, our address of interest starts with 19Gmgg.)

Figure 10-3: Inferring owned addresses from the change address 19Gmgg.

Try this exercise. Browse to `http://bit.ly/2xn20dX`, which is Bitcoin transaction `e5838dbb8b5eb7a1a8ba532e168edb1d7fd0fe072206fb04ef24c6c6806a7682`. Can you identify the change address? See Figure 10-4.

Six addresses send around 0.127… bitcoin to two addresses:

- Output 1: 1LTShY - 0.010… bitcoin
- Output 2: 16YCvV - 0.117… bitcoin

One of the input addresses, 17Z2c3 (0.08… bitcoin), could pay the 1LTShY amount without the need for the others. This means that 16YCvV is likely the target payment, and 1LTShY is probably the change address. In fact, if you look at the other inputs, it would have been more efficient to use inputs 1 and 2 to pay for 1LTShY if it had been the primary payment (see Figure 10-4).

Figure 10-4: Working out the change address from the transaction.

Now try another exercise that's a little harder. Browse to http://bit .ly/2y8P5dR, which represents the transaction de187bb4248ffd87ced39ae 497b452756a7583fd5c7863fd95110656e144a34b. Or if you can't browse to this, just take a look at Figure 10-5.

Figure 10-5: Inferring the change address with fewer inputs and outputs.

It's trickier to figure out the change address with this one because there is just one input and two outputs, and the one amount covers both outputs. How can you try and infer the change address and the primary payment? Change addresses are often dynamic in that they are generated by a modern wallet when a transaction is built. If this is the case, you would expect there to be no prior transactions to the addition of the change.

If you click output 1BWRXX, you can see that there are several hundred transactions, with the address being used to both spend and receive coin over a long period of time. However, if you take a look at 1M96jh (Figure 10-6), you see just two transactions: the one you have just been looking at and a second transaction to zero the value of the address. This is normal behavior for change addresses because they are often swept into primary addresses for future transactions.

> **NOTE**   Remember that you can't be completely dogmatic about this, but the techniques are right more often than they are wrong.

Figure 10-6: Inferring change addresses by looking at how often it has been used.

There is another way to locate the change address. This is when a user who is making use of a single signature address (which, as you know, always starts with a 1 in Bitcoin) pays a company or person that is making use of a multi-signature or multisig address (which always starts with a 3). If there is an output also starting with a 1, this will be the change address. You can see an example by browsing to http://bit.ly/2CbXD5h, which represents transaction de187bb4248ffd87ce d39ae497b452756a7583fd5c7863fd95110656e144a34b. Take a look at Figure 10-7. The change address will be the 16VPPK address.

Figure 10-7: The 1 address is likely the change address.

It is the same in reverse, where a multisig address starting with 3 is the input and the outputs are a 1 and a 3 address. The change address will likely be the multisig 3 address.

Another Simple Method to Identify Clusters

Sometimes you can be looking at a transaction and just cannot decide which is the change address that belongs to your suspect. A simple technique is to look for other transactions that use one of the addresses as part of an input that includes an address you already know belongs to them.

For example, if you look at Figure 10-8, you will see a single address sending coin to two addresses. Either could be the change address, and in fact, if you clicked them both, you would see that neither address has ever been used before. So which address is the change address that belongs to your suspect? In this instance, the 1 address is likely the target and the 3 address is the change address as described in the last section; however, there is another way.

Figure 10-8: Which is the change address?

Now let's say that by looking at the other transactions, you find a later move-ment of coin from your suspect's address to a single address, likely to consolidate funds into a single address as shown in Figure 10-9. This list of input addresses are primarily the same input address from Figure 10-8 but includes an output address from Figure 10-8. This identifies this address as belonging to your sus-pect and was likely the change address in the Figure 10-8 transaction.

Figure 10-9: Output address from Figure 10-8 is now an input address with the input address from Figure 10-8.

This technique works well when other methods do not provide any definitive answers. Now you may be wondering why Figure 10-9 shows many inputs from the same address, all with different values. Although an address has a balance in the user's wallet, each transaction into the address is a separate transaction and must be transacted as a separate input. Hence, it is not unusual to see lists of the same address as an input.

Moving from Transaction to Transaction

As you most likely have discovered, you can simply click an address in blockchain.info or any of the other blockchain explorers to move from transac-tion to transaction. As I mentioned in the introduction to this chapter, you can easily get "click happy" and start clicking addresses like a mad person, which is quickly followed by "click blindness," where you get completely lost, which is then followed by closing your browser and getting a coffee (or something stronger). To create a map of activity, from one address to the next, really requires a visualization tool such as the ones I will discuss in the next chapter.

Sometimes you just want to get a mental picture of where coins came from and where they are going, so a significant map of transactions isn't always needed.

In this case, I simply grab a pad and pen and draw a tree using the first five or six characters of each address. I note which address appears to be a change address and which is the primary payment, and I've developed a sort of shorthand to quickly build a paper map of my transactions (see Figure 10-10). It is not exactly a work of art, but using this approach, I get a rapid visual view of my address of interest. In the example illustrated in the figure, my target address was 17h6C. I went back just one level and then mapped another four levels onward, noting some change addresses and when payments were grouped together.

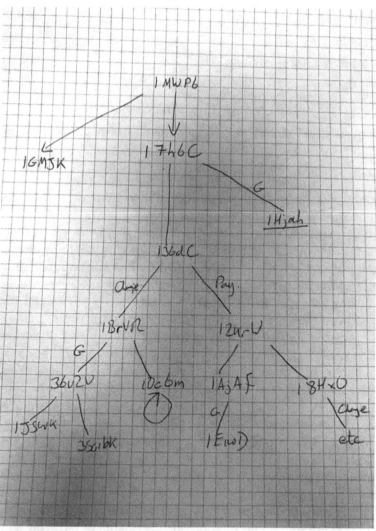

Figure 10-10: Graphing transactions on paper.

You can use your own technique, but I find this paper-map method really useful, especially if I do not have access to a visualization tool.

Putting the Techniques Together

If you'd like to practice some of the techniques you've learned thus far in this chapter, research Bitcoin address 3EGy678G659RnevCA1pmfzVrrC5DEaiqAt (which you can find on blockchain.info at http://bit.ly/2qhH9qA) and try to answer these questions:

- What can you find?
- Who does it belong to?
- How many transactions are there?
- Over what period of time?
- What happened to the coins sent to this address?
- By picking an address that sent coin to the target, can you cluster change addresses?
- Can you cluster addresses for this user?

Obtaining these answers is about as far as you want to go with this investigation. If you Googled the address, you will see that it is the donation address for charity The Turing Trust. You can see in blockchain.info that there are (at time of writing) 26 transactions including the address, 24 payments into the address, and two outbound transactions starting 4 March 2016 until 31 December 2017. Clustering change addresses is fairly straightforward for many of the people donating to The Turing Trust due to the target address belonging to the charity being a multisig address. Hence, as long as the input starts with a 1 the change address will always be the address beginning with 1.

On 2 August 2016, the address appears to likely pay 0.1 bitcoin to the address 1Q75AC, and the change is going to 3F1bAR. You know that the 3F1bAR belongs to Turing Trust because you see the address being used, along with payments to the primary address being collated into the single address 13Km9e on 28 August 2016. (See previous Figure 10-9.)

An easier way to see this cluster is to use a site that attempts to group addresses into pseudo-wallets using the same rules you have been learning. Browse to www.walletexplorer.com and search for the target address 3EGy678G659RnevCA1pmfzVrrC5DEaiqAt. (Or use http://bit.ly/2AfKne4.) This explorer will list all the transactions involving the address with the coin-received transaction color-coded in green and the outward payments in red. You will undoubtedly recognize some fields such as the transaction ID, the date, and the balance, but there is also a "wallet address" written as a 10-character hexadecimal string. Wallet addresses are not part of the blockchain but are a construct of the explorer website as it attempts to group addresses. For example, Figure 10-11 notes that the wallet address that includes `3EGy678G659RnevCA1pmfzVrrC5DEaiqAt` is `31ebe0d4f5`.

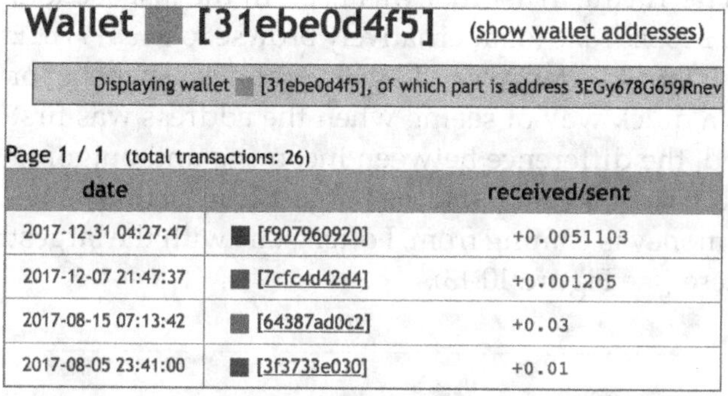

Figure 10-11: A wallet address from www.walletexplorer.com.

If you click the "show wallet addresses" link at the top of the screen, it will display the addresses that it thinks belong together. The result for this example is shown in Figure 10-12. You can clearly see the two addresses that were previously manually identified as belonging to the same person listed as part of the same wallet. The author of the site is Aleš Janda, who apparently works for Chainalysis as an analyst.

address	balance	incoming txs	last used in block
3EGy678G659RnevCA1pmfzVrrC5DEaiqAt	0.13556752	24	501834
3F1bARuLkjv4kcByhjTVHHifw4AatBWb2h	0.	1	427247

Figure 10-12: Clustered addresses are the same as we inferred manually.

Although this example only had two addresses, the technique works for almost limitless numbers of addresses from the same suspect. For example, the "wallet" for Bitcoin exchange `www.coinmotion.com` can be found at `http://bit.ly/2CyQz70`. This wallet contains almost 14,000 addresses that are all related to coinmotion. It would take a significant amount of time to cluster all of these addresses manually, so this is where explorers such as WalletExplorer.com can really help to speed up an investigation.

Although the information is not as complete as walletexplorer.com I also find bitcoinwhoswho.com is sometimes useful to identify address owners.

Other Explorer Sites

Many sites like blockchain.info exist for following transactions. Some just handle a single cryptocurrency, while others provide explorers for many different currencies. One of my favorites is `www.BTC.com`. If you browse to the site and search for the Bitcoin address of The Turing Trust that was used in the last section, `3EGy678G659RnevCA1pmfzVrrC5DEaiqAt` (or alternatively browse to `http://bit.ly/2AhyGUd`), and then click the Stats tab, you will get a graphical snapshot of the address. This provides a quick way of seeing when the address was first used, how often it was used, the difference between incoming and outgoing transactions, the Average Transaction value, and the Largest Transaction value. If I want to research where money is coming from, I often start with the largest transaction and go from there (see Figure 10-13).

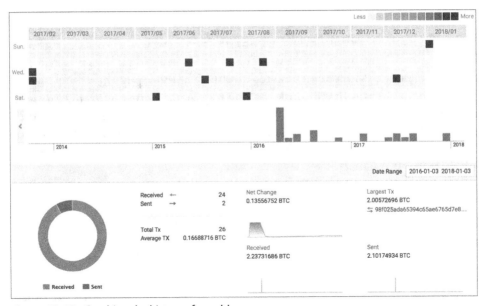

Figure 10-13: Graphing the history of an address.

This is also my favorite site for exploring the Bitcoin Cash fork. All the techniques just covered for clustering addresses work the same with Bitcoin Cash.

Blockexplorer.com is a useful explorer because it provides a live list of transactions in near real time. You can also list all the blocks mined on a specific date (see Figure 10-14).

Blocks by

Height

Waiting for blocks...

Blocks mined on:

UTC 📅

Loading Selec

#	Sun	Mon	Tue	Wed	Thu	Fri	Sat
52	31	01	02	03	04	05	06
1	07	08	09	10	11	12	13
2	14	15	16	17	18	19	20
3	21	22	23	24	25	26	27
4	28	29	30	31	01	02	03

January 2018

Figure 10-14: Filtering on all blocks mined on a specific day.

Another go-to site is chainz.cryptoid.info. It is an explorer like the others, and although it doesn't have some of the "bells and whistles" of the others, it provides blockchain viewers for many unusual cryptocurrencies. See Figure 10-15.

Crypto-currency

NPCcoin	FailCoin	Atomic Coin
Litecoin	Vcoin	KittehCoin
Dash	ReddByteCoin	Ultimate Secure Cash
BitConnect Coin	LoanOrLease	BigUp
e-Coin	CreditCashCoin	Kobocoin
Stratis	Walletbuildercoin	JouleCoin
Koruna	Loco	GapCoin
Wexcoin	ABC Blockchain	8Bit
DigiByte	AudioCoin	GlobalCoin
Experience Points	Atmos	Coino

Figure 10-15: The chainz.cryptoid.info website has explorers for more unusual cryptocurrencies.

Another site for exploring lesser-known currencies is blockexperts.com, which is a company that provides block explorer hosting as a service. Again, the currencies are not mainstream but could provide a useful capability if you stumbled across their addresses. See Figure 10-16.

Name	Abbreviation	Algorithm	Type
2GiveCoin	2GIVE	Scrypt	PoW PoS
AlphabetCoinFund	FUN	Scrypt	PoW
Ambercoin	AMBER	X13	PoW PoS
Amygws	AMY	Scrypt	PoW
AsiaBizCoin	ABZC	SHA-256	PoW
aTTis	ATT	Scrypt	PoW PoS
AvalonX	ALX	X11	PoW PoS
BeezerCoin	BEEZ	Scrypt	PoS
BestChain	BEST	Scrypt	PoW

Figure 10-16: Blockexperts.com.

I also quite like the following sites for Bitcoin:

- `www.blockcypher.com`
- `www.blockchair.com` (has a powerful export engine)
- `www.chain.so` (has a nice, simple layout)

You may ask, "How would you know what cryptocurrency an odd-looking address belongs to?" Simply googling the address will usually provide an answer. For example, if you found an address `AN7x4fANwLWXBDobqdjgNnqwKmVvHEac4p`, you would see that the prefix character `A` is neither Bitcoin nor Ethereum. If you googled the address, you would find links to the AlphabetCoinFund cryptocurrency blockchain (see Figure 10-17).

AlphabetCoinFund Block #80467 | BlockExperts
https://www.blockexperts.com/fun/height/80467 ▾
20 Jun 2017 - View detailed information about AlphabetCoinFund block #80467.

AlphabetCoinFund Block #80466 | BlockExperts
https://www.blockexperts.com/fun/height/80466
View detailed information about AlphabetCoinFund block #80466.

AlphabetCoinFund Block #80894 | BlockExperts
https://www.blockexperts.com/fun/height/80894 ▾
30 Jul 2017 - View detailed information about AlphabetCoinFund block #80894.

Figure 10-17: Google an address if you do not recognize it.

If you want a site for exploring any of the primary cryptocurrencies, I recommend bitinfocharts.com, which provides blockchain explorers for the following (among others):

- Bitcoin
- Bitcoin Cash
- Ethereum
- Ripple
- Litecoin
- Dash
- Monero

Following Ethereum Transactions

Most cryptocurrency blockchain explorers work in similar ways to Bitcoin as the fundamental technology is very comparable. However, cryptocurrencies like Ethereum are different in a number of fundamental ways, and this determines the way that you follow the money. As previously discussed, Ethereum can either trade a currency in the form of Ether or can trade a contract such as a coin offering. This means that you may not be following money but rather following the path of a contract or looking for the investors into an ICO (Initial Coin Offering).

Although a number of sites will allow you to explore the Ethereum blockchain, such as bitinfocharts.com, my go-to site is still etherscan.io with its associated API to access the raw data. The same general rules apply as any cryptocurrency. Public addresses are posted on the blockchain with a value or content that can be transacted with another address. This will then be entered onto the blockchain and distributed to all nodes on the network.

One difference with Ethereum is that you are generally only sending a transaction to one address at a time, but it's worth noting that it is possible to define a contract that will trigger multiple transactions. When you're following a transaction, remember the difference between a "coin" transaction and a contract transaction where no currency changes hands. Although a coin transaction is still technically a contract, it's useful to understand the differences. You can see an example of an ether transaction in Figure 10-18 and a contract transaction in Figure 10-19.

From:	0x75e7f640bf6968b6f32c47a3cd82c3c2c9dcae68
To:	0x77677f9ccc4c4a7fe36f7679d7d32ce68c3854b7
Value:	0.6048 Ether ($128.09)

Figure 10-18: An Ethereum ether transaction.

From:	0x731e6cc591b055001ccb9758008f636819df6152
To:	Contract 0x4c0ff1b2c1ef5e2b3dd2c74023cbf7ae36f01391 Contract 0xd937ebe98787a0037eb94efd3e107bb574bb93d3 Internal Invoke 30 ERC20 (IBCCoin) TOKEN Transfer From 0x4c0ff1b2c1ef5e2b3dd2c... to → 0xcb93c6faf472cd7baa4b...
Value:	0 Ether ($0.00)

Figure 10-19: An Ethereum contract transaction.

Browse to etherscan.io and search for transaction `0xcc4685ff36ed8552f91b5487c963fef92e20e7c00a87d5a25d9dc9eee8c40b71`, which you can find at `http://bit.ly/2x6V845`. The layout is clear—you can easily identify the From and To addresses as well as the Value field that classifies this as an Ether transaction (see Figure 10-20).

TimeStamp:	181 days 10 hrs ago (Sep-14-2017 05:15:26 AM +UTC)
From:	0x75e7f640bf6968b6f32c47a3cd82c3c2c9dcae68
To:	0x77677f9ccc4c4a7fe36f7679d7d32ce68c3854b7
Value:	0.6048 Ether ($396.49)
Gas Limit:	21001
Gas Used By Txn:	21000
Gas Price:	0.0000000231 Ether (23.1 Gwei)
Actual Tx Cost/Fee:	0.0004851 Ether ($0.32)

Figure 10-20: Etherscan transaction layout.

If you click the To address, 0x77677, a list of all transactions involving this address will be displayed and tagged with either the transaction value "in" or "out." The major difference with Ethereum is that there are no change addresses. Instead of needing to transact the value of an address and recover the difference as change, with Ethereum, you can simply transact an exact part of the overall balance of the address. As values are transacted, you'll see the balance of the address fluctuate. This generally means that single Ethereum addresses are used rather than a large number of addresses that need to be clustered.

To be able to investigate Ethereum, you also need to recognize the different types of transactions. As I mentioned earlier in this chapter, these are primarily just value and contract transactions that can be broken down into the following four primary types:

- Value transaction (technically still a contract)
- Contract transaction that triggers another contract that moves a coin value

- Contract transaction that acts as an agreement
- Contract transaction that transacts a token

You could argue that the third and fourth bullet items are essentially the same, but it is important to understand the differences. If you glance back to Figure 10-18, you can see an example of a straight value transaction: just a From address, a To address, and a Value. Figure 10-19, on the other hand, shows an example of a contract transaction that moves a token or "coin that does not have any inherent value." You see a From address, but the To address is a contract that triggers a second contract that moves 30 ERC20-compliant tokens, described as IBCCoin, from one address to another. The value is stated as zero. If you are interested in looking at a particular coin or token transaction, you can search on the contract address or search etherscan.io for the token name.

For example, if you search etherscan.io for the token name Ethos, you'll get a list of information on the Ethos token, the contract address used, and the token transactions that have taken place. At the time of writing, there were well over 80,000 transactions of Ethos tokens. If you were investigating a fraudulent ICO (Initial Coin Offering), then this would be a good place to start. Although you can click each and every transaction and try to start de-anonymizing each purchaser, or try to figure out the owner of the ICO, a few tools are available that can help you.

If you have browsed to the Ethos page as described previously, you will see four tabs above the list of transfers. The Token Holders tab provides a list of all Ethereum addresses that hold Ethos tokens. This list only has 12,000 holders, which is somewhat less than the 80,000 transactions. Obviously, there are more transactions than holders because it is likely that coins are traded, bought, and sold by the same address, but with a lower number of actual coin owners. This list can actually be much smaller if a fraudulent ICO carries out a large number of internal transfers to make the token offering look popular.

The page also has a TokenHolders Chart button. This can help you to see how tokens are distributed and whether the majority are in the hands of a single owner (see Figure 10-21).

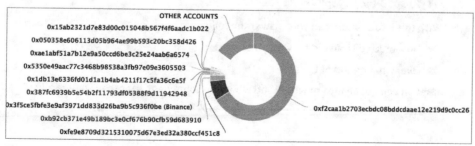

Figure 10-21: Graphing the owners of tokens.

The next tab is Read Smart Contract. This is the raw contract for the token and provides the name, the total supply of tokens, and the address that belongs to the ICO owner (see Figure 10-22). This can help you to focus on one address to investigate if there is any doubt as to the physical owner of the token offering.

11. > owner → 0xe0d4f1ac2ae186da9cd8dc56502d3faea13c9976 *address*	
12. > symbol → ETHOS *string*	
13. > released → True *bool*	
14. > canUpgrade → True *bool*	

Figure 10-22: Part of a raw contract with the owner's address.

There is also a Comments tab. In this example, you see a posting that directs you to a story on medium.com about Ethos rebranding from an earlier name, Bitsequence. Comments can be a useful resource to understand the history of a token, thoughts of other traders, bad experiences, or even people reporting what they consider to be fraudulent activity.

If you clicked the Contract Address at the top of the screen to the right of the Total Supply field, you would be presented with a tab that enables you to read actual source code of the contract. Clicking Contract Source will provide a listing of the code that can be interpreted by a programmer to figure out exactly what the contract is doing. (I will not pursue that level of detail in this book.)

EXERCISE

The WannaCry virus of 2017 was a cryptovirus that infected computers, encrypted their hard drives, and demanded bitcoin in exchange for an unlock key. It is thought that there were over 300,000 computers affected.

The Bitcoin addresses used by the attackers were as follows:

■ 13AM4VW2dhxYgXeQepoHkHSQuy6NgaEb94

■ 12t9YDPgwueZ9NyMgw519p7AA8isjr6SMw

■ 115p7UMMngoj1pMvkpHijcRdfJNXj6LrLn

With this information, can you answer the following questions?

■ How much bitcoin did they receive?

■ Over what period of time?

■ Can you get an idea of where and when the coins went after they were received?

Monitoring Addresses

Being able to monitor an address can be very useful. Perhaps you are investigating a live kidnapping, a ransomware virus has published an address, or a company has been specifically targeted and the attackers have provided a Bitcoin address. This can also be useful when you have a large number of addresses that you wish to monitor. Rather than sitting and watching a blockchain site for movement, you can have a site watch an address and notify you of any activity.

Blockonomics.co

One of my favorite sites to monitor addresses is www.blockonomics.co. You need to have a Google ID to log in, so if you don't have one, or you don't want to use an existing ID, head to Google and set up a new ID.

Although you can add multiple addresses, which is useful if you have recovered the xPub key from a device, you can monitor all of their public key addresses just by adding the xPub address. When you add an address, you can also add an ID tag to help you identify the owner of the address, which is especially useful if you are running multiple investigations.

Choose any Bitcoin address you may have on hand, or browse to a blockchain explorer and find an address to monitor. Click New Address + (Add). You can now click the History link, and you will see transaction history for the address or addresses over the period of time you select (see Figure 10-23 and Figure 10-24).

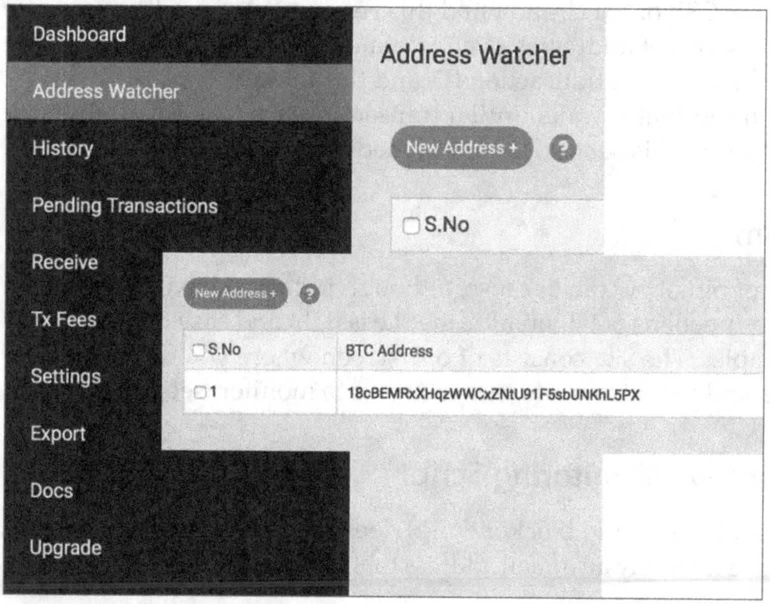

Figure 10-23: Adding an address to monitor.

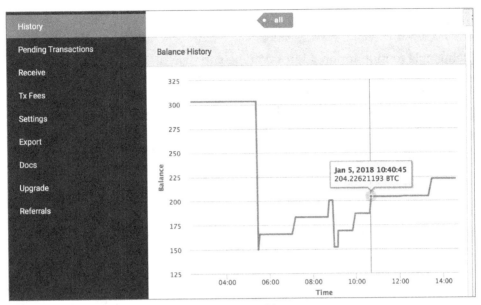

Figure 10-24: Graphing the history of a monitored address.

If you click the Settings link, you can choose to subscribe to a transaction notification e-mail. This is very useful if you are monitoring addresses over a long period.

Lastly, by clicking the Export link, you can export the transactions just from the addresses you are watching and specify the date range. You have options to export as either CSV or Excel, and I find this very useful to produce evidence about a specific series of addresses over a defined time period. It exports the date, time, the hyperlinked transaction ID, and the amount.

Just bear in mind that it waits until a transaction has two notifications or blocks before an e-mail is sent, so it's not immediate.

Bitnotify.com

I am a big fan of bitnotify.com because, although it doesn't have the excellent capabilities and functions of bitonomics, the site is light and easy to use. It really couldn't be simpler. The site consists of one screen where you can enter your e-mail address and the Bitcoin address you want to monitor (see Figure 10-25).

Writing Your Own Monitoring Script

Using sites like bitnotify and blockonomics does mean losing a little privacy, because you have to supply an e-mail address that can likely be linked to your IP address that is also linked to the addresses you are monitoring. It could be that this is too much information supplied to a third party during your investigation. For most investigations, I set up my own monitor using the API supplied by blockcypher.com. If you would like to do this as well, follow these steps:

1. Open Notepad++ and add the following HTML code to a new note:

```
<iframe src="https://live.blockcypher.com/widget/btc/17h6CDrX
Ub4zVUjedkP6ibkpkieDXd116j/balance/" style="overflow:hidden;"
frameborder="0"></iframe>

<iframe src="https://live.blockcypher.com/widget/btc/18cBEMRx
XHqzWWCxZNtU91F5sbUNKhL5PX/balance/" style="overflow:hidden;"
frameborder="0"></iframe><br/>
```

Please note that each `<iframe src=...</iframe>` code sequence should all be typed on a single line. You can see the Bitcoin addresses embedded in the URL starting `17h6CD` and `18cBEM`—these can be changed to whatever addresses you want to monitor. The code in its current form will display the data side-by-side in blocks, as shown in Figure 10-26.

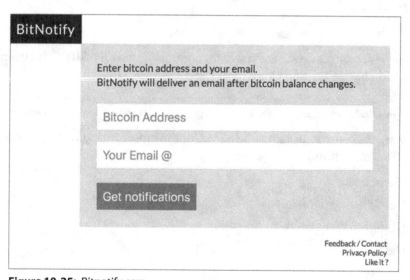

Figure 10-25: Bitnotify.com.

Figure 10-26: Monitoring two addresses.

2. Cut and paste the `iframe` line as many times as you need to monitor as many addresses as you require.

   Obviously, there is a screen limit to how many addresses you can have displayed side-by-side depending on your resolution, but adding the following to the end of a line will generate a line break and drop any subsequent results into a new line:

   ```
   <br/>
   ```

This method means that you will not need to provide an e-mail address, but remember that you will still leak your IP address to BlockCypher connected to whatever addresses you are monitoring embedded in the URL.

One of the nice things about the BlockCypher API is that you can use the same technique to monitor addresses on any of the blockchains it supports. At the time of writing, these include the following:

- Bitcoin
- Litecoin
- Dogecoin
- Dash

If you want to adjust your web page to monitor a Litecoin address, for example, you would change the `btc` element in the code to `ltc` like this:

```
<iframe src="https://live.blockcypher.com/widget/ltc/<Address to
monitor>/balance/" style="overflow:hidden;" frameborder="0"></iframe>
```

Here are the codes to use after `/widget/` for the most common cryptocurrencies (at the time of writing):

- Bitcoin: `btc`
- Litecoin: `ltc`
- Dogecoin: `doge`
- Dash: `dash`

Monitoring Ethereum Addresses

You can monitor Ethereum addresses in the same way as other cryptocurrencies using the standard etherscan.io because it has a built-in capability. Browse to etherscan.io and find an address to analyze or browse to the example at `http://bit.ly/21XEHjD`. If you look in the header part of the address information, you will find the field Address Watch and a button marked Add To Watch List. Clicking this button will require that you log in to etherscan.io, but it sets up a list of watched addresses that you can tag with a description and specify whether you wish to receive e-mail notifications (see Figure 10-27).

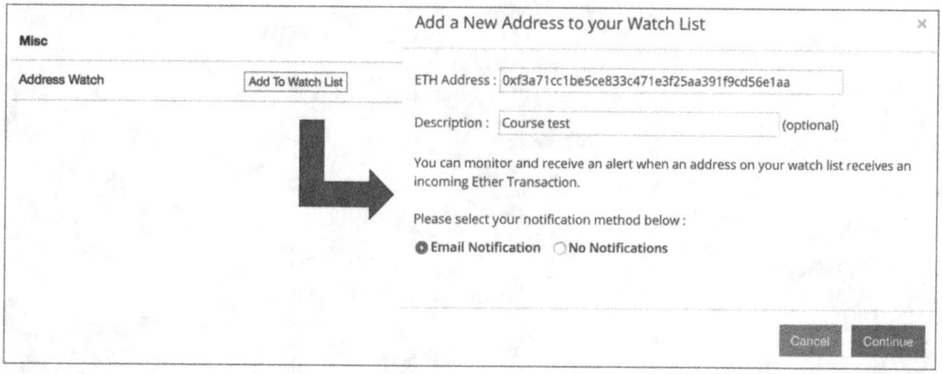

Figure 10-27: Setting up an Ethereum address monitor.

Summary

As I discussed in this chapter, following the money across a blockchain can be a daunting task—the mechanics of following transactions are as simple as clicking an address, but it can be very easy to get lost, fast! So, as we learned, it is important for the investigator to focus on what can be achieved with each target address. Identifying change addresses, send addresses, and others can help you cluster addresses together under a single owner. This in turn enables you to set up monitoring on those addresses to know when they are used. Being able to look at the balance of addresses to try to ascertain the primary storage address, if used, can help you target the right address should you get to the point of asset seizure.

I often speak to investigators who feel that following the money is all about clicking from address to address, but this method ignores the huge amount of data that can be recovered and inferred by just looking at a transaction, a balance, or the relationships between addresses to find ownership patterns.

If you really want to follow the money from address to address to eventually discover storage addresses, currency conversion addresses, or payments to vendors, it is considerably easier to use the visualization tool that's discussed in the next chapter.

CHAPTER 11

Visualization Systems

In Chapter 10, "Following the Money," you learned how to follow coin or even contract transactions by clicking destination addresses in a transaction and finding where coins were transferred. To do this manually and just by eye can be extremely difficult even if you take detailed notes. Visualization software helps you by graphically displaying the paths from transaction to transaction, making it easier to analyze the transmission of coins. I have always been a big fan of visualizing data—"seeing" data seems to help with comprehension. Our brains naturally see patterns to help us identify things.

However, visualization systems can still leave you lost and confused in a map of addresses. You need to use such systems thoughtfully and, perhaps, creatively.

In this chapter, I will introduce you to visualization tools, many of which are free to use. I will also reference the market-leading software and its benefits.

Online Blockchain Viewers

Many of the online blockchain viewers have a visualization option. These viewers are free and easy to use but have limited capabilities for searching or formatting the visual data. They can be better than nothing, but I sometimes find that I get just as lost, but even more quickly. I can create a link map, but I'm not sure what the map actually means. The key is to go slowly, always looking and thinking about what you are seeing.

Blockchain.info

The site I have referred to consistently in this book is blockchain.info, which has a reasonable visualization option. Browse to blockchain.info, perhaps to the example `http://bit.ly/2xbbS8o`. If you look under the "Summary heading," you will find a link called Visualize - View Tree Chart (see Figure 11-1).

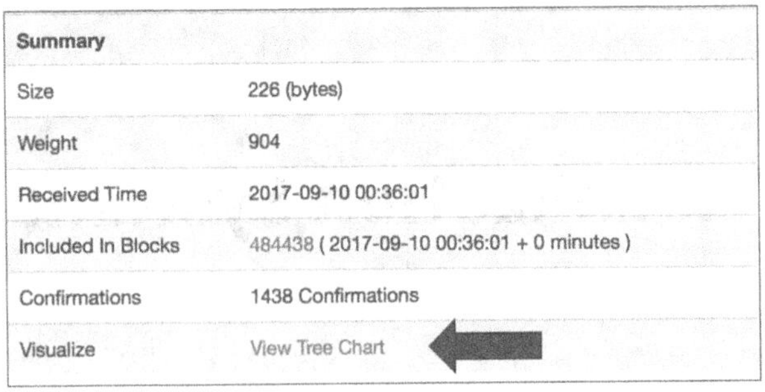

Summary	
Size	226 (bytes)
Weight	904
Received Time	2017-09-10 00:36:01
Included In Blocks	484438 (2017-09-10 00:36:01 + 0 minutes)
Confirmations	1438 Confirmations
Visualize	View Tree Chart

Figure 11-1: The View Tree Chart link on blockchain.info.

The resulting screen will graph the transaction that was on the screen when you clicked the link. In this example, the origin address (Blockchain.info doesn't display the origin address in its visualization) moves 3 bitcoin to two addresses: 18UoXw and 1TW76a. To be specific, the input address takes 3 bitcoin and outputs 2.9991 bitcoin to the two addresses plus the fees. The circles are scaled in size depending on the balance of the address. A gray circle means that the output is unspent and, therefore, has no children; an orange circle means that the value is spent and moved to another address. Clicking an orange circle will load the next transaction, and so on. Figure 11-2 shows the transaction map when you click the View Tree Chart link.

In Figure 11-3, we have followed the money that went to address 18UoXw to two levels. The majority of the value went to 1LmM4G with the rest to 1Kgh8k.

This view is useful to quickly map the transactions, but it has a number of limitations: you cannot map backward to previous transactions before the origin address, it's difficult to scale the map, and you cannot search for addresses, which can be vital in a large map. The only way I've managed to use this functionality successfully was to create the map, print it to a PDF, and then annotate it in a PDF editor. This method works, but it's not very efficient. As discussed in Chapter 4, "Transactions," all of the data is available via an API, which can make searching, organizing, and visualizing straightforward.

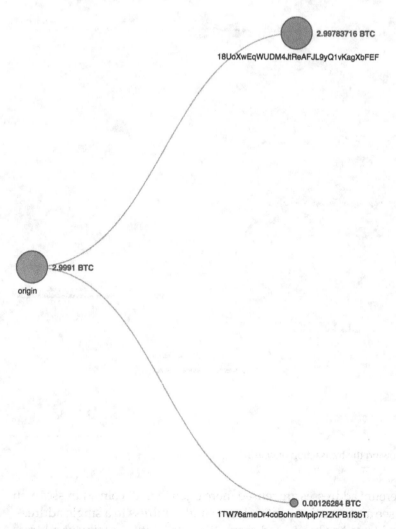

Figure 11-2: Blockchain.info visualization of the transaction.

Etherscan.io

The Ethereum blockchain viewer etherscan.io also has the functionality to be able to map transactions. At the time of writing, this is slated as a beta release function on the site, and I have had the function crash on me on more than one occasion. However, when the function works, it provides an output that is very similar to blockchain.info. The circle nodes are not sized to the amount of the transaction, because many transactions are of zero value if they are transacting a non-value contract; however, a filled circle means you can click it to see onward transactions, and an empty circle means no further transactions are available to see.

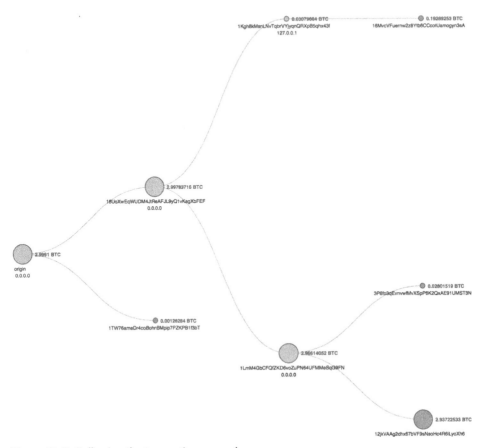

Figure 11-3: Following the transaction onward.

Because Ethereum addresses are reused more often than Bitcoin addresses, you will often just see a transaction containing a single address to a single address, but where an address has been used many times, clicking a recipient address will often generate a huge graph that lists every address. This is demonstrated in Figure 11-4 where we first see a transaction from one address to many addresses, but clicking the receive address shows every outbound transaction the address has made and so on, and with reused addresses, this can be a significant list.

As with blockchain.info, I find these online capabilities useful to a limited degree, but the software tools that are available are significantly better to use.

Numisight

Numisight is software that can be downloaded from www.numisight.com. It is currently in a Public Alpha state of release, and the software contains a number of bugs, but I still find it extremely useful (especially because it is currently a free tool). If you are able, visit the site and download and install the software.

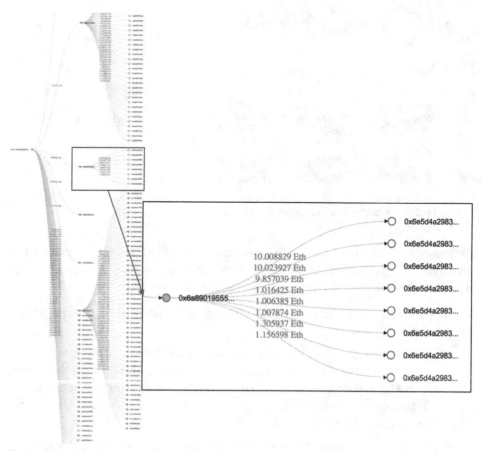

Figure 11-4: Ethereum tree of transactions.

The interface is fairly straightforward to use but can, as with most of these visualization tools, quickly become unwieldy. Just as I recommended when you're following the money manually, think about each click that you make.

When you open Numisight, you will see a blank canvas with an address search bar in the top right. Find an address of interest on a block explorer, paste it into the search bar, and press the Enter key (or the Return key on a Mac). The example I am using is the WannaCry address 13AM4VW2dhxYgXeQepoHkHSQuy6NgaEb94.

You'll see a graph appear as a series of blocks linked to other blocks as shown in Figure 11-5. Instead of a block being an address as in the online visualization tools, each orange block in Numisight is a transaction. Each green block is an unspent output in an address. The menu buttons across the top are fairly obvious, with the clock icon enabling you to search between a particular date/time frame, the i button providing more data on a transaction, and the cog icon presenting you with options. You can also select some example Bitcoin address graphs from the Samples drop-down menu.

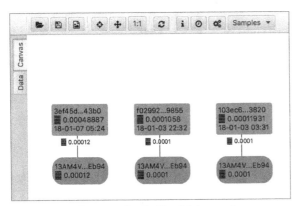

Figure 11-5: An example of a Numisight graph.

One of the most useful aspects of Numisight is the Data tab, which can be accessed from the left side of the graph view. This view collates all the recovered data from the blockchain in three very useful views:

▪ Addresses tab—This is just the address or addresses that you have searched for.

▪ Transactions tab—This view shows each transaction that the graph includes and provides the transaction ID, how many inputs and outputs there were for the transaction, how many of the outputs are unspent, the time, and the Bitcoin transacted. You can also click any of the columns to order the data, such as by time or value.

▪ Coins tab—This lists every Bitcoin address that has transacted with your target address, the value, whether it was spent, and the received and spent transaction IDs. It can be useful to sort on the addresses to see the most-active addresses related to your target or to sort on the Spent column to easily see a list of how many transactions remain unspent, for example.

If you return to the Canvas tab, click an orange transaction tab, and click the i button in the menu bar, a slide-out bar will be displayed on the left side of the canvas containing significant data about the transaction. This data includes the transaction hash, the time, the block height, the fees and values, and the input and output addresses. Looking at the example in Figure 11-6, you see that our target address from Wannacry is an output. This means that address 1Cfby8 sent bitcoin to our searched address, but there is a second address that's almost certainly a change address, which you can cluster with 1Cfby8 as belonging to the same sender.

NOTE   The value sent to the Wannacry address is just 0.00012 bitcoin, which at the time of writing is about $1.60. This is obviously not a serious attempt to obtain an unlock for an encrypted computer, but it may be a researcher or investigator injecting a micropayment for tracking purposes.

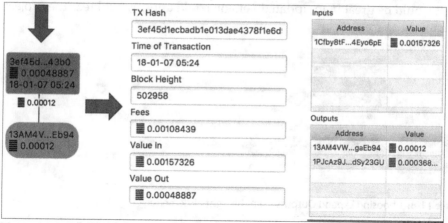

Figure 11-6: Numisight displaying information on a transaction.

About halfway along the graph, you can see a large number of transactions that are all moved in a single transaction. If you click the note below the transactions that are all payments into the target address, you'll see that a large number of paid ransoms have been moved in a single transaction to two output addresses. This can be seen in Figure 11-7.

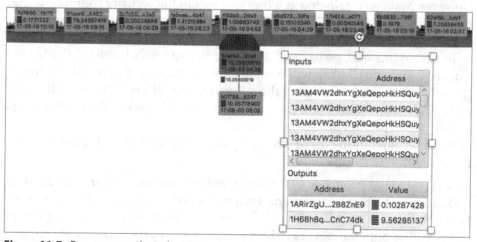

Figure 11-7: Payments made to the Wannacry address moved to two addresses.

If you right-click this transaction node and select Expand Outputs, the onward transactions for the two addresses will be displayed as shown in Figure 11-8.

You can also use the Expand Inputs option from the right-click menu to head back in time and see the transactions that were made previous to the transaction you are investigating.

As with any of these tools, you can click and click and end up with a meaningless graph. Numisight is a flawed but useful tool that is free of charge to use. It would be great if an updated version could appear, but I fear the project is currently on ice.

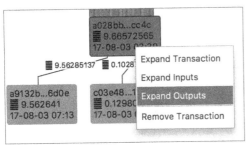

Figure 11-8: Choosing Expand Outputs from the right-click menu.

Maltego

Maltego from South African company, Paterva, is an outstanding tool built primarily for automating certain open-source investigation tasks. Although the commercial version of Maltego is not free, it is a vital part of my investigative toolkit, and I strongly recommend that you buy it if you have the means to do so. However, Maltego originated as a free tool within the security community and has always offered a free Community version of the software. Although limited in its results and abilities, it is still useful when you're investigating Bitcoin.

To obtain this tool, go to www.paterva.com and select Products ⇨ Maltego Clients ⇨ Maltego CE. You will need to register and then download and install the software. When you install the software, you will need to enter the user name and password that you used at registration. Also select Public Transform Servers when prompted.

To understand the basics of Maltego, you will need to know the definition of the following two terms:

Entities Maltego provides a number of objects and icons that you can drag and drop onto a blank canvas and then run searches on. There are entities for Domain, IP address, Alias, Twitter Name, and more. When you drag one of these entities onto the canvas (which is referred to as a *graph* in Maltego) and right-click it, a menu with search options relevant to the entity is displayed. For example, when you drag the domain name entity onto the graph, you can edit the entity to the domain name you wish to investigate.

Transforms When you hear or read the term *transform*, just think search or convert. Maltego transforms either search for data based on the input entity or convert one type of data into another type. With the previous example of a domain name entity, transforms are available to perform the following tasks and many more (see Figure 11-9):

■ Look up the DNS name

- Look up e-mail addresses associated with the domain
- Look up the website associated with the domain
- Look up the mail server associated with the domain

Many different entities exist, and each has many context-sensitive transforms, or searches, associated with it.

To carry out the search, the data is sent to Transform Servers, which can be either located at Paterva in the case of the Public Servers, or you can purchase your own Transform Servers to run in-house. The servers do the heavy lifting of the searches and pass the results data back to the Maltego client where they are mapped to the graph. Figure 11-10 shows the results of running the transform To Website [using Search Engine], from the domain csitech.co.uk. This transform looks online for wherever csitech.co.uk is mentioned, and the results are clustered into a single output for analysis.

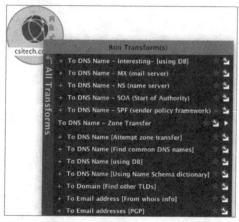

Figure 11-9: The transforms available for the Domain entity.

Using Maltego is essentially a process of providing some known information and then running transforms to generate new data mapped to the graph.

When you run Maltego for the first time, it launches a home screen with a large number of plugins available to be installed and used. Many of the plugins require payment, but others are simply made available to the community to extend and improve the tool. If you are working along with the book and have navigated beyond the home screen, it can be loaded by browsing to Windows ⇨ Home. Among the long list of transform plugins available to install there's one called Bitcoin. Find it and click the Install button (see Figure 11-11).

Open a new graph by clicking the common new page button (page with the plus symbol inside) on the menu bar or by clicking the circle (which has three smaller circles inside it) in the upper-left corner of the window and selecting New. On the left side of your graph, Maltego places all of the entities that can be dragged onto your graph, categorized in a series of headings. Under the Personal heading, you will find two Bitcoin entities: Bitcoin Address and Bitcoin Transaction. If you click and drag the Bitcoin Transaction entity onto your graph and release, it will create an icon on the graph as shown in Figure 11-12. Double-click the default transaction ID and replace it with the following:

```
Bf0da8c1f6dff13fe06056baf5b7b4406caab92a8f936aff3db5ec4e4ce47b53
```

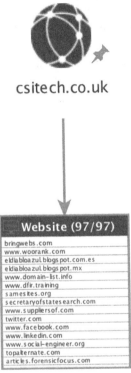

csitech.co.uk

Website (97/97)

bringwebs.com
www.woorank.com
eldiabloazul.blogspot.com.es
eldiabloazul.blogspot.mx
www.domain-list.info
www.dfir.training
samesites.org
secretaryofstatesearch.com
www.suppliersof.com
twitter.com
www.facebook.com
www.linkedin.com
www.social-engineer.org
topalternate.com
articles.forensicfocus.com

Figure 11-10: The results of running the To Website [using Search Engine] transform.

If you are following along with this example in Maltego, you can copy the transaction ID value from blockchain.info by navigating to `http://bit.ly/2D6Kija` and paste it into the default transaction ID field as described in the last paragraph.

Right-click the entity and then click the + symbol next to the Bitcoin menu item. This will display the transforms available to you, which include the following:

To INPUT Addresses   This will generate new Bitcoin address entities that were the input to the transaction.

To OUTPUT Addresses   This will generate new Bitcoin address entities that were the output of the transaction.

To IP Address of First Relay   This will attempt to locate and display the node that first relayed the transaction. This will be discussed in more detail in the next chapter.

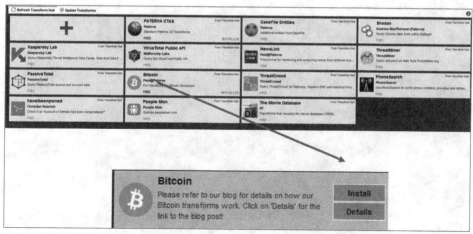

Figure 11-11: Install Bitcoin transforms and entities from the Transform Hub.

Figure 11-12: Drag the Bitcoin Transaction entity onto the graph.

If you select To OUTPUT Addresses, Maltego will work for a moment and then draw two new entities to the screen with the addresses of the outputs. You can also right-click again and run the To INPUT Addresses, which will draw the addresses to the graph that were inputs. In the example depicted in Figure 11-13, you see that address 141C65 has an arrow pointing both ways. This signifies that 141C65 is both an input and an output, meaning that it is being used as a change address.

You can now do analysis on each address. Right-clicking an address entity will provide seven transforms. Two of these no longer work since they are for the deprecated Taint Analysis capability. The remaining five provide the following analysis abilities:

Get Address Details   This transform will do a lookup on the address and return details to the Detail View pane on the right-hand side of the Maltego window. It will return the number of transactions the address has been involved in, the final balance, and the total sent and received.

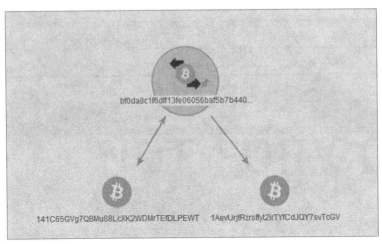

Figure 11-13: The transaction has two output addresses.

To Addresses [*Received from]   This is a very useful search. It returns addresses that were inputs to transactions where this address was an output. Essentially, it will look for the address in the entity you are searching for anywhere that this address was an output and will create new entities for all of the input addresses.

To Addresses [*Sent to]   This does the opposite of the previous transform. It returns addresses that were outputs to transactions where this address was an input.

To Transactions [where address was an input]   I find this transform very useful indeed. It returns all transactions where the address was an input, and if you then select the collection containing all the resulting transactions and run the To INPUT Addresses command, you get all the inputs back that *must* be owned by the same person. This makes finding clustered addresses very quick. You can also output this data as a CSV (which you will learn more about later in this section).

To Transactions [where address was an output]   Does what it says.

Take a look at Figure 11-14. This tells me that address 141C65 also owns 17nLha and 12x4jS.

This graph was the result of my running the following transforms in the order specified here:

1. I started with transaction ID `Bf0da8c1f6dff13fe06056baf5b7b4406caab 92a8f936aff3db5ec4e4ce47b53`.

2. I then ran the To INPUT and To OUTPUT address as described previously. This drew two new Bitcoin addresses as shown in Figure 11-13.

3. I then selected the output address 141C65 and ran the transform To Transactions [where address was an input]. This found 61 transactions where 141C65 was an input address. (The Community edition of Maltego will only find 12.)

4. Next I selected the collection/group of 61 addresses, right-clicked the entire collection, and ran To INPUT Address. This works through all 61 transactions and draws new entities for each new address it finds.

Out of the 61 transactions, it found two with multiple input addresses that were not 141C65. In Figure 11-14, the two transactions are broken out of the group at the bottom of the graph along with the two addresses 17nLha and 12x4jSa. This tells me that these three addresses are owned by the same person.

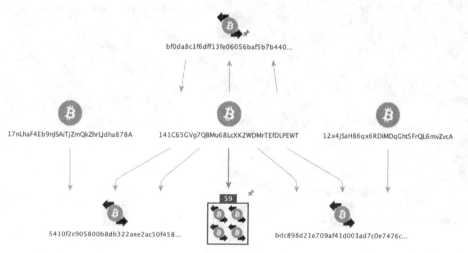

bf0da8c1f6dff13fe06056baf5b7b440...

17nLhaF4Eb9nJSAiTjZmQkZhrLJdha878A   141C65GVg7Q8Mu68LcXK2WDMrTEfDLPEWT   12x4jSaH86qx6RDiMDqGht5FrQL6mvZvcA

59

5410f2c905800b8db322aee2ac50f458...   bdc898d21e709af41d003ad7c0e7476c...

Figure 11-14: Finding clustered input addresses.

In a graph with a large number of addresses found, you could also look at the output addresses for each input and work out the change addresses, deleting the target addresses. Once you have a graph of input and change addresses, which by definition are clustered by owner, you can output them as a CSV file. To do this, click Select By Type ➪ Bitcoin Address in the top menu bar of the Investigate tab. This will select all the Bitcoin addresses left on the graph. You can now click the ball icon in the top left of the Maltego window and select Export ➪ Export Graph to Table ➪ Selection only, as shown in Figure 11-15. This will output a CSV table of the addresses, which is very useful for further investigation.

In the paid version of Maltego, you are also able to import a table of data for analysis. If you have a CSV or spreadsheet list of addresses or transaction addresses, you can import the list and apply the correct entity type to the columns. This will then import the data and map the values to entities on a graph. This can be useful if you are looking for connections between addresses, for example. You just import the list and then run the transforms To Addresses [*Received from] or To Addresses [*Sent to], and you will see any direct connections mapped between addresses.

Remember to try the different graphing options under the layout menu to the left of the graph.

From version 4.1.0.10552 Maltego also includes transaction and address entities and transforms for Ethereum.

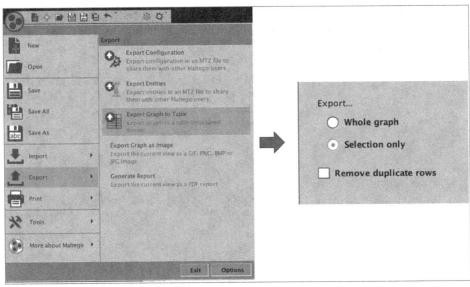

Figure 11-15: Exporting the clustered addresses as a CSV file.

Maltego is a very useful visualization tool with some searches and abilities that are very difficult to achieve using manual methods. The free version is often sufficient for limited investigations, but the power of Maltego both for Bitcoin and for broader open-source investigation work makes it a worthwhile tool to invest in.

EXERCISE

The Petya/NotPetya ransomware attack of June 2017 used the address `1Mz7153HMuxXTuR2R1t78mGSdzaAtNbBWX`. If you have installed Maltego on your system, you can use it to investigate where the paid coins were sent. Use the transforms carefully and search online for the resulting addresses. Then use that information to answer the following questions:

▪ Did they make donations to any websites?

▪ Can you produce a CSV of all the Bitcoin addresses that paid into the target address?

TIP Graph transactions where address was an OUTPUT. Select just the transactions, and look up all addresses that were the INPUTS. Then select all of those addresses and export.

Learnmeabitcoin.com

It can be very useful to be able to link addresses to try ascertaining any connections, even fairly distant. For example, imagine that you had the address of a suspect and the address of a dark website that you think he may have been trading with. You can either manually follow every transaction from the address and clustered addresses to each end point to try and find the dark web address or you can use learnmeabitcoin.com. Although the site has a less than inspiring name, it can be very helpful in automating this tricky and labor-intensive task.

Learnmeabitcoin.com is a site that attempts to teach you about Bitcoin and provide some useful tools. The site enables the user to generate a 256-bit random number, generate a SHA256 checksum, convert decimal to hexadecimal, and even swap endian. However, the most useful tool for the investigator is the Path tool, designed to find a connection between two Bitcoin addresses. It sensibly restricts the search to 20 hops, which in reality is a significant level of separation, and more hops would require considerable time and processing power.

If you browse to `http://bit.ly/2mzJlVh` and enter two Bitcoin addresses, it will strive to find any connection. Figure 11-16 shows an example of how the result is displayed.

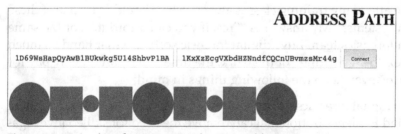

Figure 11-16: Looking for connections between addresses.

The resulting visualization depicts the link between the two addresses. Rolling your mouse over each icon displays its data, and clicking it will load the transaction in a blockchain viewer. The icons are as follows:

- Green circle: Bitcoin Address
- Grey square: Amount
- Blue circle: Transaction ID

So reading the example in Figure 11-16 from left to right would tell you the following information:

> Address 1D69Ws (the leftmost green circle) sent 10 bitcoin (leftmost gray square) as part of transaction 084667 (blue circle), which output 14.508

bitcoin (gray square) to address 17Bymc (green circle), which sent 1.047 bitcoin (gray square) as part of transaction 192719 (blue circle), which output 1 bitcoin (gray square) to target address 1KxXzE (green circle).

I use this site regularly to see if there are connections between addresses and to map those connections. Although the output is a little clunky, it works, and I will often follow the path it provides in blockchain.info or on Maltego.

Commercial Visualization Systems

A number of excellent commercial investigation systems are available, primarily Chainalysis and Elliptic. At the time of writing, both companies focus purely on Bitcoin. This is reasonable as the majority of cases that come through the door are related to Bitcoin; however, one of the reasons for this book is that there are many cryptocurrencies, some of which are becoming popular. Some cryptocurrencies such as Monero offer better anonymity than Bitcoin, so understanding the concepts of investigating on any blockchain is vital for an investigator. Also, these tools are expensive and may not be within the scope of every investigator or their unit.

People who attend my training classes always ask, "Should I buy one of these investigation systems?" My answer is, "Yes, if you can afford it." For the same reason that a forensics team buys digital forensic software that handles much of the complex "heavy-lifting" of the work, the time saved can quickly pay for the system. However, keep the following things in mind:

- As with digital forensics software, these systems are not foolproof—there is no Find Evidence button that can remove the need for skilled investigators. In other words, they are good, but not perfect.

- As mentioned at the beginning of this section, they only cover Bitcoin at the moment although one of the market-leading tools will soon offer Ethereum investigations too.

- Because the tools are often using algorithms to cluster addresses, the information is only inferred; hence, they can provide mistaken or incomplete information.

I am not recommending one product over another. However, Chainalysis software has been very helpful in providing test accounts for me to work on and I have been very impressed with its tool.

As I mentioned at the start of this section, buy the tool if you have the money—just don't rely on it utterly without question. And if a Monero job lands on your desk, it's going to require some manual work.

Summary

Visualizing blockchain data can be an invaluable way to track payments effectively. All the clustering methods that you learned in Chapter 10 still need to be used to understand ownership or addresses and track them from or to a target address. As you saw in this chapter, Maltego is very useful in finding, mapping, and exporting clustered addresses, but it won't go as far as the current crop of commercial tools that are available.

Although visualization tools are useful it is vital that when being deposed an investigator needs to understand how the visualization tool is working and how the results are inferred or discovered. This highlights the need to understand the inner workings of a cryptocurrency as covered in Part 1 of this book.

CHAPTER 12

Finding Your Suspect

In this chapter, we will examine techniques you can use to track and, hopefully, locate your suspect. We discussed clustering addresses and following transactions in Chapter 10, "Following the Money," but how can you identify a resource on a blockchain that is identifiable so that you are able—with the proper legal authorities or using open-source techniques—to obtain information on a suspect? This chapter will teach you about IP address tracing as well as its limitations, tracking to a service provider such as a currency exchange, and searching on the so-called dark web using Tor.

When investigating movement of funds on a cryptocurrency, it is easy to hit a dead end. Even with the techniques discussed in this chapter, there will be times when you will need to be patient and just watch and wait for coins to move to a traceable end point, such as a trader or exchange.

Tracing an IP Address

I sat in a presentation in 2017 where the law enforcement specialist in Bitcoin presented, among other things, a number of possible security vulnerabilities and methods for identifying users on the blockchain. Included in this list was a review of the "traceability of the IP addresses found on the Bitcoin blockchain." It was one of those uncomfortable moments when you are willing someone to stop talking because they are very wrong in what they are saying, and you feel rather embarrassed for them. Simply put, the Bitcoin blockchain does not record any IP addresses.

His mistake came from a misunderstanding about information that block-chain.info records when it detects trades on the blockchain. Blockchain.info watches a large number of Bitcoin nodes, and when it sees a transaction for the first time, it records the IP address in its database. You can see an example of this in Figure 12-1.

```
    ],
    "weight":764,
    "block_height":481874,
    "relayed_by":"139.99.131.171",
    "out":[
        {
            "spent":true,
            "tx_index":277869735,
            "type":0,
            "addr":"1D1kiFDJCEjQLk2K2RYj5nUWyTz4s42RfG",
            "value":349208,
            "n":0,
            "script":"76a91483c5ff637d7603332983cd6adadbac55394ea91288ac"
        }
    ],
    "lock_time":0,
    "size":191,
    "double_spend":false,
    "time":1503586036,
    "tx_index":277869735,
    "vin_sz":1,
    "hash":"7a5397a5c3496b77b512af53a9ab8d406beda38105c304c7f587815147e2071f",
    "vout_sz":1
}
```

Figure 12-1: Relay address on blockchain.info.

If you would like to browse to this record on blockchain.info, open a browser and go to `http://bit.ly/2he4Pbr`.

Although much of the data provided here by the website is raw information from the blockchain, the IP address is specific to its own database. Does this IP address relate to the user who sent the transaction? Perhaps, but it is unlikely. Bitcoin uses a peer-to-peer network structure to facilitate the efficient dissemination of transactions to all Bitcoin nodes around the world. When Alice creates a transaction, for example, it is sent to the peers recorded in her Bitcoin wallet software. Those peers transmit the transaction to their peers, and the process continues until every Bitcoin node is aware of the transaction. Blockchain.info watches a large number of nodes, and when one of those nodes transmits a transaction for the first time, it is that IP that is recorded. This is depicted in Figure 12-2.

Alice is using IP address 212.58.21.53 and creates a transaction. This is broadcast to her peers, one of which blockchain.info is monitoring. This relay node is using IP address 172.58.42.44, and this is the IP that blockchain.info records in its database. Hence, in this instance, the IP address recorded is not the originator of the transaction.

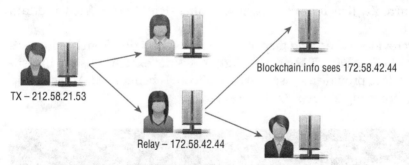

Figure 12-2: Bitcoin peer-to-peer network.

However, it is possible that the originator of the transaction was the IP address that blockchain.info saw—the problem is, there is no way of knowing.

Since the erroneous conference, I have seen other work done by researchers and even journalists where they have used the IP address in blockchain.info to "identify" and even expose what they believe to be the user of a particular Bitcoin address. But is this a dead end, or can we get closer to the IP address that generated a transaction and hence connect it to a Bitcoin address?

Back in 2011, security researcher Dan Kaminsky gave a talk at the Black Hat USA conference entitled "Black Ops of TCP/IP." During that talk, he postulated that if you could scan the Internet for every host with port 8333 open, the Bitcoin Core port, and then watch the transactions flowing from each node in real time, the IP address that first transmitted a transaction would likely be the originator of the transaction. Although this does not take into account thin clients such as Electrum or clients on mobile devices that do not have a full blockchain locally, the reasoning is sound. In fact, even if a person was using a mobile device, the transaction would still be traceable to the server that the client was connected to. In Chapter 13, "Sniffing Cryptocurrency Traffic," I will show you how to capture all the transactions coming from a full node.

Bitnodes

Using the concept voiced by Dan Kaminsky and others, a researcher named Addy Yeow set up a website named bitnodes.earn.com based on open-source code that he released on GitHub (`http://bit.ly/2EHKuVO`). The idea was to send `getaddr` or `get address messages`, starting from a set of known Bitcoin nodes to recursively map every running Bitcoin node. Bitnodes runs constantly and provides an API (application programming interface) for an investigator to be able to analyze the data. All the data is clustered into timestamps so that you can be very granular in ascertaining what nodes were live at a particular point in time. This means that if you have an IP of a suspect, you are able to use the API to know if it has ever been used as a Bitcoin node at a time in the past, or is currently live. It is also possible to filter IP addresses from a certain ISP or country.

Bitnodes provides a live world map of transactions occurring from IP addresses across the globe (see Figure 12-3). Although this is not exactly a useful investigative tool, it does provide a sense of where Bitcoin is being used. You can find this map by browsing to `http://bit.ly/2spitgM`.

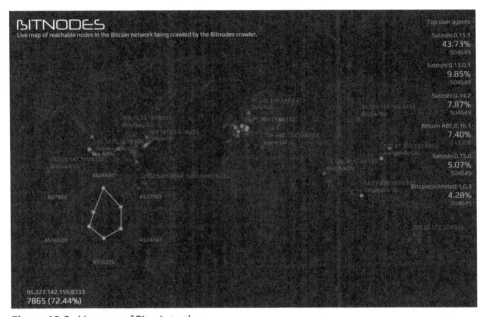

Figure 12-3: Live map of Bitcoin trades.

The site provides an interface to be able to search for any IP address and get information as to whether it is a Bitcoin node, its time live, its location, and other information (see Figure 12-4). You can find this interface at `http://bit.ly/2GfHSvz`.

You can also extract raw data on whether an IP address is currently live in JSON format. You simply browse using the following URL format:

```
https://bitnodes.earn.com/api/v1/nodes/<IP-Port>/
```

For example, the following URL will return the data in Figure 12-5:

```
https://bitnodes.earn.com/api/v1/nodes/208.118.235.190-8333/
```

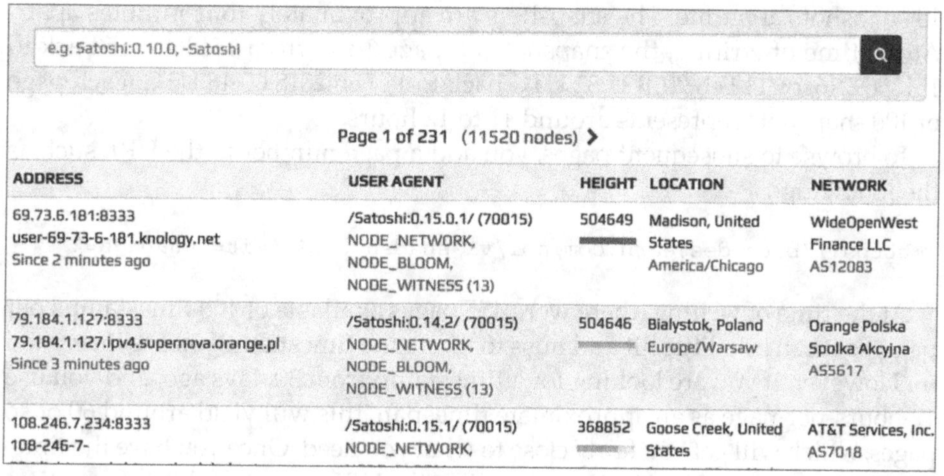

e.g. Satoshi:0.10.0, -Satoshi

Page 1 of 231 (11520 nodes) >

ADDRESS	USER AGENT	HEIGHT	LOCATION	NETWORK
69.73.6.181:8333 user-69-73-6-181.knology.net Since 2 minutes ago	/Satoshi:0.15.0.1/ (70015) NODE_NETWORK, NODE_BLOOM, NODE_WITNESS (13)	504649	Madison, United States America/Chicago	WideOpenWest Finance LLC AS12083
79.184.1.127:8333 79.184.1.127.ipv4.supernova.orange.pl Since 3 minutes ago	/Satoshi:0.14.2/ (70015) NODE_NETWORK, NODE_BLOOM, NODE_WITNESS (13)	504646	Bialystok, Poland Europe/Warsaw	Orange Polska Spolka Akcyjna AS5617
108.246.7.234:8333 108-246-7-	/Satoshi:0.15.1/ (70015) NODE_NETWORK,	368852	Goose Creek, United States	AT&T Services, Inc. AS7018

Figure 12-4: List of current Bitcoin nodes.


```
"hostname": "",
"address": "208.118.235.190",
"status": "UP",
"data": [
        70015,
        "/Satoshi:0.14.2/",
        1515053910,
        13,
        504663,
        "bitcoin1p.fsf.org",
        "Boston",
        "US",
        42.3584,
        -71.0598,
        "America/New_York",
        "AS22989",
        "Free Software Foundation, Inc."
],
"bitcoin_address": "",
"url": "",
"verified": false,
"mbps": "0.785019"
```


Figure 12-5: Metadata from a Bitcoin node.

This data includes the Bitcoin version in use, the time it was last seen (in UNIX time), the city, the country, and the host it relates to (if available).

Bitnodes performs a regular crawl of the Internet and indexes the IP addresses it finds as timestamps using the UNIX time format. You can use the following URL to list the latest snapshots:

```
https://bitnodes.earn.com/api/v1/snapshots/?limit=100
```

Note that the end of the URL is `limit=100`. This specifies the maximum number of snapshots on a single page, and without this, you would only see

10 snapshots at a time. The snapshots are approximately four minutes apart. At the time of writing, the snapshots on page 1 ran from 1518607945 back to 1518569216, or 14 Feb 2018 11:32 UTC back to 14 Feb 2018 00:46 UTC. Each page of 100 snapshots represents around 11 to 12 hours.

To browse to subsequent pages, you add a page number to the URL such as the following:

```
https://bitnodes.earn.com/api/v1/snapshots/?limit=100&page=2
```

At the time of writing, there were 455 pages available of 100 timestamps per page, so it can be a little hit and miss to locate the timestamp you are interested in. However, if you are looking for a timestamp from 30 days ago, and you use 12-hours-per-page as an approximate timespan, this will yield around 60 or so pages, which will get you fairly close to what you need. Once you have the timestamp you are interested in, you can adjust the URL to extract this information. For example, if you want to see the IP addresses live at timestamp 1515855919, you need to browse to:

```
https://bitnodes.earn.com/api/v1/snapshots/1515855919
```

This will list all the visible IPs at that time, with metadata including the version of Bitcoin being used, the city, and the ISP that the IP address belongs to (see Figure 12-6).

```
"timestamp": 1515855919,
"total_nodes": 11621,
"latest_height": 504052,
"nodes": {
        "185.25.48.184:8333": [
                70015,
                "/Satoshi:0.15.1/",
                1513754749,
                13,
                504052,
                "btc1.sqrrm.net",
                null,
                "LT",
                56,
                24,
                "Europe/Vilnius",
                "AS61272",
                "Informacines sistemos ir technologijos, UAB"
        ],
        "95.213.145.52:8333": [
                70015,
                "/Satoshi:0.13.2/",
                1514129788,
                13,
                504052,
                "95.213.145.52",
                null,
                "RU",
                55.7386,
                37.6068,
                null,
                "AS49505",
                "OOO Network of data-centers Selectel"
        ], ... ... .. .....
```

Figure 12-6: IPs and metadata of Bitcoin nodes from a snapshot.

From this list, you can see if your suspect's IP address was live as a Bitcoin node in that time frame.

Using these techniques, you may be able to confirm the following:

- If an IP address is being used as a Bitcoin node
- When the node has been live
- The approximate location of the node either via a lookup on the IP address or via its geolocation metadata
- If an IP address is confirmed as a Bitcoin node, you may be able to use legal means to request user data from the ISP that owns the address

These methods are useful, but Bitnodes provides a different view of the data that can be very useful to an investigator. Having crawled the peer-to-peer network mapping each node it can see, Bitnodes then watches the propagation of blocks and transactions through the network, recording the first 10 IP addresses it has sight of that propagated the transaction or block and then attaching a "first-seen" time to each IP address. This gets you closer to the originator of a transaction.

This capability only works on blocks and transactions over block height 400000 (after Feb 25 2016) and will only work after a block or transaction is more than 8 hours old. The statistics are calculated based on the arrival times formatted as UNIX time in milliseconds from the first 1000 nodes that propagate the data. To use the tool, find the transaction hash (TXID) for the transaction you are interested in. In blockchain.info, that is the long value above the transaction addresses. Copy and paste the TXID into the following URL:

```
https://bitnodes.earn.com/api/v1/inv/<TX_ID>/
```

This will list the IP addresses seen propagating the transaction in time order. Try the following URL to return the IP addresses for TX_ID a6350ff0c5a0cebd46518881e0486baa1145ac925fee88450fefd13fa61c31c:

```
http://bit.ly/2EFoTxn
```

This returns the following JSON values:

```
"[2a01:4f8:171:3567::2]:8333",
1499717236030
],
 [
"138.201.33.232:8333",
1499717236030
],
 [
"[2a01:4f8:a0:300a::2]:8333",
1499717236036
```

```
],
  [
"88.198.33.138:8333",
1499717236036
],
  [
"23.253.151.73:8333",
1499717236041
],
  [
"148.251.67.240:8333",
1499717236061
],
  [
"73.226.64.145:8333",
1499717236065
],
  [
"52.5.87.242:35131",
1499717236069
],
  [
"52.58.91.193:8333",
1499717236075
],
  [
"68.76.147.138:8333",
1499717236081
```

The first IP address is an IPv6 address, and the second address is an IPv4 address, but both have identical time values with the last four digits being 6030. Although we have looked at UNIX time already in this book, these times are 13 digits long rather than the standard 10 digits and represent the time in milliseconds; hence, you cannot use a standard converter to look up the times. My favorite millisecond converter can be found at `http://currentmillis.com`. The last four digits represent the seconds and milliseconds and are generally sufficient for network propagation.

These two IPs represent the first nodes to be aware of the transaction, and one of them could be the source of the transaction. Use an IP lookup website to search for the owners of the IPs and the hosts. Try using site-on-ip.com to look up the first IP: 2a01:4f8:171:3567::2. The results show three hosts on this IP:

- `dnsseed.litecoinpool.org`
- `seed.bitcoin.jonasschnelli.ch`
- `seed.bitcoinstats.com`

These sites are tagged as "seeds." The DNS Seed is a type of DNS server that returns IP addresses of full nodes on the Bitcoin network to enable a new node to find peers to propagate with. Hence, you can discern that this IP is likely not the originator, but an early peer. If you look up the details on the second IP, 138.201.33.232, you find the following hosts:

- `dnsseed.koin-project.com`
- `dnsseed.litecoinpool.org`
- `dnsseed.litecointools.com`
- `dnsseed.ltc.xurious.com`
- `seed.bitcoinstats.com`
- `x9.dnsseed.thrasher.io`
- `x9.seed.bitcoin.jonasschnelli.ch`
- `x9.seed.bitcoin.sipa.be`
- `x9.seed.btc.petertodd.org`

You cannot help but notice the similarities.

NOTE It is possible that the exact timestamps in this example are explained by the host connecting to both an IPv4 and IPv6 address simultaneously.

For example, why are some of the same URLs tagged as hosts on the IP address? These are DNS seeds and normal seeds that point to a list of known Bitcoin nodes should the DNS seeds fail for some reason. These seeds are hard-coded into the Bitcoin source code in the file `chainparams.cpp`. (This source code is available at `http://bit.ly/2HgPzmA`.) In 2018, the seed values in the source code are

- `seed.bitcoin.sipa.be`
- `dnsseed.bluematt.me`
- `dnsseed.bitcoin.dashjr.org`
- `seed.bitcoinstats.com`
- `seed.bitcoin.jonasschelli.ch`
- `seed.btc.petertodd.org`

If you see any of the values listed here, then the IP is a known long-term, reliable Bitcoin node and is a known relay. Of course, it is possible that your suspect may be a long-term relay, but this technique gets you closer to your originator.

Another example can be seen in TX_ID `f73ae4a1142a063e78087ae6d9c8d c936f222f2dc8ee477d34d531ffe852790e`. The first IP addresses are as follows:

```
"bitcoinranliixsu.onion:8333",
1518391303552
```

```
"78.129.241.145:8333",
1518391303888


"171.33.177.9:8333",
1518391303889
```

The first IP is an Onion address from the Tor network: `bitcoinranliixsu` `.onion`. If you search for this on the Bitnodes website, you'll discover that Bitnodes knows about it, but it is certainly not a reliable node (see Figure 12-7).

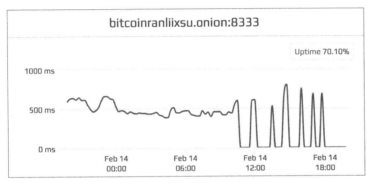

Figure 12-7: Graph of uptime of node.

As you can see, at the time of writing this node is available only 70 percent of the time. It is also not included in the list of "fall-back" nodes available on Tor (which is kept updated at `http://bit.ly/2BsRS5E`), so although you still can't be sure, it is possible that this could be the originator of the transaction.

The Bitnodes site and API can be very useful to an investigator who has an IP as part of his investigation and wants to know if it was a Bitcoin node as well as for an investigator who wants to know more about a transaction. It is just possible that the IP address could be the originator, and appropriate legal means could be used to obtain location information of the suspect.

Similar sites are available for other cryptocurrencies. For example, litenodes.net (`http://bit.ly/2CmkrOW`) is an attempt to find the IP addresses of all Litecoin nodes on the network, and ethernodes.org attempts to map all Ethereum nodes. Interestingly, Ethereum has approximately 25,000 nodes in comparison to Bitcoin's 11,000.

Other Areas Where IPs Are Stored

Although it can be difficult to trace an IP address from a transaction, plenty of other places exist where IP addresses can be stored that are related to blockchain activity. Here are some examples:

Online Stores   A suspect may purchase goods or services at an online store and pay using a cryptocurrency. In order to ship goods, the store will have to take personal details, which may include a home address, phone number, and other personal data. This is usually stored in a database and will be related to the cryptocurrency address that was used to purchase. If you can identify the store on the blockchain, you may be able to use legal means to request the release of information about the purchaser. This information should also include access to the weblogs and any other logging or analytics information that could help identify their IP address and also track their movements on the website.

Exchanges   Aside from sites such as localbitcoins.com, which allow the purchasing of coins for cash "on the street," most purchases of cryptocurrencies will be via exchanges. Exchanges are becoming increasingly regulated and are required to gather significant information on the user, which will include data such as his or her home address as well as financial information such as bank details and credit card details. If an exchange can be identified, then legal means can be used to request the information including any IP address logs that may exist.

RELEASE OF DATA BY ROGER VER

It is notable that in 2012, Roger Ver, the owner of bitcoinstore.com, had bitcoins that had been mistakenly refunded to a customer, not returned. To shame the customer into returning the coins, he published the information bitcoinstore.com held on the client, which can be seen in the following image (redacted by me).

> *Roger TODAY 04:36 PM*
>
> ▮▮▮▮▮▮▮
>
> *I looked up your address with Blockchain, and %100 for sure the funds were sent to a Bitcoin address that you control.*
>
> *Here is the proof of the link to your account corresponding with Bitcoin address: 1H4UR5M72Ybpo4zrqWe8JKKYSeN1gxqBcU*
>
> *[Wallet {email='nethead▮▮▮▮▮▮*
> *, guid='46f2b149-45c1-309c-98e0-af31be28175f'*
> *, shared_key='2ea287bc-abf8-71b1-8e45-276ac034b854'*
> *, secret_phrase=▮▮▮▮▮▮▮*
> *, alias=▮▮▮▮*
> *, created=Sat Dec 08 17:46:45 GMT 2012*
> *, updated=Wed Dec 19 01:43:47 GMT 2012*
> *, created_ip='188.95.51.84'*
> *, updated_ip='79.107.123.47'*
> *, sms_number='+44 7583383202'*
> *, country='USD'}*
>
> *You need to send back my 4.5119 BTC to:*
> *18yDbzddGVEr1Vyp4NXrP6mqAmUTesAg9a*
>
> *right away.*

Although Mr. Ver received mixed responses to his actions, it provided a good insight into the customer data that was readily available to an administrator of the exchange. As shown in the image, this data included the customer's e-mail address, secret phrase, alias, IP addresses, and most importantly, Bitcoin addresses that had been used by the account to trade with the store.

Thin Clients   Although I have focused on clients such as Bitcoin Core thus far in this book, many so-called thin clients do not store a complete copy of the blockchain, but instead connect to servers that handle the communication with the blockchain for them. The servers are called SPV (Simplified Payment Verification) servers, which handle the verifications of trades on the blockchain. These servers usually retain the IP address of the user connected to cryptocurrency addresses they use. In fact, the Bitcoin thin client Electrum uploads all the addresses from a user's wallet to the SPV server. Again, significant information can be obtained through legal means.

Online Wallets   Many exchanges also provide online wallets; however, a number of providers just provide secure storage of your private keys in the cloud. Most of these services will retain the IP address of the logged-in user, which can be requested.

Is the Suspect Using Tor?

If you have identified an IP address, it can be useful to ascertain if the address owner is using the Tor network to obfuscate his or her true location. As a concept, Tor has been around for over 20 years; however, the code was only made available publicly by the U.S. Naval Research Lab in 2004. The model is fairly simple—a user connects to one of a large pool of entry nodes, which then bounce your data through various relays before routing to the Internet at large through an exit node. All the nodes are provided by volunteers, although anecdotally, governments are thought to run many of the exit nodes. The system effectively prevents somebody watching your Internet activity and provides a good level of anonymity.

> **NOTE**   It is worth noting that data leaving an exit node can be surveilled by the owner of the node. If the destination server or website being browsed to is not SSL encrypted, traffic leaving the node will be in plain text and can be read. Care should still be taken when using Tor and sending personal or otherwise identifiable information.

Because it is not supposed to be possible to trace data traffic from an exit node, back through a random series of relays, through an entry node, and back to the originating IP address, the addresses of Tor nodes can be made public. Tor manages a list of all nodes, which is available online and enables you to check the list to see if a suspect's IP is actually a Tor exit node.

Browse to `https://torstatus.blutmagie.de`. This site maintains a list of all Tor nodes currently active. The onscreen list provides a table of the router name, the hostname, the type of nodes it provides, and other information (see Figure 12-8).

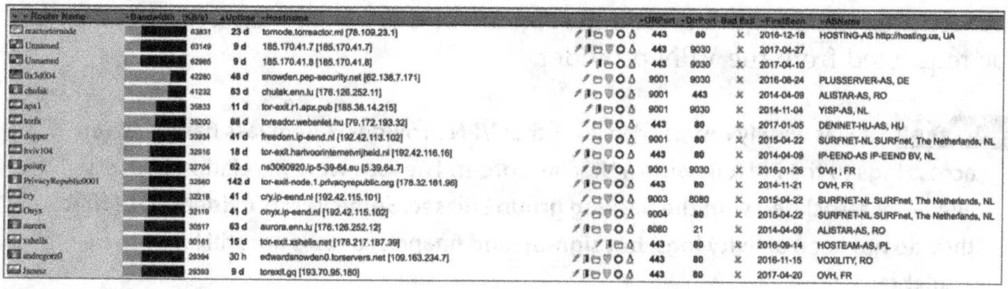

Figure 12-8: List of Tor nodes.

If you look at the top of the web page, you are able to download a series of CSV files of different nodes. One is called "CSV List of ALL Current Tor Server Exit Nodes." If you download this file, you will see that it contains a list of every current exit node. You can now simply search the list to see if your suspect's IP address exists in the list.

The problem with this is that Tor nodes change all the time, so the IP address you have may not be a live exit node on the day that you download the list. To help with this, Tor maintains a historical list of every exit node that was live during a particular month. This means that if you have an IP address, perhaps one that was used by a suspect at an online store, you can check the date that the IP address accessed the store and then locate the right Tor list and check to see if that address exists.

To find the historical lists, browse to `http://bit.ly/2EJZbYE`, where you will find monthly lists of exit nodes that stretch back as far as February 2012.

Is the Suspect Using a Proxy or a VPN?

If you obtain an IP address using any of the methods previously described, as with Tor, it can be useful to know if the suspect is using a proxy or a VPN (Virtual Private Network) to access the Internet and hide his or her true IP address.

A proxy is a remote server that acts as a jumping-off point to the Internet. This is usually effective at hiding a user's IP address and can sometimes be encrypted between the user and the proxy. Unless a proxy is run by the user or a trusted third party, public-type proxies should not be trusted as secure. As public proxies are often run by those wishing to hide their traffic and provide the capability to others, it can be difficult to obtain user logs via legal means.

A VPN creates an encrypted tunnel from the user to a remote server before breaking out onto the Internet. A VPN can be set up by a user, but this normally means paying for server space with an ISP and leaving a trail of information that can be requested. Many users will make use of a VPN provider to buy access to VPN jump-off points around the world; however, once again, sign-up procedures and logging of true IPs can mean there is still information that can be requested from the VPN provider.

> **NOTE** It was widely reported in 2011 that VPN provider Hidemyass handed over access logs to the FBI following a UK court order. The logs were in relation to users allegedly associated with the hacking group Lulzsec. Some VPN providers state that they do not keep activity logs, but sign-up and financial details are still likely to be available.

How can you work out if an IP address belongs to a VPN provider or proxy? My preferred approach is to make use of the services of ipqualityscore.com. The site provides a number of services designed to help prevent fraud, but these can be useful to the investigator. If you click the Proxy Detection link, you are able to try out the service free of charge. Simply enter the IP address of your suspect, and the site will attempt to ascertain whether the IP is from a proxy or VPN server (see Figure 12-9). In my testing, I have found it to be extremely accurate.

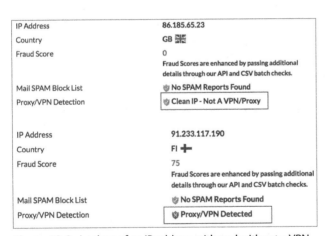

Figure 12-9: Lookup of an IP address with and without a VPN.

Ipqualityscore.com also enables you to register for free and gain access to 5000 free lookups per month—in fact, the site is quite reasonably priced at just $50 for 50,000 lookups per month. This enables you do batch lookups of a list of IP addresses. Once you are registered and logged in, browse to `http://bit .ly/2o14IAo`, and you can then easily upload a CSV file containing a list of IP addresses to check (see Figure 12-10).

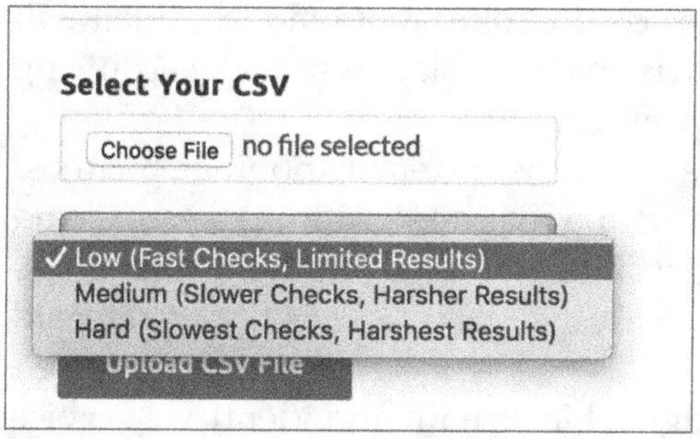

Figure 12-10: Uploading a CSV file.

Once you have identified if an IP address comes from a proxy or VPN, there is the possibility of requesting information or logs from the service provider.

Tracking to a Service Provider

Following transactions through the blockchain manually or using visualization tools is a vital skill, but an investigator needs to translate that work into real-world data, a name, IP address, or other identifiable information. Thus far, this chapter has focused on finding or researching IP addresses; however, if you can link transactions to a service provider of some type, then legal measures can be used to request stored information on a customer. When I use the term "service provider," it should probably be qualified to a legitimate service provider. A store located on the Tor network that sells drug-manufacturing equipment and only takes Bitcoin is unlikely to respond to your request for customer information, but many legitimate providers will often respond positively where a legal approach is made. A service provider could include, but is not limited to the following:

- Exchange
- Coin-mixing company
- Legitimate trader
- Thin-client server administrator

Currency exchanges are an excellent resource for information if you can identify that coins were either purchased from a particular exchange or if coins were cashed out to a fiat currency using an exchange. Getting cryptocurrency coins without leaving a trace has become increasingly difficult, especially Bitcoin, because mining would often be a way of acquiring coins with little or no attribution. However, Bitcoin now requires specialist and expensive hardware to achieve any success. Coins could be acquired by trading in person with an existing coin owner or using sites such as www.localbitcoins.com. Recently,

ATMs have appeared that enable you to acquire coins anonymously, but it will be interesting to see if and when countries pass legislation to make acquiring currency without a trace increasingly difficult.

Using a currency exchange to purchase coins is extremely popular, but most of the major exchanges are being regulated and require significant personal and financial information to complete registration and enable purchasing. Some wallet sites now actively recommend `localbitcoins.com` as their preferred purchasing route.

If you can follow transactions through a blockchain and identify a service provider of some type, then you can use legal means to request data and acquire real-world data to help your investigation. But how do you identify a service provider? It's not possible track "through" an exchange, because the coins that come out of an exchange are different from the ones that are deposited. Imagine taking a $5 bill to a bank and depositing it. If you go back the next day and ask for $5, the teller will not go and get your original bill; instead, she will provide you with the same value from a float. Exchanges and mixers work in a similar way. When a coin is transacted with an exchange, addresses are aggregated, and the majority of coins stored are kept in an offline (cold storage) wallet for safekeeping. The exchange will keep a float in an address, and as people purchase coins, they will transfer the required amount from the float and accept the rest back as change.

By far the best way to identify clusters such as exchanges, mixers, and major online traders is by using a commercial tool such as Elliptic or Chainalysis. A similar task can be achieved manually, but it will likely take longer and require more resources.

The first thing you need to be able to do is cluster addresses so that you know addresses owned by the same user, group, or organization. I discussed these techniques in detail in Chapter 10, but in simple terms, you can infer that the following addresses have the same owner:

- Input addresses belong to same owner
- Input addresses used with other input addresses in other transactions
- When you compare the input and output values of changed addresses:
  - Payment from a multisig address starting with a 3 has a 3 change address
  - Payment to a 3 address from a 1 address has a 1 address as its change address

Once you are confident with manually clustering addresses, you can make a micro-transaction to the service provider. If you then withdraw the coin value you deposited, most exchanges will expose a large number of input addresses used by the exchange and also expose a change address. You can then use clustering methods to build a picture of the exchange. If you do this regularly and to many of the primary exchanges, you will begin to see repeated addresses and can accurately identify the address as being owned by a particular service provider.

This process is often evident on the blockchain where an exchange has an address with a large float ready to transact coins with users who buy them. For example, let's say the exchange puts 100 bitcoin in an address. A person buys 0.5 bitcoin, and the exchange transacts all 100 bitcoin, with the exchange taking back 99.5 as change. Next, a person buys 1 bitcoin. The exchange uses the change address to send that person the 1 bitcoin and takes 98.5 bitcoin back to another change address. In reality, the transactions will be to multiple customers in a single transaction, but you will still see the large amount sent back as change each time. This process is called *unpeeling*. You can see a good example of this if you browse to `http://bit.ly/2GrxaD1`. This will load a record of a transaction with one input of 8892 bitcoin and with 14 outputs. The final output is for 8890 bitcoin. Is this the change address? If you are sharp-eyed, you will notice that this output address is the same as the input address—this alone shows that it is the change address (see Figure 12-11).

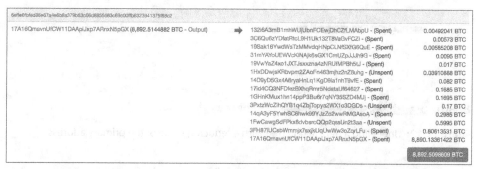

Figure 12-11: Large transaction with change address back to itself.

Next, click the View Tree Chart link and follow the output starting 17A16Q by clicking it. If you keep clicking this address, you will witness transaction after transaction as coins are "sold" to customers and the balance returned to itself. This is depicted in Figure 12-12, but I recommend that you try this for yourself if you can because it's more impressive on screen.

When you see patterns like this, you are almost always dealing with an exchange. If you now take the address 17A16Q, you can do a lookup with either www.bitcoinwhoswho.com or www.walletexplorer.com. This will identify the address as belonging to Poloniex.com. You have now identified an address used by the Poloniex exchange. If you are researching a Bitcoin address, and the input to it is 17A16Q . . ., you will know that the source was the Poloniex exchange, and you can now make a legal request for information.

Also, a large number of addresses in each of the vast number of transactions from 17A16Q contain coins originating with Poloniex. This is a good start in building a database to identify exchanges. Of course, it's a very limited start, but this demonstrates how you can identify an exchange by its pattern and then extract ownership data and addresses belonging to clients reasonably easily.

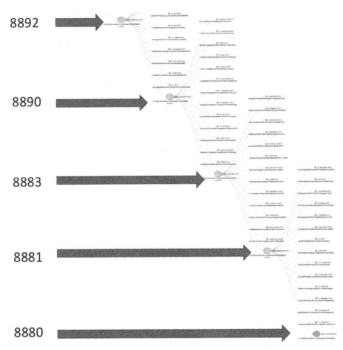

8892

8890

8883

8881

8880

Figure 12-12: Unpeeling a transaction tree with a reducing value of the primary address.

It can be useful to know what crypto and fiat currencies an exchange supports. An excellent site is www.coinlib.io/exchanges, which details each exchange and the currencies that are supported. Searching for Poloniex shows that they support a wide range of cryptocurrencies but only support U.S. dollars for payment and cashing out (see Figure 12-13).

Tracking transactions back to a store or trader can sometimes be more complex, but on many occasions, the trader will publish an address. It is then straightforward to do some online open-source research on the address to find out more about it. Once you have an address or addresses used by a trader, you can use clustering techniques to find other addresses and then extract all the inputs to those addresses to begin to identify customers. It is extraordinary how often you can find an address that belongs to a trader. Next, you extract all the input addresses, perhaps using Maltego as described in Chapter 11. Many of the input addresses belong to customers, and a good number of those will be just one hop from an exchange where they bought their bitcoin or other cryptocurrency.

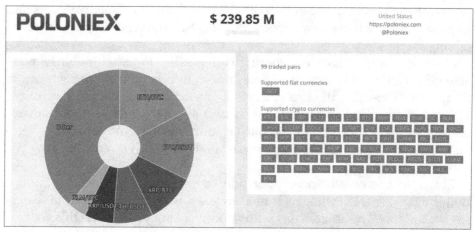

Figure 12-13: Currencies supported by Poloniex.

EXERCISES

Take a look at the following address, and then answer the questions:

`1Kqzbv4ekpJX3ohYWGEzMqzvf27VjBux35`

1. Who owns the address?

2. Can you cluster some addresses owned by the same person?

3. Can you find three addresses of users who paid for goods?

4. How much bitcoin did they receive over time?

Answers

1. The owner is likely The Pirate Bay.

2. There are too many to list, but you should be able to infer ownership of at least 10 addresses.

3. Again, there are a large number of addresses. The target address will always be an output. Looking at payment amounts may help you discern which addresses are likely customers.

4. At time of writing, they received 22.57 bitcoin.

Considering Open-Source Methods

The blockchains of most currencies are by definition open source. Their underlying code is usually publicly available—for example, the Bitcoin code can be obtained by browsing to `https://github.com/bitcoin`. The open-source nature of the code means that researchers can examine it and find security problems, improve it, or fork it to a new version. But, this isn't the type of open source I'm talking about.

Open-source intelligence gathering is the ability to search publicly available information for both explicit and implicit information about a subject. In Chapter 8, "Detecting the Use of Cryptocurrencies," you learned how to use HTTrack to download a website and then use a search tool such as Agent Ransack to use a regular expression to find Bitcoin addresses. But, you cannot use regular expressions to search the Internet, so you have to be clever in the way you construct search terms.

I teach a class on advanced open-source intelligence gathering, and one of the first things I tell students is that Google is there to stop you from searching the Internet. This is often met with opposition, but you can test this yourself by browsing to Google and searching for the name of a movie that is currently showing at theaters. Google will generally display the movie times at your local cinema. But what if you were not looking for that? What if you were looking for the movie's cast, where it was filmed, or even showings in another city? Google hasn't ignored these possibilities, but its algorithm has looked at your search, considered where you are geographically, and has given you the information that previous searchers have clicked on recently. It's a bit more complex than that, but it means that when you are searching Google's vast index for a restaurant called "The Eatery," it somehow manages to give you the information about the café nearest to you rather than one on the other side of the world.

If you are searching as part of an investigation, you need to form searches to acquire the information you actually want rather than what Google thinks you want. To do this, there is a series of search modifiers that you can use. For example, if you know that your suspect has a Facebook page, is called Mario, and accepts bitcoin donations, you can use the modifier **site:** to just search the site that you want. For example, try the following search in Google:

site:facebook.com Mario bitcoin donations

This search will only look at pages from Facebook, because you invoked the `site:` modifier. You should be able to find the page depicted in Figure 12-14.

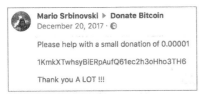

Mario Srbinovski ▶ Donate Bitcoin
December 20, 2017 · ©

Please help with a small donation of 0.00001

1KmkXTwhsyBiERpAufQ61ec2h3oHho3TH6

Thank you A LOT !!!

Figure 12-14: Results of searching using the site: modifier.

Here are some other useful modifiers:

- `intitle:` searches for a word in the web page title.
- `allintitle:` searches for all search terms in a page title.
- `intext:` searches for pages with a single search term.
- `allintext:` searches for pages with all of the subsequent search terms.
- `inURL:` searches for a word in the URL of the page.
- `allinURL:` searches for all the search terms in a page URL.
- `filetype:` searches for a specified file type (such as `.doc`, `.pdf`, `.txt`, or whatever file type you specify after the colon).

Using these modifiers, you can get more control over your searches to find information related to your suspect.

> **EXERCISE**
>
> Use the `site:` modifier to look for the Bitcoin address on spacechain.org. It's very tricky to find by browsing the site, but Google will find it if you search cleverly.

Accessing and Searching the Dark Web

The dark web isn't actually dark—it is just the name that journalists have locked onto because it sounds mysterious and dangerous. The so-called dark web has many names such as the deep web, darknet, and although a little inaccurate, often just Tor, which is the primary method of accessing this information. Dark web sites are simply Internet-based resources such as websites, forums, IRC chat channels, and others that are not accessible using a standard browser and cannot be seen using normal search engines.

Being able to access this area of the Internet is vital for an investigator because, although the dark web is not all about criminality, many sites that sell services or products that are illegal or, at best, not mainstream, exist in this space. Many of these traders use Bitcoin and other cryptocurrencies to accept payment; hence, we need to be able to investigate them effectively.

I often speak to investigators that are nervous about getting online and browsing the dark web because they are afraid of viruses, hackers, mistakenly downloading illegal material such as child images, and many other concerns. Unfortunately, they are right to be nervous, but this should not be an excuse to avoid travelling to the online version of the rough side of town.

You can take precautions by using a virtual machine to browse rather than your primary computer and by being very cautious where you click and what you download. Of course, these concerns will differ for a law enforcement officer and a civilian investigator, as laws may apply differently depending on what you are investigating. A law enforcement officer may be looking for illegal images, while a person investigating ransomware may be actively trying to be infected in order to be able to examine the malware.

When it comes to investigating traders, the investigator is primarily looking for what services or products are being offered and any published cryptocurrency addresses. If a shopping-cart type of system is being used, an investigator may want to make a purchase to be able to follow the payment on the blockchain and see where it ends up.

Being able to browse the dark web is very easy. Numerous software tools can help you, but perhaps the easiest method is to download and install the Tor Browser from `torproject.org`. The URL you need is `http://bit.ly/1jdsLFC`. Alternatively, you can Google for **Tor Browser**, and it is generally the first result.

Once you have installed the browser, run it, and you will see that it looks very much like a standard Firefox web browser. On the left side is a small icon that looks like a green onion—click this icon to change security and connection settings for controlling your access to the network (see Figure 12-15).

Figure 12-15: Options on the Tor Browser.

One of the largest search engines on the dark web is called Torch (see Figure 12-16). You can access it by typing **http://xmh57jrzrnw6insl.onion** into the address bar of your Tor Browser.

Try searching for **Laundry** or **Mixer** to find Tor-based services that will offer to store and "launder" your coins by joining and splitting them. A good example is OnionWallet, which you can browse to at `http://laundryfju74rt34.onion/`, or EasyCoin at `http://walletbjvdecnjgp.onion/1/login.php`.

It's a good idea to get used to working in this environment. It can feel very different from the standard web—sites are often down, connections fail, and the sites feel very basic and not dissimilar to the Internet of the 1990s. However, once you have spent some time browsing the environment, it will quickly feel like home. I suggest that you spend some time searching for the following items:

- Bitcoin addresses
- Aliases
- Sites
- Forums
- Chat sites

Figure 12-16: Torch search engine.

A great resource for knowing what sites are available on the dark web is www.hunch.ly. In addition to the Hunchly software sold at the site (which is excellent OSI-management software) the site provides a daily spreadsheet of what dark web sites are live, what is new, and what is currently down (see Figure 12-17). I highly recommend it. If you browse to https://darkweb.hunch.ly, you can request the daily e-mail from there.

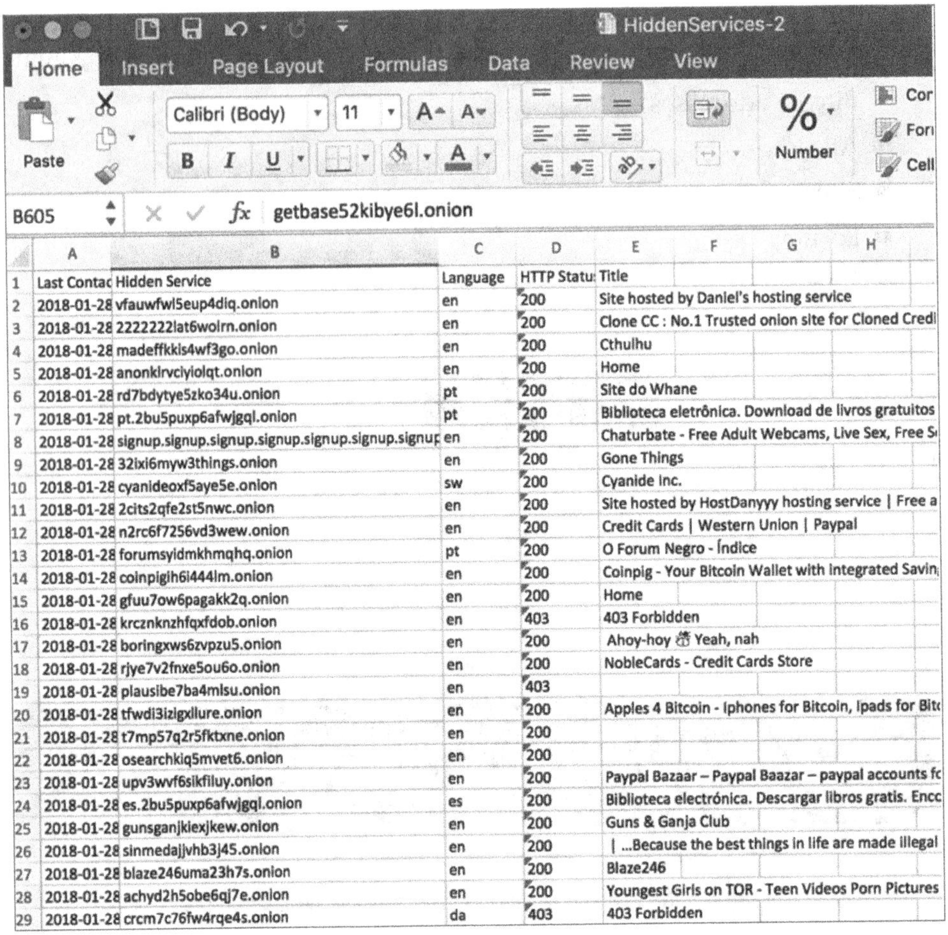

	A	B	C	D	E
1	Last Contac	Hidden Service	Language	HTTP Statu	Title
2	2018-01-28	vfauwfwl5eup4diq.onion	en	200	Site hosted by Daniel's hosting service
3	2018-01-28	2222222lat6wolrn.onion	en	200	Clone CC : No.1 Trusted onion site for Cloned Credi
4	2018-01-28	madeffkkls4wf3go.onion	en	200	Cthulhu
5	2018-01-28	anonklrvciyiolqt.onion	en	200	Home
6	2018-01-28	rd7bdytye5zko34u.onion	pt	200	Site do Whane
7	2018-01-28	pt.2bu5puxp6afwjgql.onion	pt	200	Biblioteca eletrônica. Download de livros gratuitos
8	2018-01-28	signup.signup.signup.signup.signup.signup.signup	en	200	Chaturbate - Free Adult Webcams, Live Sex, Free S
9	2018-01-28	32ixi6myw3things.onion	en	200	Gone Things
10	2018-01-28	cyanideoxf5aye5e.onion	sw	200	Cyanide Inc.
11	2018-01-28	2cits2qfe2st5nwc.onion	en	200	Site hosted by HostDanyyy hosting service | Free a
12	2018-01-28	n2rc6f7256vd3wew.onion	en	200	Credit Cards | Western Union | Paypal
13	2018-01-28	forumsyidmkhmqhq.onion	pt	200	O Forum Negro - Índice
14	2018-01-28	coinpigih6i444im.onion	en	200	Coinpig - Your Bitcoin Wallet with Integrated Savin
15	2018-01-28	gfuu7ow6pagakk2q.onion	en	200	Home
16	2018-01-28	krcznknzhfqxfdob.onion	en	403	403 Forbidden
17	2018-01-28	boringxws6zvpzu5.onion	en	200	Ahoy-hoy Yeah, nah
18	2018-01-28	rjye7v2fnxe5ou6o.onion	en	200	NobleCards - Credit Cards Store
19	2018-01-28	plausibe7ba4mlsu.onion	en	403	
20	2018-01-28	tfwdi3izigxllure.onion	en	200	Apples 4 Bitcoin - Iphones for Bitcoin, Ipads for Bitc
21	2018-01-28	t7mp57q2r5fktxne.onion	en	200	
22	2018-01-28	osearchkiq5mvet6.onion	en	200	
23	2018-01-28	upv3wvf6sikfiluy.onion	en	200	Paypal Bazaar – Paypal Baazar – paypal accounts fc
24	2018-01-28	es.2bu5puxp6afwjgql.onion	es	200	Biblioteca electrónica. Descargar libros gratis. Encc
25	2018-01-28	gunsganjkiexjkew.onion	en	200	Guns & Ganja Club
26	2018-01-28	sinmedajjvhb3j45.onion	en	200	| ...Because the best things in life are made illegal
27	2018-01-28	blaze246uma23h7s.onion	en	200	Blaze246
28	2018-01-28	achyd2h5obe6qj7e.onion	en	200	Youngest Girls on TOR - Teen Videos Porn Pictures
29	2018-01-28	crcm7c76fw4rqe4s.onion	da	403	403 Forbidden

Figure 12-17: Dark web spreadsheet at hunch.ly.

Investigators need to be able to confidently search and browse on the dark web in order to follow traders and services that exist in that online space.

Getting real-world information on a trader on the dark web or a customer using its services is certainly difficult. There have been some successes by using the following techniques:

- Using OSI techniques to search on the standard Internet for names and aliases used by traders on the dark web

  The same aliases as are found in the dark web often crop up on World Wide Web–based forums, gambling sites, and other web resources that may provide an easier path to identifying the person.

- Monitoring addresses

   Traders may advertise their cryptocurrency address on their dark web site. Monitoring the address for payments made to other addresses or traders may lead you to a legitimate trader or service such as an exchange that may enable a legal request for information.

- A law enforcement department or team with appropriate legal warrants exploiting vulnerabilities in the code of a dark web site to extract information

   This could include exposing standard IP addresses, downloading databases, or providing remote access to the server.

- Purchasing goods from a dark web site to reveal other information

   One trader even put a return address on a package containing the ordered goods.

- Using false identities to join and engage with dark web forums and chat groups to become trusted

   This may eventually result in real-world information being shared. This takes skill, planning, and care.

Detecting and Reading Micromessages

The first transaction done by Satoshi Nakamoto on Bitcoin carried a message hidden in the code of the transaction that read, "The Times 03/Jan/2009 Chancellor on brink of second bailout for banks." This demonstrated an ability to carry micromessages within the structure of a transaction and could be useful in identifying the owner of an address.

Due to the high fees of Bitcoin at the present time, sending these types of messages is not sustainable as a widely used messaging system. However, any message encoded in a transaction exists on the blockchain forever and hence is a sound way of making a statement that literally lasts until Bitcoin is no more. Although Bitcoin is too expensive as a communication tool, other cryptocurrencies with lower transaction fees could appear as a viable solution—perhaps as a blockchain-based Twitter-type tool.

In fact, because we can encode anything into hexadecimal and inject it into a transaction, it is possible to place any type of file, whether a document or an image, onto the blockchain, and it can never be removed. Good examples of this are files from Wikileaks. Although they're not easy to extract, if you browse to transaction ID `6c53cd987119ef797d5adccd76241247988a0a5ef783572a9972e7371c5fb0cc` or via `http://bit.ly/2Hh73zj`, you will note a series of outputs that cannot be decoded. This forms code for a download tool that can then be used to extract the raw Wikileaks files from the blockchain (see Figure 12-18).

Name	Size
squelettes-dist	167
Brasil-rejeitou-prisioneiros-de.html	32 789
Cablegate-Brazil-frames-suspected.html	33 340
Cablegate-Telegramas-das.html	34 665
De-olho-nas-Olimpiadas-US-faz.html	33 664
Em-segredo-Brasil-monitora-e.html	37 275
Embaixada-se-aproxima-de.html	32 549
EUA-criticam-Plano-Nacional-de.html	33 446
Groups-to-contact-for-comment.html	33 915
Har-blir-vi-blasta.html	35 925
index.html	2 799
Iraq-Inquiry-told-to-protect-US.html	30 113

Figure 12-18: Wikileaks files downloaded from Bitcoin.

I have included this section in this chapter about finding your suspect, because micromessages from addresses you have identified could contain information that will be useful in helping you make a real-world identification. For example, there could be a message starting with a real name (for example, "Hi Mike") or containing a credit card number, or myriad other possibilities.

A number of different ways exist to embed a message into a transaction, but I will cover just one primary method here. Creating a message to embed into a transaction can be done very easily by following these steps:

1. Construct a message that is less than 20 characters long.

2. Encode the message into hexadecimal. You can use the tool available at `http://bit.ly/2nqHKBM`.

3. Convert the resulting hex string into a Bitcoin address. You can use the tool found at `https://blockchain.info/q/hashtoaddress/<Your_Hex_Value>`.

4. Insert the hex value you created at the end of the URL.

   This will generate a Bitcoin address. Send a few satoshis to the address, and the transaction will appear on the blockchain with your message to the world encoded in it.

To see a good example of this, browse to `http://bit.ly/2BDI01T`. This transaction has many very small inputs with all but the change address unspent. This is a clue that this may be a micromessage. Scroll down to the Output Scripts at the bottom of the page as shown in Figure 12-19.

Copy each block of hex between the square brackets from each output script into the hex box in the tool at `http://bit.ly/2nqHKBM`. Figure 12-19 shows the hex you need to copy with the first block starting `22339`. Once copied into the hex editor it reveals the start of the message "There is not." Work your way through each hex block to eventually reveal the entire message.

Output Scripts

DUP HASH160 PUSHDATA(20)[223339365ce2809c5468657265206973206e6f74]	EQUALVERIFY CHECKSIG
DUP HASH160 PUSHDATA(20)[68696e67206c696b652072657475726e696e6720]	EQUALVERIFY CHECKSIG
DUP HASH160 PUSHDATA(20)[746f206120706c6163650d0a2074686174207265]	EQUALVERIFY CHECKSIG
DUP HASH160 PUSHDATA(20)[6d61696e7320756e6368616e67656420746f2066]	EQUALVERIFY CHECKSIG
DUP HASH160 PUSHDATA(20)[696e64207468652077761797320696e6200d0a2077]	EQUALVERIFY CHECKSIG
DUP HASH160 PUSHDATA(20)[6869636820796f7520796f757273656c66206861]	EQUALVERIFY CHECKSIG
DUP HASH160 PUSHDATA(20)[766520616c6c74657265642ee2809d0d0a202d4e65]	EQUALVERIFY CHECKSIG

Figure 12-19: Output scripts containing a message.

If you would like to watch messages and images being encoded to the Bitcoin blockchain in near real time, browse to Cryptograffiti at `http://bit.ly/1mn8H5h`. You can see some of my recent favorites in Figure 12-20.

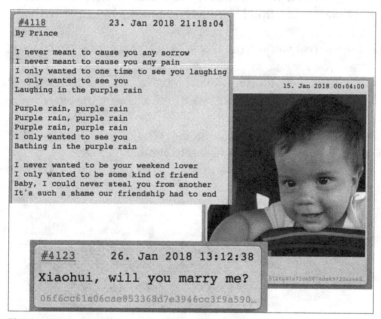

Figure 12-20: Messages on the blockchain.

If you see a transaction where the outputs are very small values and all but one of them are unspent, it is a possible micromessage.

Ethereum has an add-on called a Dapp in alpha stage that allows encrypted peer-to-peer chat over the Ethereum blockchain. It is interesting in that it enables features such as messages that expire after a period of time, and users that only exist as a non-attributable hash provide completely anonymous communications. For example, a journalist could anonymously publish a hash for a whistle-blower to communicate with. Both sides would remain anonymous and protected.

If you can identify messages used by a suspect, and you see odd transactions such as previously described, this may be a message that contains useful information.

Summary

In this chapter, we have looked at ways by which you can take cryptocurrency addresses and use that data to try to locate your suspect in the real world. We have considered methods where you can use IP addresses to try to find the source of a transaction, learned ways you can track transactions to or from a service provider, and how you can find information using open-source methods including on the dark web.

Finding a suspect in the real world from blockchain transactions can be very challenging, and unless you are able to make legal requests for information from service providers, it can be almost impossible. However, the techniques you learned in this chapter can help you to make sense of the data on the blockchain and try to relate it to real-world services.

You also learned about micromessages. Although they're not widely used at present, you can use them to send and receive attributable messages.

Some of these techniques are complex and need to be practiced. Take your time and document everything.

CHAPTER 13

Sniffing Cryptocurrency Traffic

If you work as an investigator, I feel sure that when you read the title of this chapter regarding sniffing network traffic, you will think of the potential issues involved that could make it difficult or impossible. If you work within government or law enforcement, you will immediately think of the application of wiretap and intercept legislation—here in the UK, this type of activity requires an intercept warrant, which can be difficult to obtain. If you are a civilian investigator, you may assume that this type of activity is illegal and outside your sphere of expertise.

It is true that most countries have laws against intercepting any type of communications—whether it's voice, radio, or data—and parts of this chapter assume that you have the legal right to acquire data. I will make it clear when I'm talking about a technique that is likely covered by legislation, but it is your responsibility to check the local laws in your country and follow them. This also applies to government and law enforcement officers that will need to consider what approvals are needed.

This brief chapter will teach you how to monitor a specific Bitcoin node, wherever it may be in the world, and will also look at analyzing data packets for Bitcoin traces.

What Is Intercept?

Intercept legislation is usually described as intercepting and storing communications that are destined for a specific destination. Using mobile phone intercept as an example, let's say Alice calls Bob. Alice and Bob have an expectation of privacy, and the voice traffic is between two specific end-points: the voice from Alice is destined for Bob and vice versa. To listen to that phone call means positioning a receiver between the two endpoints, and it is this detail that is usually classed as intercept and hence illegal.

However, if Alice stood in the street and shouted across a road to Bob, Alice is broadcasting, so there are no defined endpoints and no expectation of privacy. Listening in to that conversation would not be illegal.

We can apply the same principle to data packets. If IP address 192.168.1.2 is sending data to 192.168.2.3, there are defined endpoints, and if we used technical measures to put a receiver between them and intercept that data, then this would likely be illegal. However, there are data packets that are broadcast to everyone, such as very specific broadcast packets from WiFi routers that broadcast the WiFi access point name. If I look at my phone and see a number of WiFi access points close by, it is because the phone has received broadcast packets announcing their existence. This is not intercept.

LAW ENFORCEMENT APPLYING INTERCEPT LEGISLATION

Some countries' intercept laws are designed to provide clarity to law enforcement and require an agency to apply for an appropriate warrant or approval before collecting and storing broadcast-style packets even if a civilian could do the same legally.

Another area that is *not* intercept is requesting data from a server of some type and receiving a response. This chapter will teach you how to watch a Bitcoin node and record the transactions and block information that is flowing out of it. It can feel a bit like intercepting the data, but because you are simply watching a flow of data making up the publicly available blockchain, this is not intercept.

Blockchain data for most cryptocurrencies is unencrypted because the data is public and there is no need to protect the data flow over the Internet. This means that it is possible to set up a WiFi-based or wire-based wiretap and watch the data flowing to and from peers on the blockchain network. Other cryptocurrencies such as ZCash are taking a different approach and encrypting their data. Please remember that a WiFi or wire-based wiretap on an Internet connection not owned by you *would* be classed as intercept in most territories.

If a suspect is using a thin client such as Electrum that does not run a full node, any transactions that are intercepted from the suspect can be considered the originator of the transaction. This can be very useful in watching the movement of coins and the attribution of public addresses. It is worth noting that the private key will never be broadcast.

Watching a Bitcoin Node

You can watch any Bitcoin node simply by connecting to it and requesting the flow of transactions. You are then able to see and record all of the blocks and transactions that are broadcast by the node to its peers.

The first thing you need to find is your target node IP address. This may be something you already have as part of an investigation, but for demonstration purposes, browse to `http://bit.ly/2GfHSvz` on the Bitnodes website. This page lists all of the current live Bitcoin nodes. Choose a node that was seen recently with its block height as close as possible to the up-to-date block number. Record the IP address and port number, which is usually 8333 as shown in Figure 13-1.

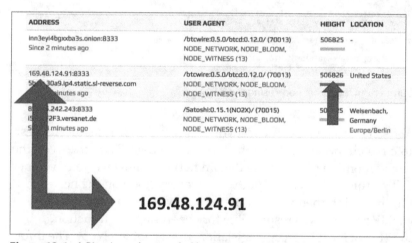

Figure 13-1: A Bitcoin node recorded by Bitnodes.

Once you have a target IP address, a great tool is available to enable you to watch transactions and blocks coming from the node. It's called the Bitcoin P2P Network Sniffer, and it's available at `http://bit.ly/2o4VL9s`. You just need to download the Python file `sniffer.py`.

Open `sniffer.py` in your chosen text editor (such as Notepad++). In the section titled "Default Settings if no configuration file is given," find the line that begins with `"host"` followed by an IP address as shown in Figure 13-2. Adjust the IP address and port to your target address and save the `sniffer.py` file.

Next, open a terminal or a command shell in the folder where `sniffer.py` is located and type the following:

```
python sniffer.py
```

```
# Default Settings if no configuration file is given
settings = {
    "host": "169.48.124.91",
    "port": 8333,
    "debug": False
}
```

Figure 13-2: Change the IP address to the target node.

The command shell will connect to the remote terminal and start to write out each block hash as well as each transaction with the TX Hash and the output addresses and their values in satoshis. The output will look similar to Figure 13-3.

```
Bitcoin Network Sniffer v0.0.2
--------------------------------------------------------------------------
Connecting to Bitcoin Node IP # 169.48.124.91:8333
Connected & Sniffing :)

- Valid Block: 00000000000000000000373c5722c35c9b0bff64899eb78922ac6dc67b673492e5

- Valid TX: b91ee5c188b1f3afdf37fc07261b1ec49d619c20984a4101c7bcf2c92f8220cd

    To: 1JjzcHJ6chwkaZzYBnQi3TX6FpcbUtzs8D  BTC: 0.00013952
    To: 1H5Au749bJrFGosDYndR6KaoXEoytQt3TS  BTC: 0.00023520

- Valid TX: 141bb768b7d07f5e99bd637f0f5f7213664647047e658f75cd0a737ea1414fcf

    To: 1LRbswLkdtvuF99UVYNGJDU44oDTpZUMU1  BTC: 0.00194305
    To: 12CJB1QDmtS8erX1i9wgu5dtDWY12yZAbE  BTC: 0.00929878
```

Figure 13-3: Output from the target node using sniffer.py.

This isn't the same as a network intercept or packet sniffing; this is just requesting the remote Bitcoin node for its public transaction data. This gives you the ability to watch an online node on the Bitcoin network; however, a developer could also utilize this code to attempt to watch every node on the network. If you can get to this point, then you can figure out, with a reasonable degree of certainty, what IP address was responsible for generating a transaction.

By the definition of most intercept legislation, this is not intercept. The information is publicly available—anyone can be a node on the peer-to-peer network and there is no expectation of privacy of this data.

Sniffing Data on the Wire

This book is not the forum to teach you how to set up a wired or wireless intercept. Most modernized countries have the capability to enable approved government agents or law-enforcement officers to watch data flowing to and from a particular IP address via agreements with Internet service providers (ISPs) or some central monitoring location. Tools in the public domain also enable equipment to be connected to a network in an attempt to intercept specific traffic or all the available traffic. It should be noted that trying to achieve full network intercept can cause many problems including bandwidth considerations and storage of the data in real time.

Intercept of WiFi-based traffic is considerably easier to achieve, and plenty of commercial and open-source tools are available to set up a WiFi-based tap. With a WiFi intercept, the limitations of antennas and the fact that it must be in listening mode only means that received packets are not acknowledged. The result of this is that there will almost certainly be missed packets that can add up to significant data loss over time.

As discussed at the start of the chapter, both of these intercept methods, WiFi and wired, are likely illegal in your country unless you own the traffic or have legal approval to do so.

Bitcoin traffic generally flows over port 8333 and is a fairly simple protocol. You can find the entire protocol documentation at `http://bit.ly/2tZgcYw`.

Perhaps the best way to learn and practice this technique is by monitoring the traffic that flows from your own Bitcoin node if you set up Bitcoin Core as discussed in Chapter 1. I recommend downloading and installing Wireshark, which you can find at `http://bit.ly/1OKJhf7`. Wireshark is an outstanding network protocol analyzer, and although it's a freely downloadable tool, it's arguably the best software available for packet analysis. When prompted, you will also need to accept the installation of the WinPCAP driver to enable Wireshark to capture traffic from your network.

Once Wireshark is installed, browse to the Capture Interfaces window by selecting Capture ⟴ Options. As you can see in Figure 13-4, this displays all of the available network adapters on your computer. In this example, I selected Ethernet0 to capture data via the wired Ethernet port on my system. (Your system may have WiFi as an option too.) Ensure that the Enable Promiscuous Mode On All Interfaces box is selected and then click Start.

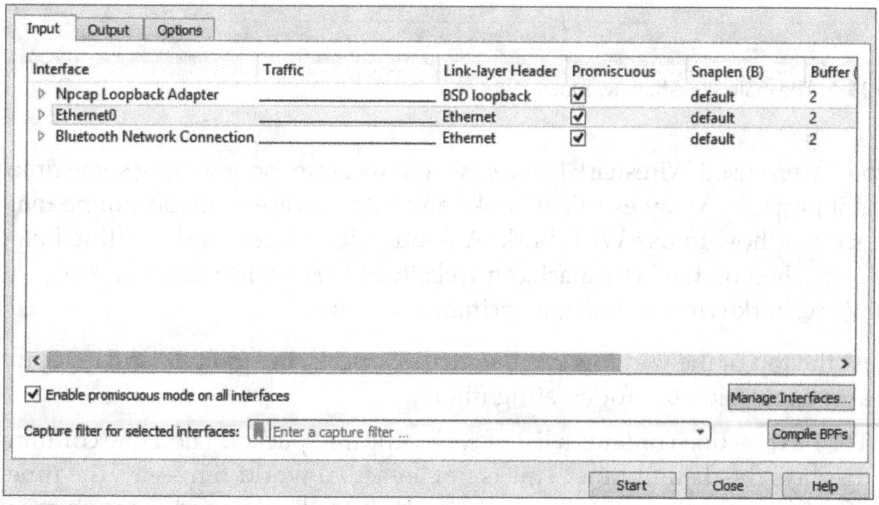

Figure 13-4: Wireshark capture options.

Wireshark will begin to capture all data packets from all ports flowing through your chosen network adapter. Ensure that Bitcoin Core is running so that Bitcoin transactions and blocks are syncing with your node.

The main Wireshark window will begin to fill up very quickly, especially if you have other network-connected services running (such as e-mail, web browser, Skype, or anything that signals the network). The window should start to resemble the example in Figure 13-5.

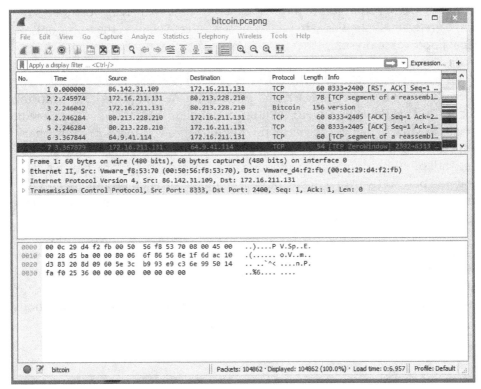

Figure 13-5: The main Wireshark window.

If you haven't used Wireshark before, I would recommend investing some time to learn it properly. Many excellent books and tutorials are available online that can teach you how to use Wireshark. A good place to start is the online help guide published on the Wireshark.org website at `http://bit.ly/2CujtAf`.

The Wireshark window has four primary sections:

- At the top of the window are the menu options, the toolbar, and an editable expression bar for creating filters.

- The next section contains a list of each captured packet. The Time column displays the default time. This is not an actual world time—it's the time offset from the first captured packet, which can be changed. The columns to the right of the Time column are Source, which displays the source

IP address; the Destination, which displays the destination IP address; Protocol, which displays the protocol used; Length, which displays the length of the packet; and Info, which is an interpretation of the packet content.

■ The third section breaks down the selected packet into its constituent parts. This is known as the packet details section. You can expand each part to view detailed raw and interpreted data about the packet.

■ The bottom section provides the raw hex that makes up the selected packet, with the ACSII interpretation on the right. Each line displays the data offset, then 16 hex bytes, followed by 16 ASCII bytes.

You can filter the packets to just show Bitcoin-related packets. You can do this while Wireshark is running or stop the packet capture first by clicking using the round red Stop button (can be square in some versions) at the bottom-left corner of the window. You have a number of ways to apply a filter:

■ Using the filter bar near the top of the Wireshark window, type the following:

tcp.port == 8333

Running this filter will just leave all the packets that use port 8333 (the port used by Bitcoin Core) as shown in Figure 13-6.

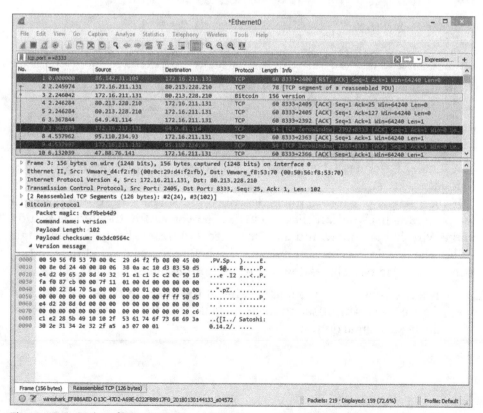

Figure 13-6: Packets filtered to just port 8333.

- ▪ Wireshark also has a built-in filter for Bitcoin. To use it, you simply type **Bitcoin** into the filter.

- ▪ You can also filter just the packets that are part of the Bitcoin network. For example, you can filter just on the Bitcoin magic value that corresponds to the first 4 bytes of the packet by typing

bitcoin.magic == 0xf9beb4d9

- ▪ Alternatively, you can filter on frames containing the IP addresses of peers on the peer-to-peer network by typing

bitcoin.services.network

You can decode transactions using the protocol documentation found at `http://bit.ly/2EOjCDI`. Figure 13-7 shows the raw hex that can be decoded using the protocol documentation. (Some decoding of the raw hex was discussed in Part 1 of the book).

```
000000   F9 BE B4 D9 74 78 00 00   00 00 00 00 00 00 00 00   ....tx..........
000010   02 01 00 00 E2 93 CD BE   01 00 00 00 01 6D BD DB   .............m..
000020   08 5B 1D 8A F7 51 84 F0   BC 01 FA D5 8D 12 66 E9   .[...Q........f.
000030   B6 3B 50 88 19 90 E4 B4   0D 6A EE 36 29 00 00 00   .;P......j.6)...
000040   00 8B 48 30 45 02 21 00   F3 58 1E 19 72 AE 8A C7   ..H0E.!..X..r...
000050   C7 36 7A 7A 25 3B C1 13   52 23 AD B9 A4 68 BB 3A   .6zz%;..R#...h.:
000060   59 23 3F 45 BC 57 83 80   02 20 59 AF 01 CA 17 D0   Y#?E.W... Y.....
000070   0E 41 83 7A 1D 58 E9 7A   A3 1B AE 58 4E DE C2 8D   .A.z.X.z...XN...
000080   35 BD 96 92 36 90 91 3B   AE 9A 01 41 04 9C 02 BF   5...6..;...A....
000090   C9 7E F2 36 CE 6D 8F E5   D9 40 13 C7 21 E9 15 98   .~.6.m...@..!...
0000A0   2A CD 2B 12 B6 5D 9B 7D   59 E2 0A 84 20 05 F8 FC   *.+..].}Y... ...
0000B0   4E 02 53 2E 87 3D 37 B9   6F 09 D6 D4 51 1A DA 8F   N.S..=7.o...Q...
0000C0   14 04 2F 46 61 4A 4C 70   C0 F1 4B EF F5 FF FF FF   ../FaJLp..K.....
0000D0   FF 02 40 4B 4C 00 00 00   00 00 19 76 A9 14 1A A0   ..@KL......v....
0000E0   CD 1C BE A6 E7 45 8A 7A   BA D5 12 A9 D9 EA 1A FB   .....E.z........
0000F0   22 5E 88 AC 80 FA E9 C7   00 00 00 00 19 76 A9 14   "^...........v..
000100   0E AB 5B EA 43 6A 04 84   CF AB 12 48 5E FD A0 B7   ..[.Cj.....H^...
000110   8B 4E CC 52 88 AC 00 00   00 00                     .N.R......
```

Figure 13-7: Raw transaction packet.

A standard packet will begin with a packet header that includes IP addresses, Mac addresses, and so on.

If you use any of `bitcoin` filters described in the last three bullet points in the preceding list, you can click the `Bitcoin protocol` in the middle section of the Wireshark window, and the offset zero will shift to be the Bitcoin magic value. The Bitcoin header is 24 bytes in size before the payload of the transactions begins. Here is a breakdown of what those 24 bytes contain:

- ▪ The first 4 bytes are the magic value at the offset zero (F9 BE B4 D9 in Figure 13-8). The offset, in this case 000000, is the number to the left of the hexadecimal output.

```
000000  F9 BE B4 D9 74  78 00 00   00 00 00 00 00 00 00 00   ....tx..........
000010  02 01 00 00 E2 93 CD BE   01 00 00 00 01 6D BD DB   .............m..
000020  08 5B 1D 8A F7 51 84 F0   BC 01 FA D5 8D 12 66 E9   .[...Q........f.
000030  B6 3B 50 88 19 90 E4 B4   0D 6A EE 36 29 00 00 00   .;P......j.6)...
```

Figure 13-8: Identifying the Bitcoin magic value.

■ The next 12 bytes identify the packet type. In Figure 13-9, the value 74 78 with 20 zeros (which is tx in ASCII) identifies this as a transaction packet.

```
000000  F9 BE B4 D9 74  78 00 00   00 00 00 00 00 00 00 00   ....tx..........
000010  02 01 00 00 E2 93 CD BE   01 00 00 00 01 6D BD DB   .............m..
000020  08 5B 1D 8A F7 51 84 F0   BC 01 FA D5 8D 12 66 E9   .[...Q........f.
000030  B6 3B 50 88 19 90 E4 B4   0D 6A EE 36 29 00 00 00   .;P......j.6)...
000040  00 8B 48 30 45 02 21 00   F3 58 1E 19 72 AE 8A C7   ..H0E.!..X..r...
```

Figure 13-9: The packet type.

■ The next 4 bytes are the length of the payload in bytes. This can be found at offset 000010 and are 02 01. This is formatted in internal byte order, so 01 02 in hex corresponds to a payload of 258 bytes. See Figure 13-10.

```
000000  F9 BE B4 D9 74 78 00 00   00 00 00 00 00 00 00 00   ....tx..........
000010  02 01 00 00 E2 93 CD BE   01 00 00 00 01 6D BD DB   .............m..
000020  08 5B 1D 8A F7 51 84 F0   BC 01 FA D5 8D 12 66 E9   .[...Q........f.
000030  B6 3B 50 88 19 90 E4 B4   0D 6A EE 36 29 00 00 00   .;P......j.6)...
000040  00 8B 48 30 45 02 21 00   F3 58 1E 19 72 AE 8A C7   ..H0E.!..X..r...
```

Figure 13-10: The size of the payload in bytes.

■ The last 4 bytes are a checksum, which is a double 256 hash of the payload: sha256(sha256(payload)). In the example in Figure 13-11, they are E2 93 CD BE.

```
000000  F9 BE B4 D9 74 78 00 00   00 00 00 00 00 00 00 00   ....tx..........
000010  02 01 00 00 E2 93 CD BE   01 00 00 00 01 6D BD DB   .............m..
000020  08 5B 1D 8A F7 51 84 F0   BC 01 FA D5 8D 12 66 E9   .[...Q........f.
000030  B6 3B 50 88 19 90 E4 B4   0D 6A EE 36 29 00 00 00   .;P......j.6)...
000040  00 8B 48 30 45 02 21 00   F3 58 1E 19 72 AE 8A C7   ..H0E.!..X..r...
```

Figure 13-11: The checksum value.

Following these 24 bytes is the payload, which consists of the transaction input and output addresses, values, and so on.

Other Bitcoin clients may use different ports. For example, Electrum uses port 50002 for Bitcoin transactions. Ethereum runs a listener on TCP port 30303 and also a discovery service on UDP port 30303. As described earlier in this chapter, you can filter on these ports by using tcp.port == <port_Number>.

Where a thin client is being used, it may still be possible to intercept traffic by identifying the ports being used and filtering accordingly. However, some thin clients use encryption to encrypt the data from the client to the peer, which would prevent the effective intercept of the content of the data. It is worth remembering that encryption only affects the content of a packet, not the header. Because the header contains the source and destination IP addresses and ports, you are still able to see the IP addresses that are the peers on the network, which could be useful data to an investigator.

Summary

This short chapter is not designed to be a detailed explanation of sniffing cryptocurrency traffic on a network. Instead, it provides an overview of what is possible and an example of how to achieve it. Traffic sniffing and network protocol analysis are specific skills that need to be learned and practiced.

In this chapter, I also discussed how carrying out any type of traffic intercept is probably illegal in your country unless you own the data, have approval from the owner of the data, or are working as a government or law enforcement officer. Even for an officer of the law, there will likely still be legal requirements and legislation to work in line with.

Putting those restrictions aside, because Bitcoin traffic and the traffic of other cryptocurrencies is unencrypted, the data is readable, and which could be very useful in connecting a user to specific cryptocurrency addresses and trades. If you see a need to engage in traffic analysis of any cryptocurrency, I recommend that you do significant research, practice, and get the assistance of a specialist in this field.

Seizing Coins

In this chapter, we will consider when and how to seize cryptocurrency assets. Police forces, government agencies, and private investigation firms are currently debating the correct procedures for seizure either at a live crime scene or later during an investigation. The processes in this chapter represent my recommendations but should not be interpreted as the only way to proceed in what is fundamentally a legal rather than a technical decision.

This entire book has been aimed at a technical investigator, but cryptocurrencies are changing the landscape of a financial investigation. Traditionally, Financial investigators (FI's) are long-time police officers with financial training, or forensic accountants with an eye for the unusual in bank and company account records. To trace the movement of money, investigators work with anti-fraud departments in banks and other financial institutions. They identify, track, and seize proceeds of crime and assets owned by criminals, follow the financial breadcrumbs through complex money-laundering schemes, and monitor the purchase of illegal material.

Financial investigators are a necessary breed of detective, but they are not usually technical. Of course, they will likely be adept with a spreadsheet and understand accounting software, but they are not digital forensics professionals. I was asked by an FI a few months ago how he would produce a seized bitcoin in court. I wasn't sure how to answer, so I spent some time explaining the fundamentals of blockchain technology, and he understood it quickly.

Understanding the blockchain with its inherent cryptography, the ability to carve addresses from computers and phones, and extracting private keys from wallets—all these skills are foreign to the FI. On the flip side, digital forensics professionals tend to have a very particular set of skills but will not necessarily understand financial fraud and money laundering.

For an investigation department to carry out effective cryptocurrency investigations requires a coming together of the FIs and digital forensics departments. In my opinion, this combination needs to include a reasonable level of skill sharing, the FIs need to set aside the traditional mindset of movement of money through banks, and the digital forensics person needs to gain a reasonable understanding of fraud. After a few cases have been completed, the result should be investigators that understand each other, comprehend technical terms, and can effectively apply their skills to this field.

Asset Seizure

Different countries use different terminology for the seizure of assets—some mean the same thing, while others have a variety of connotations. Phrases such as *freezing assets, seizing assets, civil forfeiture, assets holding, proceeds of crime appropriation,* and *cashing out* are all terms I hear from different investigators. However, you just need to remember that cryptocurrency is an asset and an asset equals money. Although some specific considerations exist when gaining control of cryptocurrency, there is normally sufficient legislation available in a country's law books to be able to effectively gain access to these assets. For example:

- In the UK, the Proceeds of Crime Act 2002 (POCA), Section 47 (`http://bit.ly/2rUpHt8`) describes the mechanism for seizure of intangible assets for criminal investigations.
- In the United States, civil forfeiture laws allow police to keep money and other valuables that are "used or intended to be used" to buy or sell property as part of criminal activity.

The same fundamental processes and laws need to apply to the seizure of crypto-assets as they do to standard asset seizure. The differences are only technical.

Cashing Out

One of the biggest concerns about the seizure of cryptocurrency is what to do with the coins once you have control of them. Do you "cash out" and convert the coins into fiat currency or hold them as they are? The issues are significant:

Secure Storage   Unlike traditional currencies where monies can be seized and banked securely, the seized coins remain on the blockchain protected by the new private key or keys. If anyone gains sight of the recovery key or private key string (for example, by taking a photo of it using a smartphone), they could potentially gain access to the funds.

Insurance   Getting an insurance company to insure the assets is extremely difficult because of value fluctuation. What are they insuring and for what value? This is almost impossible to answer with the significant value changes that could exist throughout the duration of an investigation.

Valuation Fluctuations   Investigations and possibly subsequent court cases can last several years. In just over one year, Bitcoin increased from a value of $1000 to around $20,000. Imagine a situation where coins are seized with a value of $20,000, and by the time the suspect is found not guilty, the value has plummeted to $500. Is there a possibility of a lawsuit for the lost value? Who takes responsibility for that?

In some cases, investigators have asked a judge to rule on the question of whether to convert coins to a fiat currency. Perhaps the suspect can be asked if he wants the coins to be cashed out at the current value and placed in a bank account, or just transferred to a cryptocurrency address controlled by the investigator and held until the end of the case. Suspects may distance themselves from the coins, alleging that they have nothing to do with them. This may be true or the suspect may just wish to separate himself from what may be determined to be crime. In this instance, the investigator can decide what action to take without fear of any recourse. Of course, a suspect's story can change as the case progresses.

Some investigation teams have suggested that the best course of action is to cash out coins at the point of seizure as it is possible that copies of a suspects private key may be held by others. This could be done during a live response at a suspect's premises or later in the lab, but either way, preparation and processes are needed. If this is to be done live on a suspect's computer, care needs to be taken to ensure that other evidence on the computer or device is not overwritten.

Cashing out either live on-premises or later in the process requires significant preparation. This preparation should include the following:

- Determining which exchange you will use—The investigation team should set up a relationship with a trusted exchange that knows they are dealing with coins involved in an investigation and will expedite the transaction and perhaps agree to lower fees.

- Understanding the exchange's process for cashing out—The investigation team should have authentication on hand and/or addresses to transfer the coins to.

▪ Setting up a bank account for the exchange of funds—A bank account needs to be in place to receive the funds from the exchange. Some banks are showing resistance to working with some exchanges, and although this is primarily related to purchasing cryptocurrency, the bank needs to understand the needs of the investigator. As soon as the coins are cashed out, this is now a normal situation for an FI, and the retention and management of the funds can be carried out as usual.

Cashing-Out Process

If you have decided to cash out live, the process is fairly simple. As long as you have the exchange and bank accounts in place to accept the money, then the following is the recommended procedure. I recommend always working in pairs to ensure procedural accuracy and reduce errors in copying addresses, for example:

1. Access the suspect's computer. If there are passwords to the computer or to the wallet software, these will need to be obtained from the suspect. Be aware of local laws regarding asking a suspect for information that could be incriminating.

2. Ensure that the computer is connected to the Internet. Most wallets enable you to generate a transaction without being online, and the transaction will be sent to the network only when connected. Before you connect to the Internet, it is worth checking the wallet to ensure that there are no transactions waiting to be transmitted.

3. Access the wallet software.

4. Send the complete value of the wallet for all addresses with a balance to the address that has been set up on the exchange. With most wallets, this is a straightforward process, but make sure to check and double-check the address before you click Send! Involve another person on your investigative team to check the address.

5. Check the address on the blockchain to ensure the transfer has occurred. Use a trusted computer for this, *not* the suspect's computer.

6. Access the exchange on a trusted computer and complete the transaction of coins to the bank account that you have set up for this.

Seizing Coins without Cashing Out

If the decision has been made to seize coins by simply transferring them to another address, then the process is almost identical to the cashing-out process in the previous section, but without an exchange being involved. Seizure and storage of coins requires a little more preparation, as involves the following steps:

1. Select wallet software that you will use to manage seized coins.

   A number of options exist, but I recommend that you use a wallet that enables you to set up multisig addresses. When funds are transferred from the suspect's wallet to a multisig address with two or more signatories, it means that the funds cannot be moved without the keys of the other keyholders of the address. This protects an investigator if coins go missing. Some online wallet providers also offer highly secure storage of keys offline.

2. Create a storage wallet with multisig addresses.

NOTE   It is possible to create a multisig address offline, but it is a complex process.

3. Create a wallet to import the suspect's private key.

4. Import the suspect's private key to the wallet you created in the previous step.

5. Transfer all funds to the multisig wallet.

6. Back up the storage wallet to cold storage (for example, paper).

7. Store the private key backup securely.

Setting Up a Storage Wallet

To provide an example as to how you would apply the previous instructions, I'll walk you through the process using the Electrum Wallet software for Bitcoin. Electrum is a thin client and does not require the downloading of the full Bitcoin blockchain, so it can be set up quickly. It is also fairly straightforward to create multisig addresses:

1. First, create the storage wallet that will receive the suspect's keys.

2. Download Electrum from `http://bit.ly/2EKtxXI`. Run the software and select New/Restore from the File menu. The software will ask you to name the wallet, and it's logical to use the case number or a similar identifier.

3. The next screen will ask what type of wallet should be created (see Figure 14-1). Select the Multi-signature Wallet option, and then choose how many cosigners you require.

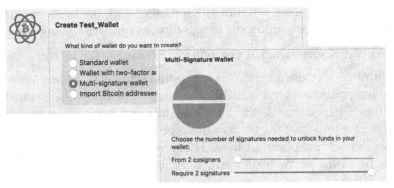

Figure 14-1: Select the Multi-signature Wallet option.

4. On the next screen, select the Create A New Seed option, which will generate the 12-word recovery mnemonic code. Electrum then forces you to rekey the code. You cannot copy or paste it here or into any other document—you must manually type it in.

   As you can see in Figure 14-2, these steps will generate a Master Public Key that you can give to your cosigners if needed.

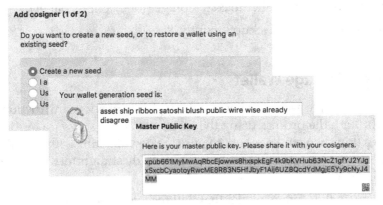

Figure 14-2: Seed generation and public key.

5. Next, enter the public keys of the cosigners to the address. This will then generate addresses that begin with 3 to indicate that they are a multisig address (see Figure 14-3).

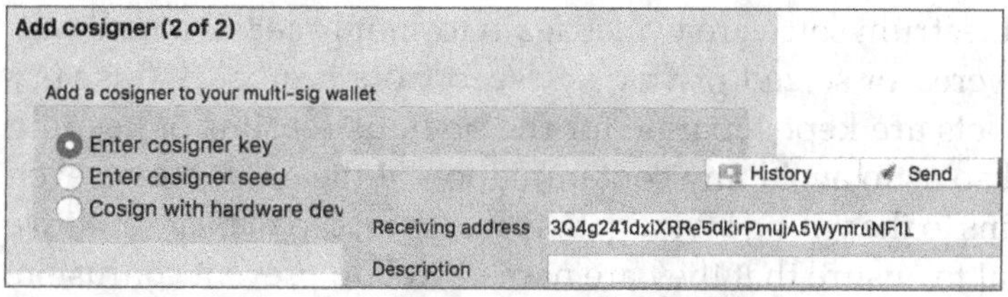

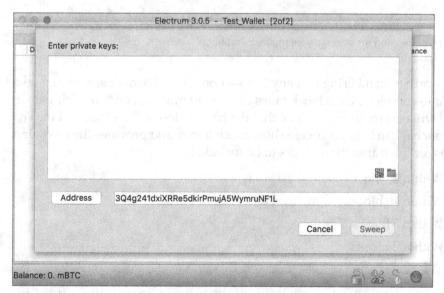

Figure 14-3: Enter cosigner address and key generation.

Once these steps are completed, you have an address ready to receive seized coins.

Importing a Suspect's Private Key

You have two ways to move the coins from a suspect's wallet into your new multisig address. The first is very easy using Electrum. From your multisig wallet, select Wallet ⇨ Private Keys ⇨ Sweep. From this window, you can enter the private key or keys of the suspect, and all the funds managed by the suspect will be moved into your new multisig address (see Figure 14-4).

Figure 14-4: Enter private keys to Sweep coins.

This method is quick and efficient but only works if you have been able to acquire the raw private key from the suspect or by dumping it from his wallet. If you have a recovery seed, then a different approach is needed.

You can use the Electrum software wallet again to simply set up a new wallet based on a recovered or seized private key seed from a suspect. It is very important that wallets are kept separate for the obvious reasons of keeping evidence separated so as to avoid any contamination of the evidence or, even worse, assigning coins to the wrong investigation. Electrum can manage multiple wallets, but it is vital to ensure that they are named well to prevent confusion.

Set up another wallet, but this time, choose the I Already Have A Seed option. You will be prompted to enter the recovery words, and the wallet will then complete its set up, contact the blockchain, and provide you with the balance and used addresses. Next, send the entire wallet to your multisig address using the Max button as shown in Figure 14-5. Remember to double-check the address you are sending to and have it checked by another person on the investigative team.

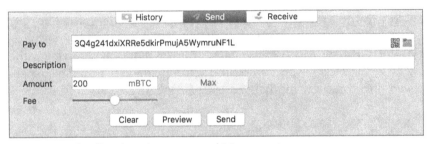

Figure 14-5: Sending the coins to your multisig account.

It is worth remembering that any transaction on the Bitcoin network can take a while to complete. Each block takes around 10 minutes, and to a fair extent, the fee will control the next block that the transaction will be included in. The Fee slider bar can help you decide how much to pay and provides the following options for the transaction blocks to be included:

- Within 25 blocks
- Within 10 blocks
- Within 5 blocks
- Within 2 blocks
- The next block

If you are doing a cash-out at the suspect's computer, you will want to wait until the transaction has confirmed at least one block before leaving. In this case, it may be worth paying the extra fee to have the transaction included in the next block. However, there will be a cost for this that may have to be repaid to the suspect in the event that the assets are returned.

Storage and Security

Assuming that you have decided not to cash out to a fiat currency and allow a bank to care for the funds, you now have to decide how best to secure the storage of the funds. Of course, you cannot actually store cryptocurrency coins because they exist only on the blockchain, but the secure storage of the private key that controls the coins is absolutely paramount. Here are some best practices to follow:

- Each signatory to the multisig address should export the recovery seed by copying the words to a file. Do not save the file.

  Remember that the computer you use should be secure because the document could be recovered forensically at a later date. Not saving the document helps, but the temporary file could still be cached to disk or in computer memory.

- Print the document twice.

  The printer should be in a secure location because the printed document could be recovered from most modern printers.

- Each document should be stored in a separate safe in different locations.

- Do *not* store the keys from all multisig accounts together.

To create a backup recovery seed with Electrum, select Seed from the Wallet menu, copy the values, and secure them as described previously (see Figure 14-6).

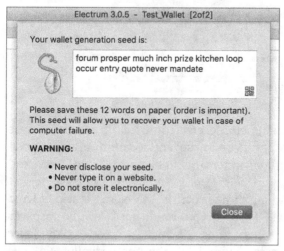

Figure 14-6: Seed values to copy.

Alternatively, you can electronically store the seed in a file by copying the seed to a document, saving the document, writing to two encrypted hard drives, and storing them separately. I am not a fan of this method, because the saved file can be recovered easily from the computer, even if it's deleted, and hard drives have a horrible tendency of failing just when you need them. In addition, many computers have live snapshots or real-time backups, so even if the file containing the seed was deleted from the primary computer, there is the risk that it will be available on backups. You may feel that this level of security in a police station or secure lab is not needed; however, the lure of easy access to perhaps millions of dollars of hard-to-trace cryptocurrency may be a significant temptation to some.

It is also possible to export the raw private keys, although again, these are written to a file, so I would not recommend this approach for the reasons previously detailed. To export the keys in Electrum select Seed from the Wallet menu, and you can then save each key pair to a CSV file for storage (see Figure 14-7).

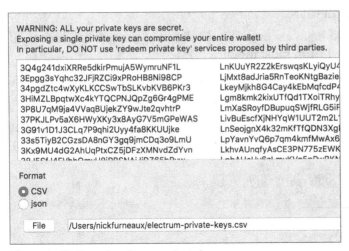

Figure 14-7: Exporting the raw private keys.

Again, I do not recommend using stored electronic media to retain these seeds or keys. Cold storage, on paper, stored in several locations is a much better solution. Remember this saying as it pertains to backups: "Two is one and one is none!"

The last thing you should do to maximize security is delete the wallet from the computer you have been using. Of course, you should *not* delete the suspect's wallet from his computer or any forensic image—which is considered evidence tampering and changing data—instead, you delete the storage wallets you just made. In my "Cryptocurency for Investigators" class, I've had students who were really worried about this step. Deleting anything is generally a bad idea in an investigation, but if the wallets remain on computers, then the possibility exists that someone could exploit that weakness and transfer the coins. However, the students have a good reason to be hesitant—an investigator never wants to lose control of the keys, so double-checking everything first is vital.

The principles are the same for the seizure of other currencies using different software wallets. Although not all of them support seed code words, most enable the dumping of the private key, so you can follow the same basic steps and end up with cold storage of the private keys or backup seeds.

Seizure from an Online Wallet

Many companies offer online wallets, including specialist high-security storage companies and exchanges that offer wallet services. The blockchain.info site that has been referred to a significant amount of times in this book is one of these companies.

Seizure of funds can be achieved in the following ways:

- Make a legal approach to the company requesting either the release of cryptocurrency funds or access to the suspect's account. Some companies say that they have no way of accessing an account, and the only solution is to go through a password-recovery process. However, a password-recovery process usually includes an e-mail verification step, and you should have access to the suspect's e-mail in many cases. This may also involve security questions, but my experience is that the exchanges often store the answers in the clear on their customer databases. Either way, access should be achievable.

- Locate the user name and password for the account. This can be easier than you may think. Here are some possible ways to get this information:

  - Ask the suspect for his password. (This actually works sometimes.)

  - Carry out a forensic analysis on the suspect's computer, looking for passwords to other resources. If you find one of the suspect's passwords, try derivatives of it to gain access elsewhere. Most people use variations of just three base passwords or phrases.

Once you have access to the online account, just transfer the funds to your storage wallet as previously outlined, and store it appropriately.

Practice, Practice, Practice

These steps may seem daunting and, to be honest, the first time I had to move coins from a suspect's live wallet to my storage wallet and then out to paper, I was really nervous! The only way to get comfortable with the process is to practice and practice some more.

Set up a training environment in your lab or office, and train the key people so that the steps become second nature. Purchase a small amount of cryptocurrency, and then role-play different types of seizures using different wallets. You may want to re-create some of the suggestions in Chapter 8, "Detecting the Use of Cryptocurrencies," to find addresses hidden in a room, or use forensic means to search a computer for public and private keys or backup seeds. Then go through the motions of cashing out, or seizing to your storage address.

Once you have copied a backup seed to paper and then deleted the storage account, use the seed to re-create the wallet. It will really help boost your confidence in the process when you see all the coins return once the seed is imported.

After you're done following the steps to move and back up the practice coins, the storage wallet can become the pretend suspect's wallet, and you can repeat the training over and over, just losing small amounts in fees during the transactions.

Summary

Everything that was covered in previous chapters of this book leads to this chapter. If you can understand cryptocurrencies, locate private key backups, track money though the blockchain, and locate service providers, it is still all for nothing if you cannot seize the assets once they are located.

Aside from the processes described in this chapter, try to get digital forensics and financial investigators to work together and share their knowledge rather than working in silos of information and abilities. This small step can mean the difference between technical solutions being ignored or successfully exploited and financial tricks overlooked or investigated.

The methods described in this chapter are not meant to be the *only* ones that you can use to gain control of cryptocurrency assets. They are just the methods and processes that have worked for me and the people I work with and train.

And don't forget to practice, practice, and then practice some more!

CHAPTER 15

Putting It All Together

This book has the subtitle "Understanding, Extracting, and Analyzing Blockchain Evidence," and it has attempted to provide an appropriate level of theoretical understanding while teaching practical techniques for carrying out an investigation involving cryptocurrencies. Although Bitcoin is still the biggest cryptocurrency, it is arguably not the best, and new pretenders to the throne are being released every day. Although this book has had a Bitcoin focus, I hope it has prepared you and given you the necessary tools to be able to research and develop techniques for any new cryptocurrency that may need your attention.

The different types of crimes that may involve cryptocurrency use are virtually unending and eventually could find their way into almost any category of crime. A few years ago, I gave a talk at a local school about my job as a digital investigator, and before I started, the teacher asked what crimes involved computers. She had assumed it was all hacking and viruses, so she was surprised when I listed burglary, murders, drug dealing, and all the other "real world" crimes. The fact is that in the past 10 years, virtually every crime has some type of digital aspect to it—whether it's cell phone call data, searches made about a crime on Google, or digital CCTV systems—the list is endless. In the United States, a man killed his wife and dumped her body in a lake, and he was convicted partially on the basis of googling "the deepest place in the lake" the previous day. In my hometown, a man murdered his neighbor and was convicted partially on his Google Street View history, which showed him pre-planning the route from his home to the place the body was left.

My point is that cryptocurrencies are here to stay. I predict that within five years, an app will go viral that allows untraceable, cheap micropayments to be made via the blockchain, and that is how people, especially the young, will transact small amounts of money on a daily basis both online and in the real world. It is just a matter of time. This will also mean that investigation of cryptocurrencies will permeate into every type of crime, and investigators need to be ready with the skills and capability to follow the money.

So where do you start applying all you have learned in this book? Practice and get involved in investigations as soon as you can, remembering that they will all be different and no single process will cover each situation. In this final chapter, we'll look at a few examples.

Examples of Cryptocurrency Crimes

Almost every day, I hear of new ways that cryptocurrencies have crept into different types of crimes, but the five examples described in this section will provide you with a reasonable sample of the possibilities that you may encounter.

Buying Illegal Goods

A person may be using a cryptocurrency to buy goods online that are illegal. (They could use cryptocurrency payment methods to buy on the street, but at the moment, Bitcoin in particular is no good for that due to the time for transactions to be included in a block and confirmed.) Where might you start with this investigation? This all depends on how the suspect came to your attention.

Was the online store shut down by a police force, and log files and customer data have been found and provided to you? If so, you will already have Bitcoin addresses connected to real-world data. Taking the Bitcoin address or addresses and using clustering techniques may enable you to find other sites where the person has bought goods. Seizing computer equipment from the suspect may enable you to extract a wallet with payment history.

Alternatively, if a computer has been obtained by a suspect, you can use carving and searching techniques to find and extract wallets and addresses before attempting to track payments on the blockchain.

Selling Illegal Goods

In the same manner as someone buying illegal goods, a trader in illegal merchandise may come to the attention of the authorities for different reasons other than using cryptocurrency payments. For example, there might be databases that link names and addresses to goods supplied and perhaps cryptocurrency addresses. In this case, you would not need to track the addresses since you have the owner's information. However, it may be useful to cluster addresses to find other purchases made and to track any cashing-out the trader may have done, and then use a financial investigator (FI) to trace the fiat currencies and seize any assets. Any cryptocurrency funds that are still on the blockchain can also be seized or cashed out and securely stored.

Stealing Cryptocurrency

Many ways to steal a cryptocurrency exist that are not related to technological crime. In January 2018, Ottawa police sought two men after an attempted armed robbery at a cryptocurrency exchange. In that same month, four men in the UK attempted to steal a cryptotrader's bitcoins by gaining access to his home and forcing him to transact his wallet to another address. In December of 2017, the managing director of a cryptocurrency exchange in Kiev was kidnapped, and money was extorted for his release. Criminals will follow the money, and if they find investors or traders with cryptocurrency, they become a new target. Investigating crimes such as these requires both a traditional investigation into robbery or extortion as well as the need to follow transactions on the blockchain until the criminal cashes out to an exchange or trader.

Of course, technological means to steal cryptocurrencies also exist. Many exchanges have fallen foul of hackers and well-organized teams either gaining access to private keys or social engineering attacks to fraudulently engineer the transfer of funds to criminals addresses. In early 2018, Japanese authorities investigated the theft of $530 million of NEM coins from an exchange. This was one of the largest digital-currency thefts, similar in size to the Bitcoin theft from the Tokyo-based Mt. Gox exchange in 2014.

Investigating these thefts may seem extremely complex, but in fact, they're just like any theft with clues left behind for an investigator to follow. Hacks of exchanges will likely leave entries in log files, and social engineering attacks often come from spear-phishing incidents via e-mail, which again provides an ability to trace back to possible perpetrators. This is before an investigator starts to follow the money on the blockchain, watching for the use of mixers, exchanges, and traders that can then be approached using legal methods for real-world information.

Money Laundering

This is complex area and goes back to the need to combine the skills of FIs and digital forensics specialists. Money laundering is the process of taking the proceeds of crime and combining those funds with legitimate funds and transactions to obfuscate their origins. On a blockchain, money can be laundered by moving coin through mixers and exchanges, buying and selling goods without leaving the cryptocurrency, as well as on gambling sites, which are a surprisingly popular choice for many criminals looking to move their funds. A white paper written by the Center on Sanctions and Illicit Finance (`http://bit.ly/2HfT4tC`) concluded that "In general, mixers and online gambling sites have the biggest bitcoin laundering problem—they process far and away the highest proportion of dirty bitcoins."

Following the money can be a complex issue where criminals are deliberately trying to hide their tracks. Having a team of both technical and financial investigators can give you the best chance of finding services that can be approached to request a real-world suspect's details.

Kidnap and Extortion

The days of leaving a suitcase full of cash on some remote rough ground in order to secure the release of a kidnap victim are probably long gone. Cash was often tagged so it could be traced and the drop site surveilled, which meant that picking up the bag was fraught with dangers of being caught. Asking for money to be transferred through the banking system also exposed the kidnapper to many opportunities for the authorities to track the payment. Bitcoin and other cryptocurrencies have provided a method to request payment that at least has the pretense of being anonymous and untraceable. Depending on the cryptocurrency, the payments are usually traceable and the parties involved can often be identified. We are also seeing cryptocurrencies being the payment method of choice for ransomware and other extortion scams. These crimes are not cryptocurrency crimes specifically, but they need to be treated as a standard extortion investigation with assistance from specialist investigators to monitor or follow any payments made on the blockchain.

What Have You Learned?

This book has attempted to teach you how cryptocurrencies work and, to some degree, how they don't work. The phone call I received from an investigator asking me to carve bitcoins from a hard drive would not have been made if they had understood the underlying technology more clearly.

Here is a quick summary of some of the main points covered in this book:

Understanding How Public and Private Keys Relate to Each Other   A Bitcoin address, for example, is fundamentally a public key that anyone who has the private key can transact. This knowledge means that as an investigator, you need to look really hard for the private key, because it will give you control of all of the assets that may be stored in addresses on the blockchain.

Knowing How the Blockchain Works   A reasonable understanding of blockchain technology enables you to apply that knowledge to virtually any cryptocurrency that may be used by a suspect. The relationship between transactions being bundled and hashed into blocks helps you to understand the security and dependability of a blockchain as well as how the transactions can potentially be relied upon in court.

Considering Dates, Times, and IP Addresses   There is much confusion regarding dates and times of transactions, and digital investigators often rely on the solidity of timestamps in re-creating actions of a suspect online or at their computer. The limitations of the timestamps on a blockchain such as Bitcoin enable an investigator to build a case with appropriate levels of confidence on the dates and times that are involved. In the same way, IP addresses saved by sites such as blockchain.info have been mistakenly relied upon to de-anonymize particular transactions. You have learned that these are just relay addresses, and it is much more complex to attribute an IP address to a specific transaction.

Searching Premises   You learned how to search premises for evidence of cryptocurrency use with a particular focus on finding a private key. You considered the different types of paper wallets, hardware devices, mnemonic keys or seed words, and addresses jotted on scraps of paper. The list of possibilities is endless, but front-line officers need to know what they are looking for.

Working on a Live Computer   This book described methods of working on a live computer at a suspect's premises, how you could search for addresses, dump wallets with their private keys, and even cash out a wallet from the live scene. To do this, you have to know that cryptocurrency wallet software is running and how important it is that a live investigator understands the different wallet types available.

Exporting Wallets   You learned how to import a found and exported wallet onto a lab computer, and then how to analyze the contents of the wallet such as the used addresses and the current balance.

Building Information about an Address   The book detailed how to build up information about an identified address, such as the number of transactions the address has been involved with, the dates of those transactions, exporting the raw data, extracting micromessages, and even basic temporal analysis of the times that transactions were done.

Clustering Addresses   Following the money is a complex process. Although some commercial products are available to help, it is vital that an investigator know how to take a single address and apply clustering techniques to infer other addresses owned by a single user, and then follow those addresses to hopefully expose further evidence. If you are unsure about certain aspects of clustering, I urge you to reread the sections in Chapter 12 that deal with those aspects.

Understanding how to cluster addresses will help you understand what the commercial tools are doing as well as their pros and cons.

Following the Money   You learned how to use blockchain viewers to surf from transaction to transaction and experienced how quickly you can get lost in the complexities of the blockchain. You learned to take the process slowly and carefully, take detailed notes, and annotate just the first 6 digits of addresses to make notes easier to read and follow.

Using Visualization Tools   To help with the complexities of following transactions, we looked at a number of open-source visualization software tools that help the investigator see connections more clearly. These tools are not a panacea, because they too can quickly become complex if not used with caution. The commercial tools carry out clustering in the same way as you learned to do manually. This means that these tools can infer connections wrongly and their limitations must be understood.

Finding Real-World Services   You studied how to identify real-world resources such as exchanges, mixers, and traders. This provides you with a target to apply legal means to try and acquire data on your suspect. I described how to use open source investigation techniques to search for addresses online, perhaps in forums or other sites and then using clustering to connect backward or forward in the blockchain to a service provider. I also wrote about making micro-payments and withdrawals to service providers to attempt to expose more addresses that could form a cluster of a known entity. Commercial software providers do this regularly.

I also discussed methods by which coins could be seized from a suspect and deliberated on the benefits and negatives of holding seized coins securely or cashing them out to a fiat currency. There is a need to consider this carefully and agree to a methodology with management to ensure that it is practical, achievable, and in line with applicable laws. Storage wallets, preferably multi-signature, or accounts with an exchange need to be agreed upon and set up, and the process needs to be practiced over and over. This planning needs to be done before you start any job that may require work on seizing coins—don't wait until you're sitting at the suspect's keyboard. Remember that once coins are moved to your storage wallet, they should be backed up to cold storage such as paper, multiple copies made, and electronic copies securely deleted.

I will not be so short-sighted as to pretend that this book has covered everything, or that the processes suggested are always going to be the most efficient way to proceed. This is a collection of recommendations based on several years of investigating cryptocurrencies and having to regularly find my own solutions to problems when the solutions had not been written down anywhere else. White papers and conference talks have begun to focus on cryptocurrency investigations, but it has only really been since 2015 and 2016 that large police and government investigators have begun to turn their attention to the issues with investigating the technology. Even now in 2018, the level of skills is very low within both the FI world and the digital forensics sphere. I hope that this will change and that this book helps with the dissemination of information.

Although blockchain technology, and Bitcoin specifically, is not actually new, it has only been in the last three years or so that the anonymization features have become more widely used by criminals. In addition, it has only been since the extraordinary growth of Bitcoin values in 2017 that criminals with large amounts of cash saw an opportunity to launder money while also increasing their overall value. This means that standard drug-dealing cases or organized-crime investigations are unveiling the use of cryptocurrencies, and many are unsure how to proceed with this element of the analysis. I hope that I have demonstrated to you that these examinations, although complex and often time-consuming, are achievable and worthwhile.

Where Do You Go from Here?

The information in this book is designed to start your journey into investigating cryptocurrencies, but it is not an end in itself. You should now understand the fundamentals of the technology, but new forks are appearing all the time in different currencies. Bitcoin Cash differs from Bitcoin in subtle ways, Ethereum is changing the way you mine coins, and ZCash has security features very different to the others.

A researcher recently said to me that she believes Bitcoin will be "the MySpace of cryptocurrencies." Although MySpace was a hugely successful social media platform, it couldn't sustain its own success and eventually paved the way for Facebook and others that have learned from its mistakes and found a way to be relevant in the long term.

Bitcoin has problems with its comparatively high fees, the length of time it takes for confirmations, and wildly fluctuating values. This may, or may not, open the way for other cryptocurrencies to learn from Bitcoin's mistakes and fill the gap in the market for a readily tradable currency. Any new cryptocurrencies that begin to find traction with users, especially criminals, need to be understood by the investigator—preferably before facing the currency in an investigation. I recommend that you make this area a subject of continuous research, watch the cryptocurrency forums, follow the right people on Twitter, and download and try new tools designed to simplify the investigative process.

I have avoided any cryptocurrency investments, apart from small deposits in many of the front-runners, because I am waiting to see what the future holds. This means I missed the Bitcoin value explosion of 2017, but I have been able to think about cryptocurrencies as an investigator rather than an investor.

However, I do recommend that you spend a few dollars (or whatever your local currency is) to buy coins on the primary blockchains, transact them, move them around, buy something, and get a feel for how they work, what is good, and what is bad. Then investigate your own transactions and try to answer questions such as these:

- What can you find on your own computer?
- Can you locate magic values and carve transactions?
- Are you able to sniff traffic and locate data in the packet stream?
- What does a blockchain viewer tell you that would be interesting in a live examination?

In the foreseeable future, in order to be good at investigating cryptocurrencies, you will need to be fairly self-sufficient, be able to do some of your own research, work with your colleagues to design processes and methods that work for you, and work within the laws of your country.

Since Sarah Meiklejohn and colleagues wrote arguably the first Bitcoin forensics paper, "A Fistful of Bitcoins," in 2013 (`https://bit.ly/2J4Rg7A`), the development of investigation techniques surrounding cryptocurrencies has been slow. I recommend researching and developing your own methods and where possible, share them with the community. It is only this way that internationally accepted investigation standards will be achieved.

Feel free to keep your eye on the `www.investigatingcryptocurrencies.com` website, which is based on this book. This site will, from time to time, publish updates or corrections to information in the book. It also contains a discount code to take my online or live course.

Happy investigating!

Index